From Multi-Modal Systems Thinking to Community Development

MCCD

From Multi-Modal Systems Thinking to Community Development

Regaining our Humanity through Community

J. D. R. de Raadt

and

Veronica D. de Raadt

Melbourne Centre for Community Development

From Multi-Modal Systems Thinking
to Community Development

Melbourne Centre for Community Development
Australia • 2014
ISBN-13: 978-1500236465
ISBN-10: 1500236462

www.melbourneccd.com

Em celebração

ao 10º Congresso Anual do Capítulo Brasileiro
da Sociedade Internacional para as Ciências dos Sistemas

e pelo

bom trabalho de nossos colegas brasileiros
de sistemas liderados pelo

Prof. Dr. Dante Pinheiro Martinelli

In celebration of

the 10th Annual Congress of the Brazilian Systems Chapter of
the International Society for the Systems Sciences

and of

the fine work of our Brazilian systems colleagues led by

Prof. Dr. Dante Pinheiro Martinelli

Table of Contents

Acknowledgements

Some material in this book has been extracted from the following previously published papers:

de Raadt, J. D. R. (1996) What the Prophet and the Philosopher Told their Nations: a Multi-Modal Systems View of Norms and Civilisation. *World Futures*, 47: 53-68.

de Raadt, J. D. R. (1997b) A Sketch for Humane Operational Research in a Technological Society. *Systems Practice*, 10: 421-441.

de Raadt, J. D. R. (1997d) Faith and the Normative Foundation of Systems Science. *Systems Practice*, 10:13-35.

de Raadt, Veronica D. (2001a) Multi-Modal Systems Method: The Impact of Normative Factors on Community Viability. *Systems Research and Behavioral Science*, 18: 171–180.

de Raadt, J. D. R. and de Raadt, Veronica D. (2004) Normative Evaluation of Community Projects: A Multimodal Systems Approach. *Systemic Practice and Action Research*, 17: 83-102.

de Raadt, J. D. R. and de Raadt, Veronica D. (2004) Where there is No Vision the People Perish: Ethical Vision and Community Sustainability. *Systems Research and Behavioral Science*, 22: 233-247.

de Raadt, J. D. R. and de Raadt, Veronica D. (2008) Arresting the Collapse of the City Through Systemic Education: A Case Study of Melbourne. *Systemic Practice and Action Research*, 21: 299-322.

de Raadt, J. D. R. (2006) Samaritan Ethics, Systems Science and Society. *Systemic Practice and Action Research*, 19: 489-500.

de Raadt, J. D. R. (2010) Community Development and Renaissance Social Humanism - Some Lessons for Systems Science. *Systemic Practice and Action Research*, 24: 509- 521.

We thank the publishers for their permission to re-publish this material.

Preface

The 17th century painting on the cover of this book is by Johannes Vermeer; it is originally entitled *Gezicht op Delft* and commonly translated into English as *A View of Delft*. When examining a masterpiece such as this, art critics often focus on the geometry of its different sections, the combination of colours and the grain of the paint and other similar details representing masterful technique. Yet, they seldom note the philosophy that inspired the painting, which is perhaps a greater and more relevant masterpiece and which renders *A Vision of Delft* as a more appropriate translation of its original title. For Vermeer presented us with Delft as an embodiment of the *City of God*. Half of the painting is occupied by the sky, which the prophet called God's "throne"[1]. The other half depicts God's "footstool" which his people have adorned with their city so that he may rest his feet and regard it all as very good. It is a city that was built upon the foundation of Erasmus' *Philosophia Christi*. It is clean, ordered and graceful. It radiates peace. In the foreground, a few of its citizens, men and women, wait for transport in a relaxed manner that would be rare in other parts of Europe at the time. Women in Holland could safely travel without male escort and could freely engage in everyday chit-chat with men while they awaited the boat to carry them to their destination.

Delft may have lacked the splendid imperial palaces of Shönbrunn in Vienna and Versailles in France that were built for their nobility. But here, within its walls, lived a different kind of nobility, a community of ordinary people who serve God with diligence, talent and intelligence. Among this nobility were the great admirals Pieter Hein and Maarten Tromp, Antony van Leeuwenhoek the "father of microbiology", Hugo Grotius the great jurist and father of international law and the famous painters Fabritius, Maas and Vermeer himself. But also included were van Buyten the baker, Arnold Bold the printer and other ordinary citizens who served their fellow men with the same dedication and integrity. They were all part of Delft's nobility as is evinced – also in paintings of the time – in Dutch homes where maid-servants dressed as neatly as their mistresses and were as literate.

---

[1] Isaiah 66:1.

Let us not think that this was a perfect city or a perfect time. The 17th Century was an era full of conflicts and violence. The Netherlands were continuously besieged by the army of Spain, which claimed it as part of its empire. It was also threatened by France and fought three wars at sea against England to defend its freedom to navigate the seas and trade with lands afar. Internally, republicans were accosted by the monarchical ambitions of the house of Orange. These ambitions led to the imprisonment of Grotius and the murders of statesmen such as van Oldenbarnevelt and the brothers de Witt. That is why Vermeer's painting is a vision rather than a view. For it is an image of what the people of Delft were trying to build in their century. And to build they needed an all-embracing philosophy – in today's language we would call it *systemic* – that integrated all the relevant sciences and the education to impart it to its citizens, so that men and women would be equipped to serve in their calling with intelligence, diligence, love for their neighbour and a clear sense of civic direction. Sadly, this philosophy was crushed down in the next century by the violent French revolution and the Napoleonic wars, inaugurating a new era driven by modernism – a misnamed philosophy that should have been more appropriately called primitivism. This is the root of our predicament; we teachers – at schools, universities and other educational institutions – have been stripped by modernism of the vision to inspire our students to live as good citizens and exercise their vocation with love and selfless dedication in order to build up their communities. We have been left with no science to show them an alternative path to the morally destructive pursuit of money and pleasure. True, although today's view of Delft has been changed by the hand of modernism, its vision is still with us as is Vermeer's painting.

However, although the vision of humanity remains the same, ours is a different historical time with different problems and challenges that demand new scientific tools and educational programmes to equip today's students. Thus years ago, we made it our mission to search for this science and develop a syllabi to teach it and this book documents our progress over a period of two decades. At times, this required us to look to the past as much

as to the future and when we turned to the past, we were aston-
ished to discover fine works largely ignored by the academic community of our day. We learned not only about the early development of the natural sciences, but also the amazing unfolding of the
humanities and, among them, the fine arts of which Vermeer's *Gezicht op Delft* is only one illustration. He and his contemporaries
bequeathed on us more than an inheritance of staggering beauty;
they left a valuable record of a social and cultural reform that was
most enlightening to us and, we hope, other social scientists. We
believed that by emulating the philosophy behind this vision of society and after an appropriate adaptation to our times, we could
hand to students a science that is wholesome and beautiful and
that inspires them to live and serve others wisely in their chosen
professions and, through this, engage in true community development. Now in our mature years, it is time to transfer this mission
to the next generation and it is our hope that this book may help
them carry it far beyond where we have left off.

Introduction

J. D. R. de Raadt

In November 1992 I took a professorial appointment in Sweden, an event that was to bring considerable change not only to our family's personal life but also to the professional lives of my wife, Veronica, and I. We arrived in Sweden with a vision based on our Christian convictions and that vision and our understanding of it went through an ongoing process of change and, we would like to think, a maturation to what constitutes the core of our believing and thinking today. The collection of papers in this book – scattered among journals and conference proceedings or half forgotten in our filing cabinet – represents a record of this process. Most of their content went into the books we wrote, especially as pedagogical tools for our students. These books are useful, but due to the necessity of simplifying their material, ideas must be presented in a static manner, as if they have never changed. The gestation of the ideas as well as the important role played in their development by the influence of students, colleagues and other people, as well as the institutions with which we were deeply involved were, of necessity, left out. This is unfortunate, because the very dynamic process of shaping one's thoughts and beliefs is of as much importance as the thoughts and beliefs themselves. In addition to learning ideas, it is useful for students to learn the intellectual creativity that gives them birth and gradually reshapes them. Only then can they learn to engage in truly analytical and original thinking. This is the purpose of this book.

The papers describe the progressive unfolding of our vision. By vision I mean the concept in the Bible that is commonly translated into the English word *faith*, a word that must yet be understood in the context of its Hebrew background. Hebrew faith incites action or, as Ortega y Gasset would put it, it is a *living* and *vital faith*[1].

---

[1] Ortega y Gasset (2004). A detailed discussion of this concept of faith as well as my disregard for Christian theology in favour of the Erasmian Christian philosophy is given in my latest book – de Raadt, J. D. R. (2013). This book ought to be considered a companion to the present, for it discusses in-depth, the biblical ideas presented here taking into account their historical setting and original language (Hebrew and Greek).

2 Introduction ♣

Now the civilised person must live by this faith[2] to remain civilised; when he loses this faith, he dies to civilisation; he stops living in the civic and spiritual sense and turns to vegetating. And this is the predicament of post-modern man: he does not live, but vegetates. He cannot reach the level of animal life, for animals struggle to live, they seek their food, hunt, fight to defend their territory and take care of their young. Post-modern man is incapable of carrying out such a struggle; he depends on corporations and the state for money and consumer goods. He is unable to self-sustain; jobs must be created for him. And as for his young, he neither cares nor nurtures them but scatters them on the ground like seeds to fend for themselves and turn into generations x, y, z or whatever. Inside, post-modern man has become deadened and he can only be brought back to life by vision; therefore, vision has been the first aim of our endeavour, not only for ourselves, but especially for our students, the young seed scattered on the sterile ground of our societies.

Vision, however, does not come alone, but is part of the totality of our humanity and thus needs to be understood systemically as being interconnected with every aspect that makes us human. Unable of course to consider everything, we focused on five of the most important factors that interact with vision and proceeded to develop our research and educational agenda around them. That is, in addition to being focused on vision, our concern extended to its relation to the civic, ethical, thought and educational aspects. By civic I mean that our vision must be communal and social and not be limited to one individual scope. As I have written before, we are not like cats, we are pack creatures like wolves that live and hunt together to be viable. This demands that our vision for life must not be purely individual but rather, be held in common with our fellow citizens. Without such commonality, our pack disintegrates. Moreover, not only should the vision be held communally but the objectives it seeks must be for the benefit of the social group as a whole; our pursuits in life should not be limited to self, but include others in its blessings. This demands an ethic from each citizen that goes beyond our contemporary understanding of the

---

[2] Habakkuk 2:4.

word *ethic*. Today, by ethics people have in mind what is strictly justice; that is, doing what is one's duty. As we shall see, given the predicament of humanity, we need to push our ethics beyond the line of duty in order for us to civilise the world; we need to carry a cross that stands not for our problems, but other people's problems. And if our aim is to reintegrate people to lead a fully civic life, a life extending itself over the complete civilised and cultural spectrum, mere charity will not suffice. We will require to change the way we think; we will require a different philosophy to the one we have today and, moreover, a different concept of philosophy itself. We must return philosophy to its original quest for wisdom and to an overarching integration of every discipline – from logic and mathematics to history, sociology, aesthetics and ethics – into a systemic totality that will aid us in attaining such wisdom. We need a civilised philosophy and science. Finally, we must pattern our lives in accordance with this wisdom; that is, we must implement it and the only form of implementation that honours our humanity is education. Without education as their foundation, government policies, laws, institutions and even democracy become mere coercive weapons that violate our humanity and impose ideas without giving us the chance to think about or understand them. I call them weapons because, although they do not draw blood, by their nature they are no different to guns. They may not kill the body but they kill the soul[3]; these new weapons are the bane of post-modernity.

These five interconnected factors – vision, civilisation, ethics, thought and education – emerged in our research as core targets to bring change into society and to develop a university curriculum. The papers that are included in this book represent the path which we trod in order to reach an understanding of this core. Before we begin the account of our progress of this endeavour, I must make clear that in all of these works we reject modernity in all its manifestations, both post and before post[4]. This includes the secularism

---

[3] Matthew 10:28.

[4] The terms *post-modernity* and *post-modern* suggest that modernity is now past, but we do not agree with this. Modernity has not come to an end; on the contrary we now live in an era in which it has reached its fulfilment just as a boil is the final eruption of an infection that has been brewing for some time

upon which modernity has been built. This has not been an easy task, for it has meant that we have had to operate in an environment where beliefs and convictions have been arbitrarily and unjustly banned. It has been done in a furtive and intimidating manner, so that many scholars, perhaps the large majority who share our beliefs and convictions, have acquiesced to the secular methodology as the conventional way of doing science. We have not acquiesced, for it would not only be dishonest to practise a methodology in which we do not believe, but irresponsible to practise it especially when we are convinced it is detrimental to humanity. Therefore, we have not just defended our intellectual territory; we have also been spurred by a sense of responsibility to other people, especially our young students.

This is the theme of the first paper – *The Prophet and the Philosopher* – bearing my presidential address to the ISSS[5] conference that took place at the Free University, Amsterdam, in 1995. I argued that modernity had robbed us of the normative part of science – that is, the norms that tell us how things *ought to be* – and left us only with an understanding of how things *are*. Furthermore, I stated that our civilisation depended upon such norms and that, whether we looked at our Hebrew or Greek heritage, respectively represented by the prophet and the philosopher, such norms were regarded from the very beginning as given to us by God. When God was excluded from culture, these norms went out with him. The paper then goes on to sketch a systems philosophy – i.e. philosophy in the Erasmian sense – mainly based on the theory of modalities of Hermann Dooyeweerd, whose Alma Mater happened to be the Free University and where he also taught and was dean of its Faculty of Philosophy. This philosophy, which I termed *multi-modal systems thinking*[6], endeavoured to bring the diverse

---

under the skin. It would be more accurate to use the prefix *full* or *hyper* rather than *post*, but we will adhere to the commonly used terms in order to avoid introducing more sociological jargon.

[5] International Society for the Systems Sciences.

[6] By choosing this name, I did not intend to change the original focus given by von Bertalannfy's *General Systems Theory;* on the contrary, my intention was to stress that from its very origin, systems thinking was meant to be multimodal; see von Bertalanffy (1971, p. 48).

disciplines into a systemic totality and, at the same time, to connect this collective group of disciplines to the natural and cultural
world. Dooyeweerd had defined fifteen modalities, but my work in
information systems had led me to make a distinction between
knowledge and information, on the one hand, and knowledge and
logic on the other. Thus I added a sixteenth modality – epistemic –
dealing with knowledge. I also diverged from Dooyeweerd, who
classified the lower modalities as being determinative and the
higher modalities as normative. I took a different perspective to
the modalities and regarded them not as aspects that existed in the
world but aspects that emerged in our interaction with the world. I
adopted this perspective on the basis that I was seeking a science
that did not merely describe the world but which also told us how
to interact responsibly with it. I was already then, without realising
it, gradually changing from an epistemology based on logic to one
based on history, but some years had yet to pass to be able to ar-
ticulate in writing this historical way of thinking. The implementation of this philosophy, even at this embryonic stage, meant reor-
ganising almost every science and then the development of educational programmes to teach it, if we were to remain true to our objective of using teaching as the chief instrument of humane social
intervention, a mammoth task.

Given that we had to reorganise every department of knowledge, where should we start? Since finishing my undergraduate
studies I had regarded management as one of the most influential
professions in our times. Therefore I decided to direct my efforts
to its science and also sought academic posts within its scope. In
my quest to build a new science of management I was greatly
helped by the work of Stafford Beer in cybernetics and systems
science and particularly by his *Viable System Model*[7]. Thus, when
in 1992 I was appointed to a chair in informatics and systems science I aimed to give our department a managerial slant. In 1995
we were already busy at our university in Luleå developing an undergraduate programme which opened its doors in 1996 and to
celebrate the occasion, we hosted an international conference of
the Swedish Operational Research Society, of which I was presid-

---

[7] (1994a; 1995).

ent. Among our invited speakers was Stafford Beer himself[8] who, despite having suffered a recent stroke, made a great effort to travel and join us in Luleå. He had recently turned 70 years old, therefore we made the occasion also a celebration of his birthday and published a special issue of Systems Practice in his honour[9]. In my presidential address – the second paper, *Humane Operational Research* – I integrated Beer's model into a multi-modal framework endeavouring to reverse the managerial dominance upon work, exercised both in capitalist as well as socialist societies. I added an extra modality – operational – representing *work* and based on Beer's operational system. I argued, using the understanding of management in living systems that Beer had elucidated for us, in addition to Dooyeweerd's idea of sovereignty that humans should be allowed to exercise control over the work they perform, that management should be subservient to work, and not the other way around. This was rather a subversive idea, one I bluntly defended as the way that God had arranged matters for humanity and on the biblical teaching that, in a contemporary context – would place him on the side of the workers rather than their managers. As I expected, attempts to apply it in my own university brought me a good deal of trouble from the bureaucracy.

But this trouble was still in the future and at that time we were busy introducing our informatics and systems science programme to our first batch of students. To leave a record of this experience I wrote an account – the third paper, *Design of an Undergraduate Programme* – explaining its principles. Reflecting on the argument in the prior paper, that management be subservient to work, I introduced a change in the modalities by placing the operational above the economic, thus regarding the former as more normative than the latter. Since the science the student would learn was normative, this was a programme that not only sought to educate the mind of the student but also his heart. By heart I do not mean just emotions, although these are not excluded, but the seat of their conviction and vision for life. In addition to circulating this

---

[8] The other guest speakers were John van Gigch and Robert Flood. Sadly, both Stafford and John have passed away.
[9] de Raadt, J. D. R. (1997e).

paper to systems colleagues, an opportunity arose to present it at the WACRA conference in Madrid in 1997. It aroused considerable interest both at the conference and among fellow systems colleagues, and I was invited to present it at two other conferences in Neuchatel, Switzerland and Cortona, Italy[10].

Addressing education of the heart proved far less difficult than I had expected and I was aided in this by a shift of mind and spirit in Sweden. Having been the most secular country in the world and enjoying, at the same time, an almost utopian "cradle to the grave" welfare system, the 1990's brought to Swedes both an economic and cultural shock that led to a re-examination of its welfare mentality and, especially among the young people, a gradual rejection of it. To cite an example, this change materialised in Sweden joining the European Union and its educational system recognising the pivotal role that Christianity had historically played in shaping what was authentically Swedish culture, allowing us to bring to the classroom ethical and social conceptions of Christianity with almost no prejudicial resistance. However, we faced a different problem; a peculiar combination of subjectivism on the one hand with utilitarian positivism on the other. This combination gave people the impression that they could be ethical and yet do as they pleased. In reality, their pleasure was dictated - through psychological manipulation – by the capitalists, who were serving their own interests.

Within the systems movement, subjectivism found its home in Soft Systems Methodology, something which I regard neither as systemic nor methodological. Beginning with its introduction in the early 1980's, this approach rapidly spread and by the 1990's it had gained the widest acceptance within systems research and its applications. Regretfully, my predecessor in Luleå was a supporter of this approach and the research students I inherited from him were already deeply immersed in its ideas.

---

[10] This paper was first presented and published in the proceedings of the 14th International Conference of WACRA EUROPE, Universidad Complutense de Madrid, 1997. It was again presented by invitation at the 5th Ecole Européene de Systémique, Université de Neuchâtel, 1998 and, also by invitation, at the 1999 Cortona Week Seminary in Italy organised by the Swiss Federal Institute of Technology, Zurich.

To introduce multi-modal systems thinking in the face of a much more popular approach among systems researchers and practitioners – it had by this time become almost synonymous with systems thinking – was not an easy task. Thus, I went back into the history of thought to seek the roots of secular thinking and expose how it clouded, or made "soft", convictions that were essential for us to live in a humane manner. My findings are summarised in the fourth paper – *Vision and Normative Science*. The paper starts with Augustine's link between faith and thought and traces the split of this systemic link to medieval scholasticism. Although faith and thought were once more brought together during the Renaissance and Reformation, their connection was again severed by the rise of modernism. Modernism thrust God away from scientific methodology and with God's exit, out went normative thought and our ability to think seriously about how we ought to live. And regaining our knowledge of how to live became my chief systemic aim: to lay the foundations of a normative science which I could teach to my students (and myself) to live well; that is, live a responsible and ethical life dedicated to serving others in their chosen profession.

These thoughts must have had some impact beyond my classroom, for the then president of the International Society for the Systems Sciences, the late G. A. Swanson, asked me to deliver an address on a global system of ethics at the 1998 annual conference of the society in Atlanta. While I liked the theme of ethics, the word g*lobal* did not appeal to me; it strongly reflected the infatuation with globalisation that spread throughout the 1990's and the idea that we all lived in a global village. Thus I argued – in the fifth paper, *Ethics for a Civilised Life* – that the capitalistic motives behind globalisation were fundamentally unethical, for they aimed to bring producers in the poor countries closer to the consumers in the rich ones which benefited the rich rather than the poor, despite the arguments of the "trickle-down" economists. Furthermore, systemic principles showed that globalisation was hard to stabilise and thus unviable in the long term. I proposed that the place to inject ethics in society was at its base, that is, in marriage[11] and the family, from where it could spread in a recursive manner over all other units of society. I also rejected the conventional concept of ethics as representing mere justice which, while being in itself good and necessary, was insufficient to make our societies viable. More was needed and this was supplied by the Christian concept of ethics, an ethic based on a special notion of love (*agape*) that required us to go beyond justice to act for the benefit of our fellow men without expectation of recompense. I argued that such an ethic was indispensable in viable social systems.

However, I also realised that talking about ethics was useless unless it was applied. It required developing a method to implement it, for my aim was not only to teach students how to think ethically, but also to equip them with professional competence to analyse social systems from a normative point of view and identify the threats to their viability. The sixth paper – *Qualitative Operational Research* – describes my first efforts to produce a qualitative modelling approach for multi-modal systems using a variety of data, both empirical and non-empirical. The paper also describes the original version of a computer package I especially designed to model the interaction between social systems. Later on, I was able to enhance this package – which I called *SmCube*[12] – with the help of funding provided by the Swedish Defence Forces.

The first application of this method and SmCube was carried out by my wife Veronica, who by this time had joined me in developing our undergraduate programme and in teaching qualitative methods. We had been approached for help by one of the leaders of Rosvik, a nearby village. The local municipality had plans to eliminate the last grade of the village's local primary school in an effort to centralise education and reduce costs. This was a challenge to a long-held belief in most Swedish villages that it is best

---

[11] By marriage I mean the union of one man and one woman as defined by Christianity and most cultures, except for some sectors of Western modernity. However apart from these cultural considerations, from a systemic point of view, this ethic needs the complement of masculine and feminine qualities bonded in marital love to be socially effective.

[12] I published a manual for the original version of SmCube; de Raadt, J. D. R. (2001).

for children be educated in their own villages for as long as it is pedagogically beneficial for them. In the seventh paper – *Normative Factors and Viable Community* – Veronica proposed to Rosvik's leaders a systemic perspective which would shift viewing the school problem as a single issue and would focus on the long-term viability of the village community as a whole. This idea was welcomed by the village leadership and started an association between Rosvik and us that lasted until our departure from northern Sweden. The village became a case study for our students to apply the skills they had learned in class and we arranged field visits with overnight stays to collect data and organise panel discussions with different members of the community. The real-life engagement with a village helped us shift our students' eyes from industry, commerce and government as the normal sphere of application of the skills they were learning, to people living in vulnerable small communities. Rosvik confronted them with the problems of humanity rather than with how to make money.

Our involvement with the undergraduate programme eventually came to an end[13], but we continued our pedagogical mission by extending and improving our research methods and producing publications that could be used in the classroom at a later time. In this endeavour, we benefited immensely by engaging as scientific advisers to several community projects funded by the European Social Fund. These gave us real-life situations to test our ideas. The projects were chiefly aimed at unemployment and population loss in marginalised[14] areas and, as is usual for projects of this kind, their perspective was limited to the economic realm. Bureaucrats in Brussels had devised their own methods to establish the success of these projects based on a very mechanical view of economics and society. Moreover, we found that most of the funding provided did not benefit the people, but was absorbed into the administrative machinery of local governments and the ring of consultants – most of them ex-government employees – who made

---

[13] For an account of the development of this programme, see de Raadt, J. D. R. (2013).

[14] Population loss was not limited to remote rural regions, but included places much closer to metropolitan areas such as Groningen in Holland and the city of Berlin itself.

their living out of these projects. They had refined the language and method of reporting the outcomes in such a manner that they always conveyed an impression of success to Brussels. As expected, this language was not limited to the people working in projects but pervaded the whole bureaucratic system, therefore deceit was either never detected or, more likely, perceived but not exposed. In my discussions, I realised that these people were not necessarily villains, but that the cut-throat environment of neoliberalism[15] had created such a desperate situation, that even decent people now believed in the creed of "every man for himself". And in this they were helped by the lax tolerance of post-modernism that preaches that what is a lie to one person may be the truth to another.

We tried to explain to project leaders the long-term outcomes to communities if their true – truth, that is, of a non-subjective kind – predicament was ignored. We also showed them that this predicament was not inevitable if one took a systemic long-term view. Our eighth paper – *Evaluation of Community Projects* – was written while being involved in a project that comprised communities from six European countries exchanging "best-practices"[16]. We selected two of the communities, one in Provence, in the south of France and the other Norrbotten, in the north of Sweden. Both communities were becoming unviable and we chose the one in Provence to explain this lack of viability in systemic terms. We introduced the concept of positive feedback and, because the common usage of the expression conveys the wrong idea[17], we coined the term *black loop*, to represent a positive feedback leading a community to multi-modal decline, that is, eventual social, moral, economic and cultural demise. The Provence com-

---

[15] Two important apostles of neo-liberalism are Friedman (1970) and Hayek (2004).

[16] This was yet another favourite term among bureaucrats, where the word *best* proved through closer inspection to be highly inaccurate; most of the practices that were referred to as such were not the best. They were not better, not even good.

[17] Although the term *positive feedback* is commonly used to describe a favourable response, technically this type of feedback may, and often is, not at all favourable to the system that experiences it.

munity provided an illustration of a black loop. On the other hand, we selected a Swedish project with a positive feedback that could pull the community out of its predicament and contribute to its long term viability. Once more, for the purpose of conceptual clarity we labelled such feedback a *white loop*. Both loops connected a set of factors which in one case led the community to an unviable situation while in the other, the loop pulled it out of such a state. We then defined a good practice as one that embodied a white loop. The French members of the project team responded rather critically to our report branding some its statements as "dangerous and unacceptable". Their criticism may be classified in two categories. The first referred to our interpretation of the data we collected but their objections were trivial[18] and perhaps resentful of us disclosing flaws in their local government. The second objection was the inclusion of belief in our model. In the written critique we were bluntly told that "France is a laic [sic] state" and by this they expected that any reference to beliefs as an integral part of the factors that comprised the black loop should be removed. Since we had established empirically that belief played an important influence – especially in ethics, its removal would have rendered our model useless. However, I do not think that these would have greatly concerned our critics as long as their municipality looked good. Moreover, French politicians and bureaucrats strongly desire to neutralise Christianity as an influence in Europe – it is a heritage from the French Revolution. At this time, the issue had come to the forefront through the drafting of a European constitution. France was against Christianity being even acknowledged as an influence in shaping Europe's history, while naturally the Pope, with Poland and Ireland supporting him, was for it. We perceived that this attempt to exclude Christianity – even from Europe's history – was a perfect instance of post-modern license to rewrite history according to its own vested interests.

---

[18] The chief problem behind their objection was their lack of knowledge of social science, history, ethics and other relevant disciplines combined with an attitude – at least on the part of the French team members – that such knowledge was irrelevant to the analysis of the data we had collected.

Yet, the facts of history combined with Christianity appeared as a primal factor in the long term viability of the communities we were studying. In the ninth paper – *Where there is No Vision the People Perish* – we turned to another community participating in the project – Mürztal in south-east Austria – to prove the point and show what happens "where there is no vision". Our first task was to clarify what we understood as the essentials of Christianity. We provided a succinct statement of these essentials extracted from the records of the Old and New Testaments through applying a systems methodology rather than a theological one and by ignoring denominational traditions that have crept into the various conceptions of Christianity. We incorporated these essential ideas of Christianity into our model as the factor we termed *vision* and showed that, as the community shifted away from this vision – even if it had been imperfectly held in the past – and adopted a secular word-view instead, fear took its place. In turn, fear thrust people onto a utilitarian ethic that was gradually fragmenting the family and other social groups. It had also eroded educational institutions as well as undermined the motivation for work.

By this time our research had made it clear the social projects we had been involved with so far were unable to go beyond alleviating some of the immediate hardships in the communities and even this capability to alleviate was questionable. Our research confirmed the conviction that education was the only legitimate means of social change, but we also understood that the results of education could only be harvested in the long-term – long-term meaning at least one generation. When we discussed this with one of our colleagues in Austria, he pointed out that the long-term was not acceptable, neither to the local politicians nor to the municipal bureaucracy. The viability of their own positions required showing short-term results in any project intervention. This pressure to show results dictated by a time-table impossible to attain explains, at least in part, the political and bureaucratic language of deception that pervades the people who manage our societies.

Mürztal, our last community project in Europe, was followed shortly by our move to Australia. We took with us our ideas of education and a hope that the Australian church would be responsive to the desperate need of post-modern society and step in to fill the vacuum left by contemporary universities that had capitulated and become vassals of industry and capitalism. But the situation in Australia turned out to be worse and the degree of subservience to neo-liberalism we came across exceeded the European level both in the universities[19] and in the church itself. Yet we persevered and formed an independent centre for community development[20] to offer a master's programme and were eventually able to negotiate an accredited award for our students through a Sydney college. To show to community leaders in Melbourne – both church and secular – how the programme responded to threats to the city's viability, we replicated our European studies by collecting data in Melbourne and applying our model to it. The details of this study are documented in our tenth paper – *Arresting the Collapse of the City*. In Europe, our research was conducted in small communities; Melbourne on the other hand, was a large city (of more than four million inhabitants) and our findings were far more alarming than the predicament of small European towns and villages. This is why the paper's title alludes to the "collapse of a city". In the second part of the paper we presented the master's programme and the systemic principles behind its design as a response to avert this collapse.

One aim of this educational programme was to provide a diversity of professionals with a common systemic language and framework across which they could communicate and collaborate with the common objective of building up their communities. As this endeavour is strongly social and Veronica is a social worker, we also developed a seminar to be presented over one or two-days and accredited it with the Australian Association of Social Workers continuing professional education programme. We ran various seminars and were invited to speak at a plenary session of the biennial conference of the Queensland branch of the association. In it we described our systems methodology and method and how it could be applied to social work. These ideas were incorporated

---

[19] An illustration of this concerning the University of Melbourne is documented by Cain and Hewitt (2004).
[20] Melbourne Centre for Community Development.

into the eleventh paper – *Social Work and Community* – which endeavours to expand the horizon of social work beyond dealing with the immediate needs of people. Undoubtedly, these needs must be met, but this does not address the preventive measures that must be put to work in order to stop other people – especially children and youth – falling into the same predicament. These measures require us to move upstream and work for longer-term objectives that involve a variety of community aspects. The paper suggests how an educational programme for social workers with a systemic perspective could equip them to broaden the horizon of their profession.

While actively engaged in our work in Australia, other developments were taking place in Brazil in which we were also to contribute, even if more modestly. In 2005, the Brazilian chapter of the International Society for the Systems Sciences organised, under the leadership of Dante Pinheiro Martinelli, its first systems congress and I was invited to deliver its closing address and to speak about ethics. In this address – presented in the twelfth paper, *Samaritan Ethics* – I began by differentiating between ethics and justice and argued that what is commonly understood by ethics is not ethics, but justice. Ethics demands from us to go beyond our juridical duties and offer service to others without expecting reciprocation; therefore I referred to this as "Samaritan ethics", for this was precisely the point that Jesus thought to explain in his parable[21]. Furthermore, I stated that the utilitarian ethic that drove our economies has gradually spread into every aspect of society and culture and that personal life was fundamentally unethical. Finally, I argued that from a systems point of view a community can only be viable when the number of its members who are prepared to practise the Samaritan ethic is proportionate to the number who behave unjustly. I sought support for this in Ashby's law[22], thus we may also call Samaritan ethics *the law of requisite ethics*.

Despite the importance of such an ethic for the long term viability of communities, modern thought, including systems thought, has been reluctant to understand, let alone, embrace it. This in-

---

[21] Luke 10:10-37.
[22] Ashby (1976).

cludes the father of general systems theory, Ludwig von Bertalanffy himself, who regarded it as impractical. A reason for this is that modernism has denied ethics and the rest of the humanities their rightful place among the sciences. It has isolated the natural sciences from the humanities and established "physical reason"[23] as the only standard for scientific thought. By doing this, it has denied us the possibility of a civilised science – a science to serve humanity – for, without the humanities, science is unable to know neither what is civilised nor what is uniquely human. This has afflicted systems science as much as other approaches. Soft systems thinking formally classifies that part of reality that is studied by the humanities as "soft" or "fuzzy". It looks at these things through an engineer's eye without realising that what it regards as soft or fuzzy is not reality but is its own way of thinking about that reality.

When the humanist sees human suffering and poverty, he does not see a fuzzy reality but a very hard one; exactly the opposite to soft systems thinking. This was the message of the opening address I delivered at the 2010 Brazilian systems congress in Iguazu and that is documented in the last paper – *Christian Social Humanism*. I began with a summary of the hard crisis in diverse communities that Veronica and I have come across in our empirical research in various countries. To respond to this crisis, I urged my colleagues to abandon physical – as well as soft systems - reasoning and to embrace historical reason as a more appropriate systemic approach. I pointed out that historical reason is not new but played a major role in the rediscovery of the humanities during the Renaissance, especially in shaping a Christian humanism that led to the unprecedented social and cultural reform of northern Europe. Since this was attained through teaching people to think in a new way, I concluded my address by encouraging my Latin-American colleagues to take the lead and develop an appropriate way of thinking for our times and set up educational programmes to teach it to the young.

For, what we have learned through our experience and from history – and by thinking historically – is that the most effective

---

[23] Ortega y Gasset (1924).

and most humane tool of social change is education. And the social change we have aimed for is not merely the disjointed correction of diverse social problems in a community, but the full realisation of a vision of a civilised people such as the one that Vermeer painted for us in his *Gezicht op Delft*. One can only attain this by equipping the next generation to reach civility for themselves and other people through their work of service to their fellow men. For a civilised character is not built by mere contemplation, reflection and retirement from everyday life, but mostly through hard work in our chosen vocation out there in the world. Therefore, we leave this collection of papers as a record of our endeavour and of what we learned on the way, with the hope that our students, and especially our South American colleagues, may improve and further develop these ideas. May they also in turn teach them to others so that, as a new vision and a new way of thinking gradually spreads throughout their communities, they may have the satisfaction of seeing part of the vision realised in their own lives.

1 The Prophet and the Philosopher

J. D. R. de Raadt

Introduction

In ancient times the prophet and the philosopher not only re-flected and taught, but also reproved. I would like to argue that, due to our time having a resemblance to theirs, it is also our duty to add to our reflection and teaching, reproof. But, before we tackle reproof, we must be able to analyse and identify what must be reproved. Thus, I will commence by setting up a framework that will relate science to civilisation and history. This will be fol-lowed by a reflection of the times in which we live. From there we shall move on to examine what kind of reproof our generation needs and conclude by sketching, in response, how our social in-stitutions can be reformed.

Figure 1-1: Multi-Modal Systems Framework

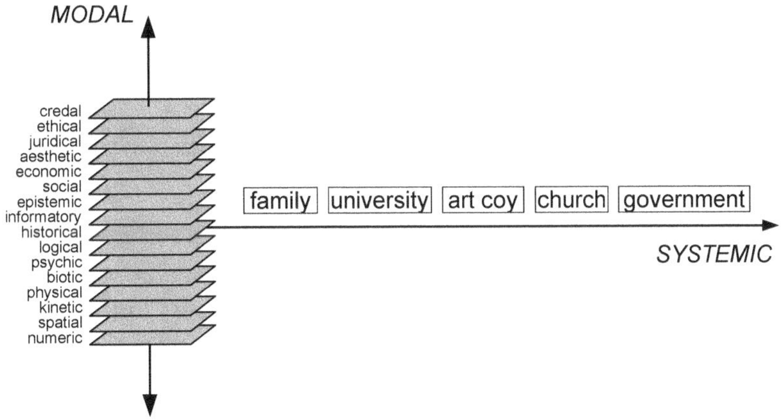

Our framework, shown in Figure 1-1, is a broad multi-modal systems map on which we place the matters that concern us in re-lation to each other and along two dimensions. The first dimension – the horizontal axis – represents the different human and natural systems and their mutual interaction. Our diagram depicts just a few of these: the family, the university, the state, the ballet company and the religious institution. My impression is that the systems research emphasis today lies mostly in this dimension and that we have somewhat neglected the second dimension – in the vertical axis – reflecting the different levels of order – or modalities – in which our lives unfold. We have borrowed much of our theory of these modalities from Herman Dooyeweerd[1]; he was a philosopher and professor of law at this university[2] and dedicated much of his efforts to study the interrelationship of the different modalities as expressions of the order ruling the universe.

In researching the modal orders in this vertical dimension, I think we also follow von Bertalanffy's[3] view of order as a multi-layered affair, or as he describes it, as a Neapolitan ice-cream with many layers: ice-cream, cream, fruits, vanilla and so on. Each one of these, according to him, reflects a unique level of order in the universe which cannot be reduced to other orders. One cannot, for example, reduce biological phenomena to physical, or social phenomena to psychological. Dooyeweerd also argues, very effectively, for the uniqueness of all these modal orders. The fifteen modalities he proposed plus a sixteenth which I have added (the epistemic modality) are: numeric, spatial, kinetic, physical, biotic, psychic, logical, historic, informatory, epistemic, social, economic, aesthetic, juridical, ethical and credal.

While Dooyeweerd insists that each modality is unique, he also recognises that each modality is not isolated and is not completely different to the others. On the contrary, all modalities are found closely inter-linked and there are strong analogies between one and the other. These analogies find their counterpart in the general systems idea of mapping or homomorphism. They are the channel through which we may work towards von Bertalanffy's hope of developing a general theory that, while recognising the multi-layered nature of order – and thus the need for specialised disciplines – provides a scientific language bridging one discipline with the other and allowing for the transferral of knowledge and the arrest of the scientific fragmentation which we experience today. The

---

[1] (1958, 1975).
[2] Free University, Amsterdam.
[3] (1971).

modalities and their homomorphisms are also useful in understanding the hierarchical arrangement and interaction of a variety of systems as has been proposed by scholars such as Miller[4] and Boulding[5].

Determinative and Normative Order

Dooyeweerd distinguishes between two types of orders in the modalities – one determinative and the other normative – and accordingly proceeds to divide the modalities into two groups. The determinative group includes the four lower modalities, from the numerical to the psychic, while the normative group comprises all others. I have taken a slightly different view from Dooyeweerd's definition of normative order. I regard as normative that type of order that directly addresses human responsibility. It is the ought that sketches for us the pattern of human virtue and nobility and the course and destiny of a civilised and cultured life. In brief, it is the vision of goodness in all its splendour.

The normative order in my view spreads through all the modalities – including the lower four – with a varying degree of intensity: stronger in the higher level and weaker in the lower levels, so that the ethical and juridical modalities are more normative than the physical and the numerical. This is shown in Figure 1-2, where the shaded and blank areas respectively represent the determinative and normative order. I think it important that we should acknowledge our normative *ought* in the natural modalities as well, especially as it concerns the environment. It is important because, from a world view that regards nature as accessible to every unbridled exploitation, we have swung to the opposite extreme that venerates nature and regards mankind as a curse upon it. Undoubtedly, and especially so in modern times, wherever we have put our foot we have produced disaster. Yet nature needs our care and this is reflected in the normative area that occupies each of the modal levels. A volcano's eruption can bring us much destruction and pollution as can modern industry. There are species that are

---

[4] (1978).
[5] (1956a).

either becoming or have become extinct without any human intervention, so that it is as much our duty to protect nature from man's
undue exploitation as from its own self-inflicted calamities. It is
this thought that has led me to deviate from Dooyeweerd's idea of
normative order.

Science and Method

It should be noted that in the classical period, that is, prior to
the Enlightenment, the foundation and the final aim of science is
normative. The ultimate concern of almost every classical thinker
is: what is man? The query is directed more to the normative than
the determinative side of our being, that is: what is a good man
and what is a good woman? This question motivates thinkers to
look not only at themselves, but also at the universe that surrounds
them, including plants, rocks, numbers and everything else that
crosses their paths. For them the answer is embedded in every
nook and cranny of this universe.

Figure 1-2: Normative and Determinative Orders

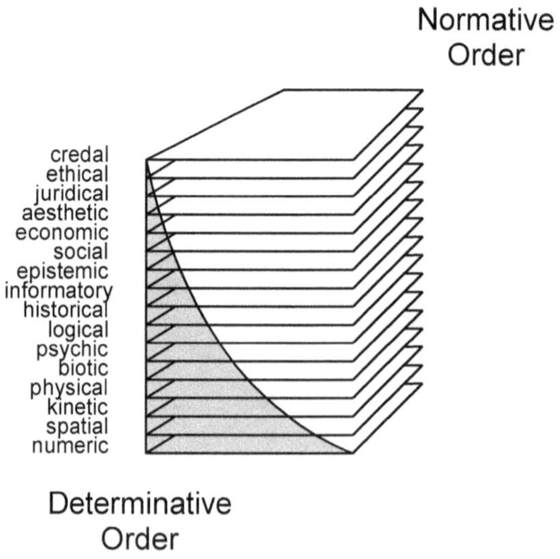

Normative
Order

credal
ethical
juridical
aesthetic
economic
social
epistemic
informatory
historical
logical
psychic
biotic
physical
kinetic
spatial
numeric

Determinative
Order

This leads us to epistemology: how can we know the answer to these questions? Here, we may find another useful application of the modalities, and yet again, I have departed from Dooyeweerd's sharp differentiation between theoretical and pre-theoretical knowledge – the latter meaning common sense experience. Dooyeweerd restricted theoretical knowledge to the logical modality. Undoubtedly theory is heavily indebted to logic, but it also uses mathematics and many other modalities. For example, all scientists know how important language is to science. Even in a strictly empirical study, those who write down its results realise that their understanding of these is polished and sometimes completely reorganised while writing down the findings, based not on tools of empirical analysis, but on rules of linguistics and rhetoric. If properly utilised, the order in these rules enhances and even modifies the theory that they are developing. Other modalities – such as aesthetic and spatial – can play a similar role.

The ability of science to employ not only logic, but other modalities as well, is due to the homomorphisms between modalities to which I referred earlier and which allow us to translate the order of one modality into the other. Let us consider a simple example and assume that we have decided to open a coffee shop in Amsterdam and that we need to settle the price we will charge for each cup. We hire an economist who introduces us to the demand function expressed as a mathematical equation. We shall use a very simple equation in this illustration. What the economist does is to abstract a small fragment of economic order – the source of our analysis – and to translate it into an equation that resides in the numerical modality. This modality becomes the idiom of our analysis (see Figure 1-3):

$$D = a - b\,P$$
where:
  P = price per cup of coffee
  D = number of cups sold
  a and b are constants

Due to the homomorphism between the economic and numeric modalities, much of the behaviour of the equation makes economic sense, but we must be on our guard, for this only occurs within the domain of the homomorphism. Beyond this, the equation suggests some absurd patterns of economic behaviour such that, above a certain price, we obtain a negative sale of coffee cups. The reason for this absurdity is that the equation does not obey economic laws but numeric laws.

Furthermore, observe that the economic modality is much more normative than the numeric. Neglecting the normative order may have even more serious consequences, for this equation does not address the quality of the coffee or the relationship between its true value and its price. Coffee is cheap in Holland and other rich countries because some poor people in Colombia or Brazil are working in the plantations for a mere subsistence level salary. Should they enjoy a decent standard of living, coffee would per-haps cost double or more, but unfavourable exchange rates reflect-ing the weakness of their economy leaves them in a disadvantaged position. If we wish to have a proper economic analysis, these as-pects should also be included by adding other modalities as idioms.

Figure 1-3 also shows that the processes of developing models is itself ordered by two modalities. The translation from one mod-ality to the other, that is from source to idiom, is regulated by the informatory modality which deals with the conversion of order into symbolic meaning. The manipulation and interpretation of symbols according to the rules of a given idiom are regulated by the epistemic modality. Out of this modality emerges the various scientific methodologies that include not only quantitative methods but also qualitative methods encompassing historical, aesthetic, theological and other types of analyses. It is this epistemic modal-ity and not the logical modality that provides us with the laws of knowledge, whether theoretical or pre-theoretical. The logical modality provides only one idiom which may be used, among many, to express knowledge.

Figure 1-3: Modalities as Idioms

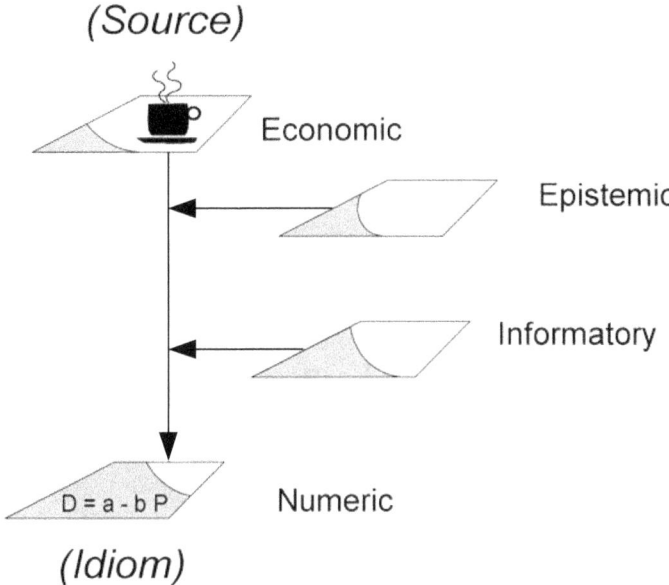

Within the epistemic modality we can establish different degrees of methodological rigour in our understanding, depending on the circumstances and purpose of our knowing, from the more scientific and strongly methodologically-based to the one which is much more loose and informal. We are thus provided with an epistemological continuum within which Dooyeweerd's categories – i.e. theoretical and pre-theoretical – are only the extreme poles. This has important implications for education. Given that the starting point of university education should be to teach students how to think, then we must ensure that the epistemological foundation of this teaching presents students not only with logic as an idiom of understanding, but with every other modality as well. Only upon such a foundation as this can one introduce them to a rich and cultured science.

Post-Modernism and Decadence

From the informatory and epistemic modalities we now move to the historical modality and review some significant events that have taken place in our intellectual life. As systems scientists we are well acquainted with the mechanistic world view that emerged during the Enlightenment and which dominated the modern period of our history. We have been deeply concerned with the fragmentation that this brought to science, but we have not paid as much attention to the brutal treatment that the normative type of order suffered at the hand of modernists such as de la Mettrie[6], who reduced it to a product of pure glandular secretions, or Comte[7], who considered it so obscure that it was not worthy to be included in the domain of science any longer. As a result, we have been left with a modern image of science that is purely determinative and strongly circumscribed by the laboratory, computers and mathematical equations. Few today think of it as dealing with norms and the ultimate questions of life.

The rejection of the normative order from the realm of science – see Figure 1-4 – leaves us with a massive intellectual void. Modern science becomes like intellectual athletics; the athlete runs for the sake of running but not for the sake of getting anywhere in particular. Modern science has no sense of direction, it offers no rigour to leads in a search for culture, nobility and virtue; on these matters it is utterly barren. No wonder that following the Enlightenment, people ignored science in their private lives and went on very much as in the past: they continued to go to church and to harbour respect for the family, the state and old values. Yet in organised life, such as in industry and in the university, a new utilitarian ethic dominated. Here, questions of norms were resolved by the arithmetical difference between pain and pleasure. Thus there emerged a society with a split personality. A relatively humane and wholesome personal world on one hand co-existed with a strictly mechanistic and utilitarian business world on the other. When one stepped from the personal to the business world, it was not only the pattern of life that changed, but all the surrounding articles

---

[6] (2009).
[7] (1896).

such as clothing, furniture and buildings assumed a mechanical mien.

Figure 1-4: Demise of the Normative Order

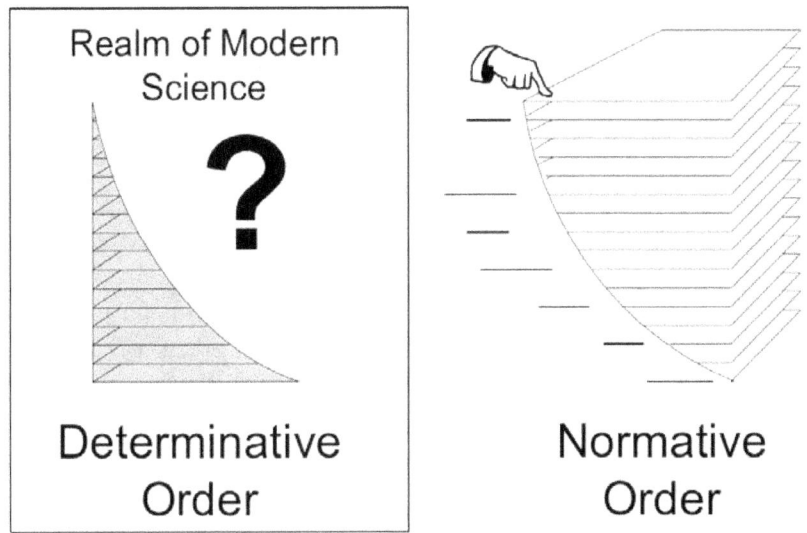

However, the space occupied by these two worlds has not remained undisputed, for the business world has progressively encroached on the personal world, though at first it was partly contained by the old norms that still survived in the community. Yet a new era, post-modernity, that was ushered in – according to some sociologists – around the 1960's burst the dam that contained the business world and inundated almost every social system with the mechanistic and utilitarian creed. Sectors of human activity that had so far been out of the reach of industry have now been incorporated into a whole new string of industries that have assimilated such things as sports, arts and now health. We speak now of the sports-industry, the arts-industry and the health-industry.

Two other industries have emerged that are of special concern: one is the state and the second is science. A strong doctrine has emerged that regards the state as a technical and economic unit that should function like a meta-industry. The major concern of modern government has become the management of the nation's economy. To this all other things – foreign relations, education and health – are made subject. The attention of voters is directed mainly to economic issues and it is according to economic success that they choose the winner. Parties from left to right have consequently distanced themselves from their original ideologies – whatever their merits – and replaced them with technological utilitarianism. As expected, most of them have become much like each other, offering to the voters a product as homogeneous as the transportation that different airlines offer their passengers.

In regard to science, there has been a subtle yet far-reaching restriction of its scope because it has been made subservient to industrial interests through the funding mechanism. A large part of research funding has been delegated to science with an industrial application; in other words, funding for the interests of industry. Industry with its utilitarian motives cares very little for science for its own sake. The funds made available are for research where the problems and questions have been already formulated, sometimes by people who are not scientists and who ignore that a large proportion of a scientist's task is asking the right question or identifying the proper problem. Thus the scientist who accepts this funding finds himself boxed into a pre-set framework of inquiry. This framework almost uniformly and uncritically assumes that technological development is good for humanity, especially when directed toward increasing industrial competitiveness. Under these circumstances, it is hard for the modern scientist to exercise and defend his professional freedom. Academic freedom is a normative question and science lost much of its normative skill when it succumbed to a mechanistic world view. Science has become yet another form of industry. We are reminded of this every time we see an advertisement for a professorial chair requesting "entrepreneurial competence" as a necessary qualification and for the new type of chairs in "Hotel Management" and "Meat Marketing" that have appeared.

All this has made industrialised societies extremely rich. The comforts that our post-modern generation takes for granted these days make the excesses and luxuries of aristocracies from the past look pale. Yet we share with these aristocracies two qualities.

Firstly, like them, we have rejected most normative obligations and supplanted them with the golden rule that we should do as we please. That is what most aristocrats did. Secondly, the privileges we enjoy today and which permit us to do as we please come from a technological system that we have inherited and which, given the state of our science, we cannot sustain indefinitely. According to Ortega y Gasset[8]:

> Technology is of the same essence and substance as science and science cannot exist if there is no interest for its purity and in its own self, and there cannot be such interest if people do not continue to show enthusiasm for the general principles of culture. If this enthusiasm declines – as it seems to be the case – technology can only survive for a time, as long as the inertia of the cultural impulse that created it lasts. One lives with technology but not of technology. (p. 106.)

Like the aristocrats, we risk to lose all because our normative ineptitude will eventually destroy our determinative competence. I have illustrated this in a graphic manner in Figure 1-5. The horizontal axis stands for time, the vertical axis for order. Along these axes are traced the normative and determinative progress – or regress – of civilisation, which in turn is represented by the surface, like an undulating floor-mat, that is formed by both orders. The graph shows that the normative order in society (the lower edge of the surface) changes through time in a sinusoidal pattern that oscillates along a steady level. That is, virtue at one time of history can be succeeded by depravity at another: it is possible for Caesar Augustus to be followed by Nero and a Roman patrician by a barbarian king.

By contrast, unless we regress so much as to utterly destroy our civilisation, a horse drawn chariot will not follow a motor car. That is, determinative knowledge and skill – the upper edge of the surface – grows unencumbered unless dragged down by moral decline. Therefore its pattern of growth – the upper edge of the surface – is also a sinusoidal pattern, but this time, oscillating around an ascending level. The combination of these two patterns gives us

---

[8] (2004b); author's translation.

a cultural surface which undulates with historical progress and the decline of virtue. Some may say, rather optimistically, that this graph shows the evolutionary path trodden by humanity on its way to ever greater achievements and which the unavoidable bumps on the road cannot stop. But there are disturbing signs in this graph which should dampen such optimism.

Figure 1-5: Civilisation Out of Balance

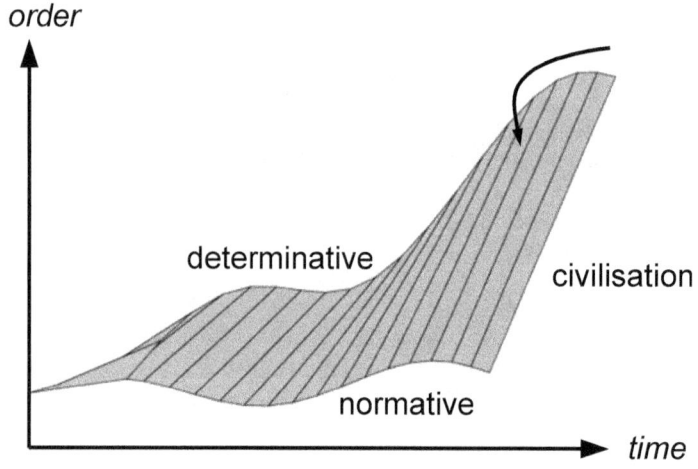

One of them is that the surface appears to be tipping over – in the direction of the curved arrow – due to the normative and determinative disparity in its structure. This disparity represents an excess of one good thing relative to another; it is a systemic instability in civilisation that may be likened to an aeroplane with poorly fitted flaps so that the lift of one of its wings is greater than the other. This has disastrous consequences: as the aeroplane accelerates down the runway, the difference of lift causes it to tip over and crash. Likewise, the disparity in human nature, reflected in an excess of our determinative science and its concomitant technological power – good things when administered in measured quantities – is not only a waste of time and resources but worse, it is a great human tragedy progressively unfolding before our eyes in the ugly shapes of pollution, unemployment, drug abuse, violence and lack of meaning that plagues our economically overdeveloped societies. Cultural decadence is, according to these, humanity tipping over because of its own excesses.

Furthermore, cybernetics[9] would tell us that the oscillations – or 'bumps' – of the system are yet another sign of instability caused by a time lag, that is, the time span between an event and the system becoming aware of that event being far too long. Cultural decadence is thus exacerbated: by the time we realise that decay has set in, it is too late to avoid it.

The Prophet and the Philosopher Revisited

The systemic time lag makes it imperative that we should speak up now, though the "tipping over" effect indicates that mere teaching will not do. One may teach primitive man but decadent man, although often making common cause with the primitive and like Rousseau praising the simplicity and spirituality of the "noble savage", is not primitive. Having been born and lived the first half of my life in a country inhabited by a large majority of primitive people and the second half in modern, western countries has convinced me of this. Primitive man is fecund soil; he has little, knows little and is naive, but he can learn much and stands to gain much. Decadent man is barren soil; he has much, knows much but is cynical; he rejects what he knows and stands to lose everything. Primitive man is humble; decadent man is destructively arrogant. Primitive man deserves to be taught; decadent man, to be rebuked.

Sadly, much of our science shares these characteristics: it does not correct, it panders. To learn how to correct this pattern we must travel into the past and meet thinkers, prophets and the philosophers, who lived when their nations were torn to pieces and who spoke out despite reprisal and persecution. In our journey we will meet Augustine, who lived through the heart-breaking experience of the sacking of his cherished Rome by Alaric the Goth in 410 AD and who as a result of this event wrote *The City of God* to counter the accusation that the blame for the fall of Rome was to be found in the abandonment of the pagan gods for Christianity. We will also meet Jeremiah who lived during the last days of Judah

---

[9] Beer (1995); de Raadt, J. D. R. (1991).

and who condemned the social oppression and immorality of his fellow citizens and witnessed the horrible destruction of Jerusalem at the hands of the Babylonians in 587 BC. There also stands Socrates and his courageous defence before the magistrates of Athens in 399 BC, also at a turbulent time in Athen's history. He was accused of teaching impiety when he was teaching normative science.

In their rebuke to fellow citizens, these men extolled virtue, understanding and faithfulness to God, all of them bound together, so that one could not posses one without possessing the others. Thus for Augustine, the fortunes of Rome were closely linked to her forsaking the pursuit of virtue. While surveying the beginning of the Roman Republic and its unfolding through time, he quotes Cato, the Roman tribune and Stoic:

> I do not think that it was by arms that our ancestors made the republic great from being small. But it was other things than this that made them great, and we have none of them: industry at home, just government without, a mind free in deliberation, addicted neither to crime nor to lust. Instead of this, we have luxury and avarice, poverty in the state, opulence among citizens; we laud riches, we follow laziness; there is no difference made between the good and the bad; all the rewards of virtue are got possession of by intrigue.[10]

For the prophets virtue was righteousness and in righteousness was embodied social justice. We have neglected to give due credit to the wisdom and insight of these men as it concerns social and economic justice, a topic about which they were far ahead of their time. Their sense of obligation to provide for the underprivileged, the poor, the orphan and the widow went far beyond that of their neighbours and it is from them that we derive most of the normative principles that have motivated modern social welfare. That famous advocate of social justice, the critical social theory of the Frankfurt school, owes much to the Jewish heritage of many of its scholars, and it has been argued that Karl Marx was strongly influenced by his Jewish background[11]. In many of the works of social critics and reformers one hears the echo of the prophet's words:

---

[10] St. Augustine (1988, I, v, 12).
[11] Tar (1985).

> Woe to him who builds his palace by
> > unrighteousness,
> > his upper room by injustice,
> making his countrymen work for
> > nothing,
> > not paying them for their labour.[12]

Virtue or righteousness, however, cannot be separated from man's intellect; virtue cannot inhabit an ignorant mind. On the contrary, it is ignorance that triggers disaster, for ignorant people are defenceless when manipulated and destroyed. It is lack of understanding, as the prophets say, that carries people into exile. This is sobering for scholars, for it impresses upon us the responsibility that we have to educate and enhance understanding.

Finally both to the philosopher and the prophet, the pursuit of virtue and understanding without devotion to God would have been monstrous. The Enlightenment's greatest mistake was its attempt at secularising – with a good measure of success – the intellect. Through my involvement in the systems science community, I have found that many of my colleagues – including some of the most illustrious scholars – harbour a very strong experience of God in their inner lives. It is a tragedy that we have to live within a scientific tradition that censors and excludes such experience from our intellectual life. One envies the freedom of past generations of philosophers, natural scientists and theologians who, up to the seventeenth century, knew nothing of the compartmentalisation of intellectual life.

Normative Order and Systems

The message of the philosopher and the prophet was not purely rebuke; in it was also a way out, a glimmer of hope. Thus it would be remiss to conclude without indicating, even briefly, how our civilisation and its social institutions should be reformed. As indicated earlier, once the normative side of order was eradicated from science, it was replaced by a utilitarianism which has dominated economics ever since. Gradually every social institution has

---

[12] Jeremiah 22:13.

yielded to the economics that turns every human endeavour into a business venture that asserts its ultimate aim in the terms of monetary utility. This obsession with utility and technology will, unless we change our course, drive our civilisation to a collapse such as is sketched in Figure 1-5.

To avoid this we must liberate our social institutions from utilitarianism and replace it with a normative mission – or "organisational vocation" – to serve humanity. Every social system has at least one modality that gives it its special quality. For a ballet company, for example, this is the aesthetic modality. It is here where the normative mission is encapsulated; the company's ultimate aim is to be a music and dance maker, for the people need music and dance to cheer them up, to inspire them and to allow them to express their feelings. This does not exclude the orchestra's financial obligations to balance its budget, to pay the musicians and dancers and to pay the interest on the capital that it has borrowed. Yet these obligations are distinct from its normative mission. We cannot say that the normative mission of the company is to pay interest.

Perhaps purely out of habit, most people today still accept this, that is, that ballet companies are not for monetary profit. Yet they would readily agree that making money is the mission of a record company. For they consider the latter a business despite it also being qualified by the aesthetic modality. In their eyes, when a social system is regarded as a business, its ultimate goal automatically becomes making money. Business is the utilitarian idea of a social system and, within this philosophy, there is no reason why we should not consider every human endeavour – including a ballet company – a business. As already mentioned, this is what post modernity is enthusiastically doing. My last diagram (Figure 1-6) shows the normative missions for the social systems originally shown in Figure 1-1. These systems are now placed around the modalities that give them their identities and their normative missions. In it, the religious institution finds its mission in the credal modality, the state in the juridical, the ballet company in the aesthetic, the university in the epistemic and the family in the ethical.

Figure 1-6: Normative Social Mission

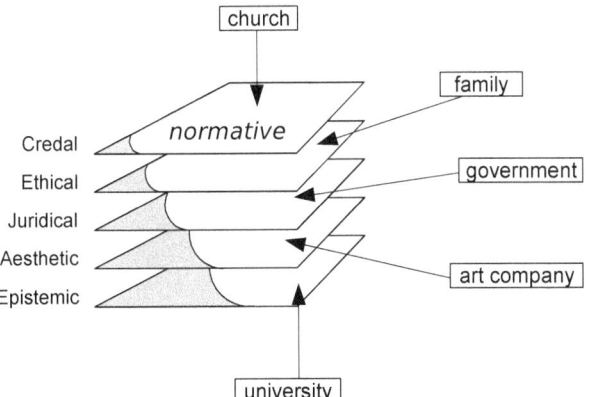

A theory of social systems management and design, different from the utilitarian theory of management and design, is needed to help us discover and unfold these missions. Multi-modal systems research is expressly aimed at developing such a theory. Out of deep concern for the predicament of our times and for the world we are passing onto our children, this research admits a standard of goodness outside itself and, like Socrates, strives to introduce it into our social institutions:

> Gentlemen, I am your very grateful and devoted servant, but I owe a greater obedience to God than to you; and so long as I draw breath and have my faculties, I shall never stop practising philosophy and exhorting you and indicating the truth for every-one that I meet... This, I do assure you, is what my God com-mands; and it is my belief that no greater good has ever befallen you in this city than my service to my God; for I spend all my time going about trying to persuade you, young and old, to make your first and chief concern not for your bodies or for your pos-sessions, but for the highest welfare of your souls, proclaiming as I go, "Wealth does not bring goodness, but goodness brings wealth and every other blessing, both to the individual and to the state".[13]

---

[13] Plato (1993, p. 53).

2 Humane Operational Research

J. D. R. de Raadt

Introduction

More than sixty years ago, the Spanish philosopher Jose Ortega y Gasset wrote:

> The common man, in encountering a world that is so technically and socially perfect, believes that this has been produced by nature. He ignores the giant effort of great individuals who have generated this world. He rejects the idea that all these facilities are dependent upon certain scarce virtues of people and that at the least failure of these, the magnificent edifice will rapidly vanish.[1]

Since then, the world has become even more technically and socially perfect, but we still do not seem to realise how immensely vulnerable it is, nor that the scarce virtues are now increasingly threatened with extinction. We have a desperate need to nurture these virtues and to channel them into the operation and management of our technological society.

How can operational research contribute to this endeavour? This is the aim of this paper and we shall do this with the help of a multi-modal systems framework that links three vital elements together: life, wisdom and management. The framework consists of two axes, see Figure 1-1 (in the previous paper). In the horizontal axis lie a string of interacting systems such as orchards, families, trades, art companies, schools, transport, courts and hospitals. Within such systems life – both biological and cultural – unfolds. Within them mankind realises its vocation and finds fulfilment.

Yet to understand these systems we must also refer to the vertical axis where we find layered a number of modalities that command all these systems: credal, ethical, juridical, aesthetic, economic, operational, social, epistemic, informatory, historical, logical, psychic, biotic, physical, kinetic, spatial and numeric[2]. Multi-modal systems thinking – as we have labelled this approach to sys-

---

[1] (1995, VI).
[2] Dooyeweerd (1958).

tems science – finds its foundation in Hebrew/Christian theism. It regards the universe as reflecting the personal character of God who has created it much as a composer devotedly composes a symphony and sustains and commands, much as a conductor directs the orchestra that performs it. While one may admire much of the work of the Greek philosophers, especially Plato, multi-modal systems thinking regards the impersonality they, especially Aristotle, ascribe to God and the order that rules the universe as impersonal. This has inevitably led to the secularisation of our modern hearts and minds and to a mechanistic and callous view of the world that regards man and nature as exploitable resources. (We already speak of men and women as human resources.) A secular mechanistic world-view also deprives us of the intellectual tools to gain control of our lives, for in the world of the machine, wisdom, love, vision and all other virtues have no place. Multi-modal systems thinking rejects all this. It believes that science – all science, including operational research – should begin by understanding virtue. But to understand virtue one must first know God and his understanding of the world.

This is the key to multi-modal systems epistemology, to imitate God's understanding. For in the Hebrew/Christian tradition God's wisdom and his command of the universe are united in his person so that one does not find the tension between epistemology and ontology present in Greek philosophy and its heirs. We understand not by some mechanical or impersonal matching of our reason to the order of the universe, wherever that may be found, but by searching God's thoughts and by imitating his understanding in the same manner that children imitate their parents while learning to speak and think. It is only here that we can find the virtues essential to human life. The impersonality of the Greek philosopher tragically led away from the very things they so passionately sought.

This wisdom and command of God, though being one, reflects nevertheless multiple aspects or modalities. This multiplicity is evinced in the variety of specialised sciences that we have. Yet, due to the scientific fragmentation that followed the Enlightenment, multi-modal systems thinking aims to stress the unity of these modalities – without denying their variety – and to provide a bridge for the integration of the sciences. Some modalities are more determinative and others more normative (see Figure 1-2). The normative side addresses our inner humanity, here we find our vocation for life. This vocation unfolds from the top of the modalities to the bottom; it starts with faith (credal modality) which spans man and God and provides the foundation of understanding. It continues with love (ethical) which gives energy to our understanding and transforms it into action.

Our age has dismissed love as impractical and even the founder of general systems theory, Ludwig von Bertalanffy had little regard for it when he wrote:

> Unfortunately, we do not live in a world where the maxim Love thy neighbour as thyself is practicable. Ours is a world governed by the struggle for existence.[3]

What von Bertalanffy seems to be saying is that we cannot live in this world in a humane way, but must submit to what the vernacular terms "the law of the jungle". I cannot but contrast this with what my mother taught me in my youth: the only hope for a civilised world rested on faith working through love. In those days we lived in the country near Viña del Mar (Chile) surrounded by poor people with inadequate health facilities. Seeing their need, my mother enrolled in the Red Cross Nursing School and after three years graduated as a Red Cross sister. She was especially concerned with the health of young mothers, so she furthered her training in obstetrics and became a matron. Like all other Red Cross staff, her work was done on a purely voluntary basis. In 1964 she told me about her dream: to build a little training clinic to teach young mothers basic hygiene, since much of the diseases that afflicted babies and young children could be prevented with more sanitary conditions at home. That same year she became pregnant and tragically contracted TB. She learned from her doctors that her life was at risk. She died a week later after my brother was born. With her also died the plan for the little clinic.

Are we to say that her love was impractical? If this were the conclusion of systems science or operational research, then we should discard them as having no place in civilised society. But this

---

[3] (1981, p. 24).

is not so; on the contrary, the right kind of systems science and operational research can greatly assist us in transferring such love into all human activities and help us to manage them and assure their viability. This is the task to which we now turn.

The Essence of a Modality

It is necessary for this, however, that we examine the modalities a little closer and describe a further element in them: their essence. The essence is the kernel or nucleus of a modality towards which the modality's order seems to be directed as the spokes of a wheel are thrust toward the hub (see Figure 2-1).

Figure 2-1: Modal Essence

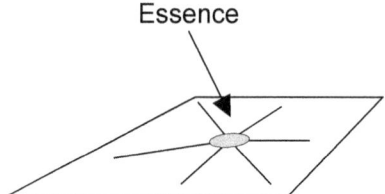

Table 2-1 lists the essence of each modality, for example, the essence of the informatory modality is symbolism. This means that all order that rules the modality has as its ultimate aim the encoding and transmission of information whether by mechanised or non-mechanised means. Like the modality itself, the essence is irreducible; one cannot reduce love (ethical) into justice (juridical) or vice-versa.

Although every social system is subject to the laws of every modality, there is at least one modality whose essential essence is endowed in the system and gives it its ultimate mission, character and uniqueness, distinguishing it from other types of systems. The family encounters this in the ethical modality, therefore the essence of the family is love; likewise for a hospital the essence is vitality, that is, the preservation of life found in the biotic modality. This essence is in turn the focus of a social system, that is, every activity in a hospital has as its ultimate mission the preservation of human life of patients. When a patient dies, there is nothing else for the hospital to do.

Table 2-1: Modal Essence

Modality	Essence
Credal	Faith
Ethical	Love
Juridical	Justice
Aesthetic	Beauty
Economic	Viability
Operational	Production
Social	Interaction
Epistemic	Wisdom
Informatory	Symbolism
Historical	Formative Power
Logical	Distinction
Psychic	Feeling
Biotic	Vitality
Physical	Energy
Kinetic	Motion
Spatial	Continuous Extension
Numeric	Discrete Quantity

Initially systems can have more than one essence in their mission, but as they develop, they become more complex and difficult to manage and therefore they split away from each other and form new social systems each with its own unique essence. For example, one may find encapsulated in the ancient tribal family such subsystems as industry – most likely agricultural – religious institution, court of justice and perhaps artistic enterprise. Yet with the passage of time each of these subsystems separates from the family and becomes an autonomous unit. Thus most social systems have only one essence. The order that rules the respective modality is the source of both authority and responsibility for the system. A system should therefore be free – except for some constraints that will be discussed shortly – to comply with these laws, for they prescribe the sphere of a system's duty as well as its rights. This sphere is thus termed the sphere of sovereignty and it is of crucial importance to today's society since an industrial totalitarianism both in private and public organisations is increasingly violating it, as we shall soon see.

The Operational System

We shall make use of Beer's Viable System Model[4] to examine the way that systems are structured. Every social system has an operational system which does the work of the system and this work is ruled by the operational modality. The essence provides the focus of this work. Let us illustrate an operation by making reference to a ballet company shown in Figure 2-2. Firstly, there is the operation itself: the ballerina's dance. This operation transforms an input into an output. The input is external to the operation, that is, it comes from the environment that surrounds the operation and which provides the ingredients to the operation: this could be the costumes and scenery for the dance – or their raw materials, if these are manufactured in-house – and the extra dancers hired to support a production. The output of this operation is both the work of art, such as a performance of Swan Lake, and also the participants in the operation itself, such as the artist. For every performance transforms the artist, hopefully into a better artist. This means that each performance ought to be an improvement over the prior one and at the same time a rehearsal of the next.

The essence of dancing is beauty residing in and governed by the aesthetic modality, therefore it is here that we find the sphere of sovereignty of the operation (S.O.S. in Figure 2-2).[5] It is in this

---

[4] (1994a; 1995).

[5] The sphere of sovereignty of a system would be the equivalent to Beer's notion of systemic autonomy found in his own theory of management and organisation.

modality that the people who perform the operation are bestowed with both authority and responsibility by their intimate understanding of the modality. That is, ballerinas are endowed with authority in their dance by their knowledge of dancing. This knowledge resides in the epistemic modality and is of two types: erudition and skill.

Figure 2-2: The Operational System

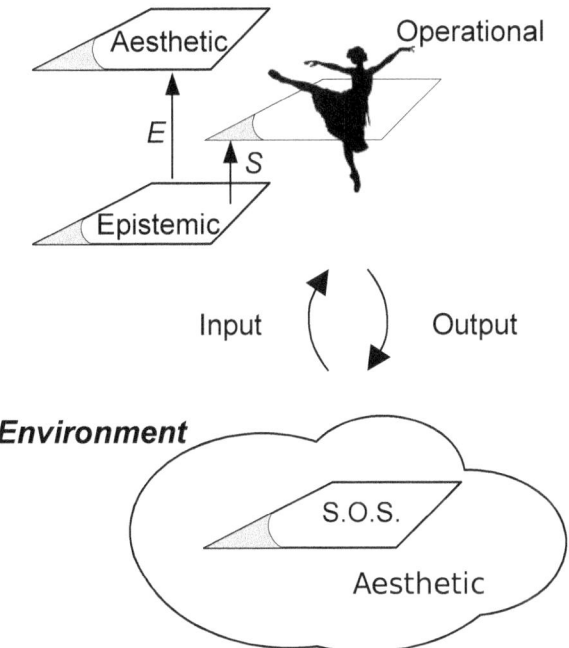

The ballerina's erudition (E in Figure 2-2) is her knowledge of aesthetics pertaining to dancing. But this is not sufficient; a person, such as a ballet critic may know almost everything there is to know about ballet, its history, choreography and lives of great dancers. Yet the critic may be utterly unable to dance at all; for this there needs to be added skill (S in Figure 2-2), such as the physical skill required to dance on the tip of one's toes. Skill or craft is primarily a knowledge that is applied in the operational modality (not to be confused with "operational system"); the Greek word for this is *techné* from which derives the modern word technology. We therefore refer to operational science as the science that studies the operational modality; it includes such things as scientific methodology, operational research, the engineering and technological sciences, crafts such as silversmithing and jewellery making, the trades and the arts. Operational science is therefore the science of engineers, craftsmen, carpenters, artists, surgeons and scientists.

Regretfully, under the influence of a mechanistic world view, the word technology has assumed in modern times a narrow meaning that implies only the mechanical tools that are used in an operation. From thence, the operation itself has been re-conceived as a mechanical process and the place of work as a factory, from which humanity has been progressively uprooted: "once the machine is in, man is out"[6].We have come to believe that machine skill is always better than human skill. Here we find the roots of modern unemployment in a world in which ironically there is so much work to do. This explains also the proliferation of material technology – or mechanistic technology – to produce things we do not need.

But this mechanistic world-view has meant not only the displacement of people by machines, but the mechanisation and consequent dehumanisation of the skill of those who have not yet been displaced. This is exemplified by advertisements for positions in information technology: employers are solely interested in the candidate's knowledge of machine and software, but seldom is there an interest in a scientific knowledge about information or the operational system where information must be supplied. Other professions, such as surgery, are also being mechanised so that the surgeon's skill is replaced by the skill to operate a computer which in turn operates on the patient.

Erudition and skill must also provide a vocation to serve our fellow man in the particular operation that we have selected for our lives. This flows out of the normative order of the modalities involved. In Figure 2-2, the normative order in the aesthetic modality provides inspiration, while the normative order of the operational modality generates a call to action, that is, to produce a

---

[6] Beer (1981, p. 15).

work of art. The combination of normative and determinative orders provides both unity and variety in human activities. The unity is provided by the normative order, inasmuch that all normative order represents the common call to humanity to seek beauty (and in other operations, love, justice and such-like). Yet at the same time, the determinative order is a source of variety. For though all dancers ought to strive toward beauty, determinative factors such as the history of the particular region, the state of advance in aesthetic knowledge, the strength of the bodies of a particular human race, will lead some women to dance ballet, others flamenco and yet another a tribal dance. Though all these dances are different, they are all united in their search for beauty.

Metasystem

An operation, whether a work of art, of craftsmanship, or science does not exist in isolation but, as Figure 2-2 points out, is coupled to the environment through the input it receives and the output it produces. It is also coupled to other allied operational systems, such as the orchestra that provides the music for the dancers and, although each operational system has its own environment, these overlap with each other and cause further interaction. All these interactions are vital for the operation and must be managed. Such management is performed by the metasystem, illustrated in Figure 2-3 where we have added an orchestra, symbolised by the violinist, as an extra operational system. We thus have not only the interconnection between dancers and their environment but also between both operational systems: dancers and orchestra. The metasystem is also a type of operation but in this case, its input and output are its interaction with the combined operational systems 1 (dancers) and 2 (orchestra). The metasystem is governed by the economic modality which, according to Table 2-1, has as its essence the viability of the operational system.   Once again, I have derived the idea of viability as the essence of the economic modality – as well the concepts of operational system and metasystem – from the work of Beer. His theory of management emerges out of his study of regulation in biology, especially in the human brain.

According to Beer[7], every living thing, whether plant, animal or man, needs a system to manage its interactions within and with its external environment to sustain its life, or make it viable. This concurs with Dooyeweerd's idea of vitality – life – being the essence of the biotic modality. Human life, however, is not restricted to the biotic: there also is life in the other modalities, such as social life and artistic life. Biological life, then, has homomorphisms in the other modalities and it is these other lives that the economic modality seeks to sustain. Thus the essence and principles of the economic modality, viability, are homomorphic with the essence and principles of the biotic, vitality. But the viability that management seeks is the viability of the operational system – a social system rather than a biological one – as it interacts with its own environment. This viability is defined by the particular mission of the social system and can be attained by the application of managerial cybernetics, a word that originates from the Greek and which signifies steward or governor. Interestingly, this is the very meaning that the word economics held prior to the rise of utilitarianism: that is, the stewardship of a household when industry and family were merged together. Management was the operation through which the ancient family was sustained or attained viability. Thus Beer calls his version of managerial cybernetics the Viable System Model.

Let us now examine the essential elements of this management cybernetics. The critical aspect in viability is stability and balance; these are the central idea in cybernetics and systems science. Much of humanity's pains is caused by extremes, in the same form that an unbalanced diet is bad for our bodies. This principle of balance, found so pervasively in nature, is also paramount to human life, where one must avoid despotism without falling into anarchy; avoid severity without over-indulging and spoiling our youth; and avoid repressive censorship without giving carte blanche to the abuses common today in our press. Stability is the ability of a system

---

[7] (1994a).

to preserve this balance; when the system is so able, then it is viable.

Figure 2-3: The Metasystem

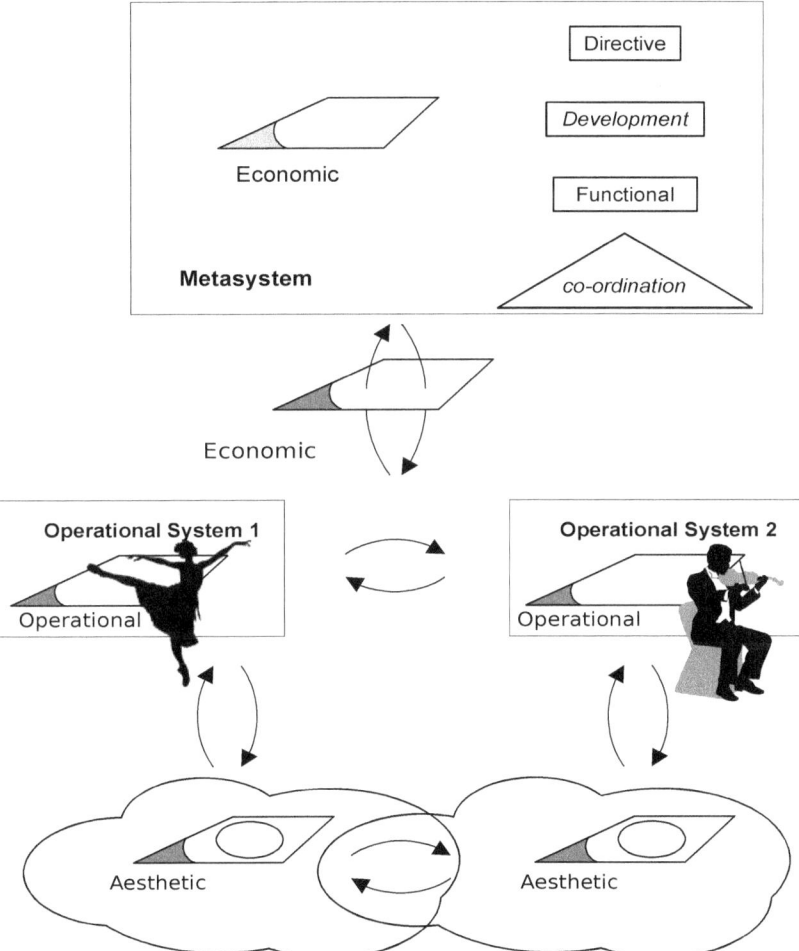

Viability is attained through four activities performed by four respective subsystems in the metasystem (see Figure 2-3). These are explained in great detail by Beer himself and only a short description is necessary here. The co-ordination subsystem co-ordinates the interactions between operational systems. For example, in

the case of the ballet company, co-ordination could entail the setting up of a rehearsal for both dancers and orchestra. The functional subsystem sustains the organisation, with a variety of functional management activities such as personnel management, maintenance of physical facilities, transport of musical instruments and
equipment and accounting, promotion and ticketing. These activities are concerned with the present or the short term of the organisation: its "here and now". The future, the "there and then", is the
concern of the development subsystem: it incorporates both planning and design such as the planning of the extension of the
theatre to accommodate a larger audience and the development of
the ballet company to include larger and more complex works in
the repertoire. Finally, the directive subsystem's activity is to balance the interactions of the functional and the development sub-
systems; that is, to decide how much effort and which resources
should be committed to the future of the company at the expense
of the present and vice versa.

The managerial activities of these four sub-systems are governed by the economic modality. While similar homomorphic activities will be performed in the operational system, they will nevertheless be in a different modality and this difference should be observed with care. For example, the conductor, operating in the
aesthetic modality, will co-ordinate the playing of the musicians
and the dancing during the performance; he will decide about the
musical standard a new player should have before being hired; he
will also plan the musical development of the orchestra and may
also have to balance future expectations against present demands,
such as when he must decide how much rehearsal time should be
dedicated to the present programme and how much to the introduction of new works. All the tasks of the conductor however,
though analogous to the managerial ones, are not governed by the
economic modality but by the artistic. Furthermore, we should be
reminded that the authority of a social system resides in the sphere
of sovereignty in which it operates. For the ballet company, this
resides in the aesthetic modality. The metasystem is only an ac-
cessory to the operational system, set up to support it and ensure
its viability. Therefore managers should not "boss" or "run" the

conductor. On the contrary, it is the conductor, as head of the operational system, who should have the final decision. If a new flute player is to be hired, the personnel department may decide upon the appropriate salary range, but it must be the conductor who ultimately decides who should be hired.

His decision should rest upon his artistic knowledge, for it is knowledge that bestows authority in social systems. Thus the importance of truth, for in truth is also found social justice. This is a most important consideration because the sphere of sovereignty of social systems has been severely violated by two managerial perspectives that tend to dominate and oppress the operational system. Both are forms of reductionism. The first is economic utilitarianism which states that any decision in the organisation should aim at maximising economic utility defined as the difference between pain and pleasure and measured in money. This means a reversal to the economic norms as they existed prior to the industrial revolution. Then it was held that the first task of any enterprise, whether it be a shoe maker or a dance company, was to serve its community. It was also considered fair that one should "not muzzle an ox while it is treading out the grain"[8], that is, that as a result of their service, producers should be justly remunerated. However, since the industrial revolution, every social institution has yielded to the new economic norms. These turn every human endeavour, including religion and dance companies, into business ventures that assert their ultimate aim in the terms of monetary utility. Thus the modern idea of treading the grain is for the owner of the ox to gobble up most of it.

We know the disaster that this utilitarian formula brought upon the underprivileged classes during the Industrial Revolution and how they were excluded from sharing the material benefits brought about by the new technology. This disaster was repeated throughout the countries of Europe in the 19th century and in Spain at the beginning of the 20th. As a reaction to the excesses of utilitarian economics, a second form of reductionism was supplied by Marx. Moved by the misery generated by the Industrial Revolution and by the hoarding of wealth by the managerial class, Marx

---

[8] Deuteronomy 25:4.

rejected management as a useless class ploy to exploit the prolet-
ariat and replaced the economic modality with the social modality
(thus the term "socialism") as the means of governing all human
activities[9]. His expectation was that the Industrial Revolution
would be overthrown by a social class revolution. Many today recognise that the social consciousness of Marx's theories and of
similar thinkers such as the Frankfurt School was borrowed from
the Old and New Testament[10]so that much of Marx's ethic of
struggle against social oppression echo the sounds of the old
prophetic themes. Yet Marx's ethic twists the prophetic message of
love into that of conflict and violence. For Marx the essence of the
social modality was social conflict rather than social interaction as
it is for Dooyeweerd and hence struggle for power becomes all important to the revolutionary process.

Marx expected that through a dialectical process, history would
eventually deliver such power to the people and thus he was content to wait for the right time. His successors such as Lenin had no
such patience and held that history must be assisted by forcefully
getting hold of power. It is out of this violent struggle that a new
system emerged in Eastern Europe and Russia. Management, as a
legitimate science and practice of viability, was rejected and the
metasystem transformed into a bureaucracy obsessed by role,
status, hierarchy, authority and privilege and as ends in themselves.
All these elements, being part of the social modality, had little to
do with viability and formed the kernel of a "gargantuan civil service" (as Solzhenitsyn called it) where:

> people don't put any effort at all into their official duties and
> have no enthusiasm for them, but cheat (and sometimes steal) as
> much as they can and spend their office hours doing private jobs
> (they are forced to, with wages as low as they are today; for
> nobody is strong enough to earn a living from wage alone).
> Everybody is trying to make more money for less work.[11]

This bureaucracy was not only corrupt, but dominated and oppressed the people as much as capitalism. The victims of this total-

---

[9] Marx and Engels (2005).
[10] Tar (1985).
[11] (1974, p. 34f.).

itarianism were people from all walks of life, both ordinary and extraordinary, tradesmen as well as great artists and scientists. Dmitri Shostakovich was forced to compose symphonies that pleased Stalin and scientists at the Soviet Academy of Science were forbidden to apply mathematical modelling to economics.

A gentler version of socialism has risen in Western European nations which are ruled by social power but are financed by restrained capitalism. In Sweden for example, internal socialism has been combined with external capitalism. Swedish industry has been intensely market oriented in its operations with the outside world, while internally it has supported a socialist system that dominates every institution. People sometimes sincerely believe that democracy is attained through the endless establishment of bureaucratic committees, often comprised of individuals who have limited managerial understanding.[12] Participation in these committees is sought mostly for social power, generating a type of distributed totalitarianism that meddles in almost every aspect of people's life: the family, the church and the university[13]. Furthermore, often people who seek membership in these committees do so after failing to show sufficient professional competence in the operational systems which they now aspire to direct. Thus many social systems are ruled by a pretty combination of managerial and professional incompetence. They face a grim future as the industrial wealth that has financed them in the past has started to dwindle.

Faced with economic disaster, countries of varying socialist intensities have begun a frantic switch towards a "market economy", trading the totalitarianism of bureaucracy for the totalitarianism of the market. The very parties that rose to power to protect people from the excesses of capitalism, the Social Democrats, the Christian Democrats and Labour now embrace the market economy and accelerated technological expansion as the panacea for all national ills. As a result, a large component of the resources previously allocated to health, education, arts and community development has been redirected toward industries.

---

[12] In fact, the Swedish language has no word that accurately translates the English term "management" or "managerial".
[13] Gould (1988).

Most politicians and managers are not too concerned about the wisdom of a market mechanism that favours the fast-food industry over education; they assume that all this is democratically decided by consumer preferences. They ignore that massive conglomerates very undemocratically manipulate such preferences to their own pleasure by exercising control through the media. Through this they not only peddle a multitude of goods we don't need and insistently pound us with the advertising of the lifestyle we ought to adopt for their sake. Devoid of a normative defence, men and women can unsuspectingly find themselves in as vulnerable a position as the country people who migrated to the big industrial centres during the industrial revolution. They are unaware that institutions that protected them in the past, such as unions, some political parties and some religious organisations either have embraced capitalism or have been swallowed up by the confusions of post-modernity.

What are we to do to stop all this? One thing we must do is to liberate our social institutions from capitalism, on the one hand, and socialism, on the other. Only wisdom and the legitimate authority it bestows in the sphere of sovereignty of every human activity can make us free. It is in wisdom where a vocation to serve humanity, rather than to overpower it, is found. This difference between a free and a bound system can be illustrated once more by referring to the ballet and a music recording company. From a multi-modal point of view, both companies find the sphere of sovereignty in the aesthetic modality. It is here where their normative vocation is encapsulated; their ultimate aim is to be a dance maker and a music maker, for the people need dance and music to cheer, inspire and allow them to express their feelings. This does not exclude both companies' obligations to balance their budgets, to pay a salary to their employees and to pay the interest on the capital that they have borrowed, but these obligations are distinct from their mission or vocation.

Here, however, is where the modern twist in our understanding and enslaving of organisations turns up. For though we may perhaps, as a left over from the past, be reluctant to say that the normative mission of the ballet is to pay interest out of profit, we are not reluctant to say that making money is the mission of a recording company. We consider the recording company to be a business and, when a social system is regarded as business, its ultimate goal automatically becomes to make money regardless of its sphere of sovereignty. It is this modern classification as a business that enslaves a social system: it forces it to give up its sphere of sovereignty and its vocation and binds it to the law of utility. According to this law every human endeavour – including a ballet company – should be regarded as a business. And, as already mentioned, this is what our political and managerial leaders are enthusiastically doing. This is what must be stopped.

Recursion

Our ballet company interacts with many other systems. This interaction also must be managed to secure the viability of all the systems involved, just as in Figure 2-3 the interaction of orchestra and dancers was managed to ensure the company's overall viability. This is made possible, according to Beer, by a recursive structure – that is, a structure that appears again and again – where all operational systems, together with the respective metasystems, are joined into one single operational system at a higher level of organisation.

This new operational system has its own metasystem sustaining it. Let us consider Figure 2-4 where there are three operational systems, each with its own sphere of sovereignty in a different modality: the ballet company (aesthetic), the school of arts (epistemic) and the railways (kinetic). Note that the ballet company, though comprised of three operational systems and one metasystem is now represented as one single operational system (1) at a higher level of recursion. Likewise, the overlapping environments of the dancers and orchestra have been merged into one environment which now overlaps with the environments of the school of arts and the railways. The reason for this merger is that the ballet company, though composed of two operational systems, is in reality one social system with one identity, such the "The Royal Ballet". This is not true however, for the combination of railways, arts school and ballet: although each one of them has an identity that envelops the various operational systems that comprise them, they are not absorbed into a single identity at the higher recursion level. Thus the interaction between the operational systems present in Figure 2-3 is not present in Figure 2-4. There are only interactions in the overlapping of environments in which are found the spheres of sovereignty of the systems. For example, the dancers' skill and knowledge (epistemic) of ballet is dependent upon the aesthetic knowledge received in the school of arts: the two modalities involved, epistemic and aesthetic, form a link between the two social systems, the ballet and the school of arts. Likewise, if the ballet plans a tour to give regional performances, it will require transportation (kinetic) by the railways and specialised service to carry, in addition to the artists, the musical instruments and costumes safely to the locations of performance. Thus the co-ordination system at this level of recursion is required to integrate these interactions. These interactions show the mutual interdependence that exists between all social systems that comprise a society. Cybernetics has taught us that these interactions are crucial[14] for the individual and that the collective viability of the social systems are each a requisite of the other. That is, no system can be viable within a recursion that is not itself viable.

The opposite is also true, a system that is not viable will eventually threaten the viability of the higher recursion within which it is an operational system. It is paramount therefore that there should be a managerial system at the higher recursion level that will sustain the various operational systems dependent on it and ensure their viability. In our example, the management system at this level of recursion may be the government of the particular community to which the ballet, the school of arts and the railways belong.

---

[14] Ashby (1976).

Figure 2-4: Recursion

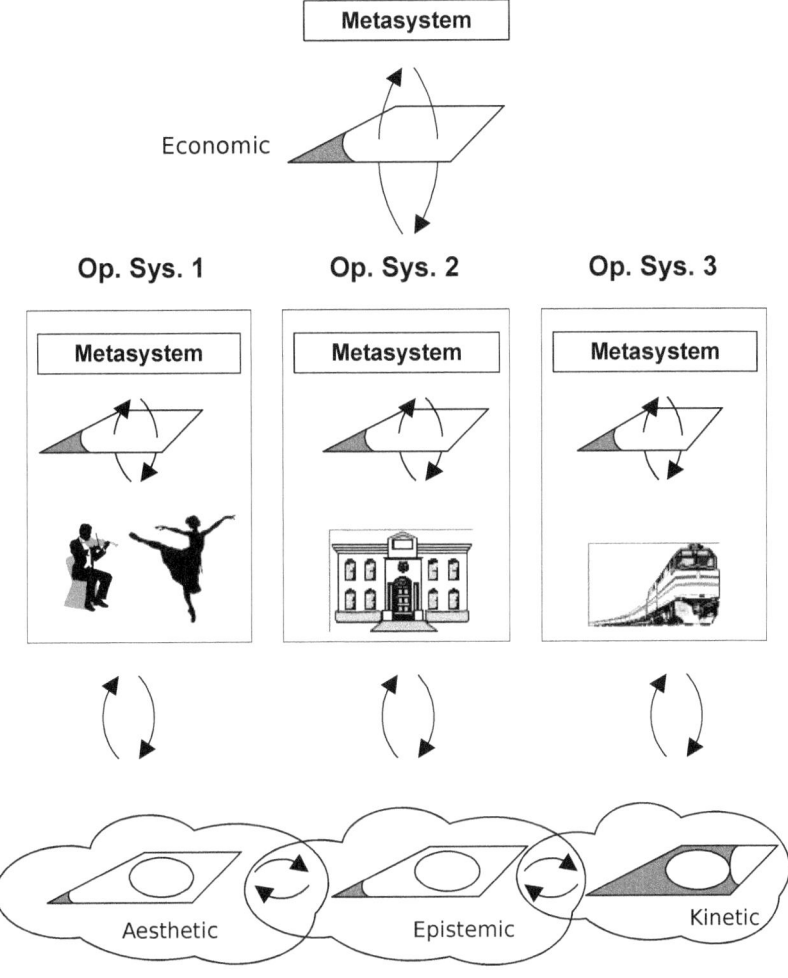

The same utilitarian or socialist distortions of management we discussed above may appear at this level of recursion. That is, there is the socialist approach to government that sees government and politics in terms of social power. The result is a government bureaucracy that owns the ballet, the school of arts, the railways and almost everything else. It controls these with great inefficiency and inefficacy and often with injustice as well. Then there is the more current solution to this: the privatising of all these institutions. Everything goes under the auctioneer's hammer, hospitals and police stations included, to be run strictly under utilitarian principles.

But our principles would dictate that government, being the metasystem at the communal level of recursion, should not intervene in the activities of each operational system but should sustain them managerially so as to ensure their continuation. This it should do in a similar manner as done with the ballet company in Figure 2-4, for in both levels of recursion the metasystem's operations are directed towards the economic modality; thus they are homomorphic with each other. This means that the upper level metasystem also has four subsystems with the same tasks as described earlier. That is, there must be a subsystem that helps to co-ordinate the interaction between each operational system, a functional system that looks after managerial things proper, a development system looking into the future and finally a system that balances the future with the present.

Management Theory and Operational Research

So far we have examined the path by which we start with wisdom and within it we find love and the other norms which comprise the human vocation and we have seen how this vocation is transformed into an activity or operation which requires to be managed. Our final task is to place management theory and operational research within the framework we have built and explain how they too can make a contribution to the realisation of our human vocation.

Management should be the concern of economics par excellence. At present, utilitarian economics makes a distinction between micro and macro-economics; micro-economics busies itself at the industrial level while macro-economics does the same at the national level. In a recursive structure such as we have discussed above, micro-economics would correspond to the management of lower recursions and macro-economics to upper recursions. However, due to the narrow nature of utilitarian economics these distinctions are accentuated, while in a multi-modal context the opposite occurs: the similarities (homomorphisms) between the two become more visible due to the emphasis on multi-modal viability rather than utility. Thus while in utilitarian economics, micro-economics is closely linked to management and macro-economics to political economy, from a multi-modal perspective management and economics may be regarded as synonymous.[15]

There is also an applied science in management – generally known as operational research – which addresses managerial practice and skill. Contemporary operations research has been severely criticised, especially by its founders, for having lost its original multi-disciplinary and systemic vision[16]. Due to the reductionistic nature of utilitarian economics and its reliance on numbers, the idiom that operational research employs today is mostly numerical. In certain quarters operational research has been identified as a branch of applied mathematics. In a prior article I have explained how there are two approaches to modelling. The first one serves the determinative form of order and uses a reductive method that isolates everything except the most important variables which are then related in a deterministic manner. The second approach is an expansive method, by which we model the normative order by trying to include the greatest number of variables we can manage in as many modalities as possible. Mathematics is an excellent idiom to produce determinative knowledge through the reductive method. But management is a highly normative science, having greater need for an expansive method. In this, operational research has proven quite barren, especially since the complex environment that managers face today renders most quantitative models for decision making quite ineffectual. Maybe as a consequence, contemporary operational research has moved away from the metasystem and its managerial scene and has increasingly occupied itself in developing models for highly mechanistic processes in the opera-

---

[15] Management and economics already are synonyms in an etymological sense.
[16] Both Russell Ackoff and C. West Churchman, among the founding fathers of OR in the USA have been critical of the development of OR and Stafford Beer, a pioneer and former president of the OR society in the UK has also expressed dissatisfaction.

tional system. This again reinforces the overall mechanistic view of social systems.

Figure 2-5: Operational Research

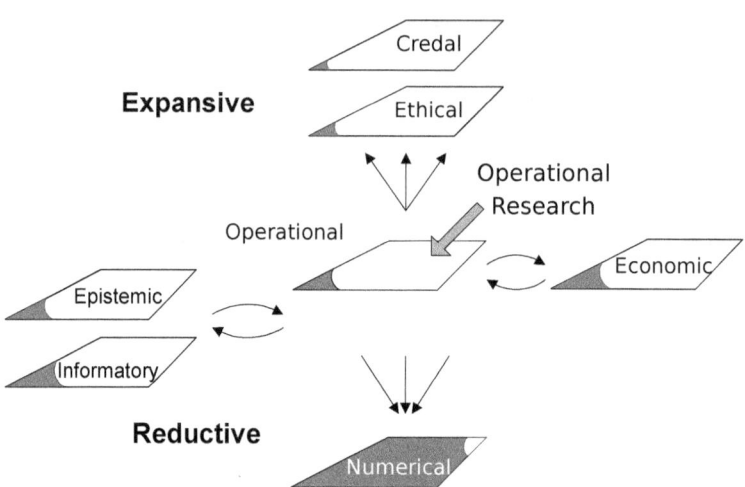

What is required is a broader operational research, one that applies both the reductive and expansive methods to build multi-modal models for each of the four sub-systems of the metasystem. This is illustrated in Figure 2-5. Here the economic problems concerning the viability of a system are being analysed from an operational perspective to guide managerial action and decision making. The analysis carried out by operational research employs two methods. A reductive method that produces quantitative models and an expansive method that produces normative models. This is the point at which our research stands at present and I would like to conclude by inviting my colleagues in operational research in all countries to join forces with us and to develop new modelling techniques that will help us bring wisdom, love and all the other virtues, so essential to humanity, into every activity we perform.

3 Design of an Undergraduate Programme

J. D. R. de Raadt

Introduction

Not long before I took my present appointment at Luleå University of Technology, I completed my book, *Information and Managerial Wisdom*[1], which was the output of about eight years of research begun in Australia and completed in the United States. The conclusions of this research regarding the contribution that computer information systems can make to management are not very optimistic. Most of information systems have been built on the assumption that an increase of power in modern information technology signifies a greater amount of information available to managers and social systems. Since the power of computers is overwhelming, we believe that we are living in an information society. However, I concluded that rather than living in an information age, we lived in an uncertainty age and that our information technology was unable to decrease significantly this uncertainty. On the contrary, in many instances the introduction of information technology increased the uncertainty in our social systems.

I also argued that our understanding of information should be based on a closer understanding of social systems and their management rather than on the machines – computers – that are supposed to produce such information. There was also a need to develop a science of information based on a non-mechanical view of the world, for it is precisely this mechanical view that leads us to confuse information with information technology. This mechanistic view was also found in modern management so that there was a correspondence between the mechanical approach to information and to management.

I also concluded that to deal with this problem, we must firstly search the epistemology that underlies our ideas of management and information and expose the naïve misconceptions that are rooted in the Enlightenment and the industrial revolution.

---

[1] de Raadt, J. D. R. (1991).

Secondly, we must establish a programme of research to rebuild our management and information thought on a sounder epistemological foundation. Thirdly, we needed a new educational curriculum for the education of managers and information professionals. So when the opportunity presented itself to develop such a curriculum at Luleå University of Technology, I took it and this paper describes what my colleagues and I built as a result.

Multi-Modal Systems Thinking

The curriculum is based on multi-modal systems thinking, a framework that links three elements together – life, wisdom and management – along two axes (see Figure 1-1). In the horizontal axis lie a string of interacting systems such as orchards, families, trades, dance companies, schools, transport, courts of justice and hospitals. Within such systems, life – both biological and cultural – unfolds. Within them mankind realises its vocation and finds its fulfilment. Yet to understand these systems we must also refer to the vertical axis where we find layered a number of modalities that command all these systems: credal, ethical, juridical, aesthetic, economic, operational, social, epistemic, informatory, historical, logical, psychic, biotic, physical, kinetic, spatial and numeric[2].

The foundation and character of multi-modal systems thinking – as we have labelled this approach to systems science – is prophetic rather than philosophic. The philosophic approach which we have inherited from the Greeks regards the universe as governed by inert, impersonal and static laws. Accordingly, the philosopher's inquiry reflects his concern with existence, he asks: what is reality? There being no satisfactory answer to this, philosophy gets bogged down. It is in this state that it is passed on to us by medieval scholasticism and modernism.

Modernism has added to this formula its own secularisation and mechanisation. There is no hope, therefore, that such an understanding of science, being built upon an inert, impersonal and static view of the universe can address the predicament of humanity. Post-modernism has attempted to escape out of this mire by

---

[2] Dooyeweerd (1958).

regarding reality as the product of our own construction and landed us with the only culture in history ever to have been called the "idiot culture". We hear about the arrogance of Rome and the cruelty of Assyria or the inability of ancient Israel to be content with its lot and getting into perennial trouble for it, but we do not hear of a whole civilisation being junk. It is the greatest insult that our generation can receive. Tragically, it is well deserved.

Therefore I have sought to follow the path of the prophet rather than the philosopher. In contrast to the philosopher, the prophet regards the world as governed by a living personal and dynamic God. Life, not existence is his chief concern. The prophet asks: how should we live? And while the philosopher struggles in his own mire, the prophet and his successors bring relief and hope to the poor, the needy and the underdog, for in contrast to philosophy, prophecy not only loves wisdom but also its practice.

God's command of the universe is thus multi-modal and is addressed in two directions (see Figure 3-1). The first is to nature in general (shaded area); in the other to the heart of man (blank area). By heart, we do not just mean emotions, but the inner centrality of our person which makes us responsible for our actions as distinct from those things that happen to us as part of nature. Though the dominion of the heart extends over all modalities, it is greatest in the higher modalities and least in the lower ones. The highest modality is the credal, the realm of faith. Faith is the foundation of all activities that are distinctively human, that is, those for which man is responsible as man. Man therefore lives by faith or by inspiration (represented by the arrow) which means that life must be anchored outside of ourselves, in God, rather than within ourselves, as in existentialism or constructivism.

Figure 3-1: Nature and the Heart of Man

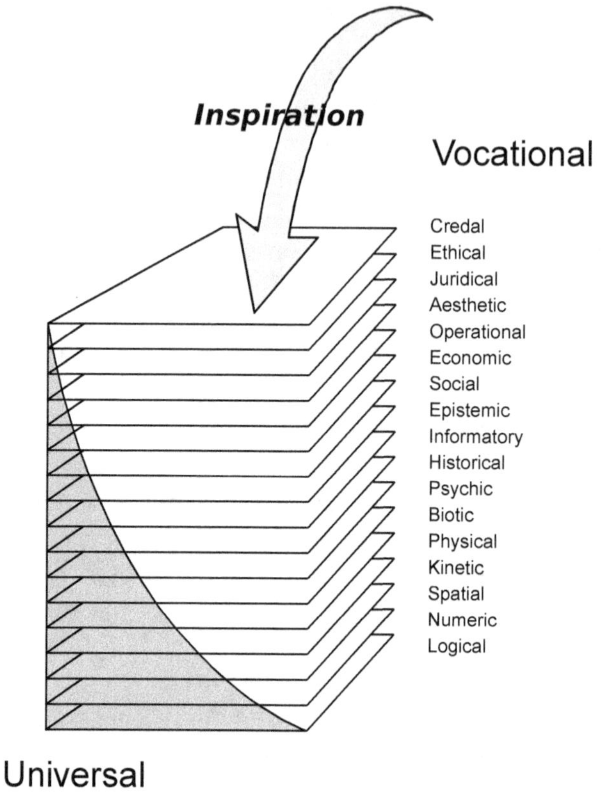

Inspiration

Vocational

Credal
Ethical
Juridical
Aesthetic
Operational
Economic
Social
Epistemic
Informatory
Historical
Psychic
Biotic
Physical
Kinetic
Spatial
Numeric
Logical

Universal

Understanding, in all its forms including scientific, is an integral part of human life and also founded on inspiration. All understanding is governed by the epistemic modality and its final goal is gaining wisdom. This wisdom, though being one, reflects nevertheless all the modalities. This multiplicity is evinced in the variety of specialised sciences that we have for each variety. For example, the credal, ethical and social modalities are respectively studied by theology, ethics and sociology. Yet, to avoid the scientific fragmentation that followed the Enlightenment, multi-modal systems thinking aims to stress the unity of these modalities – without denying their variety – and to provide a bridge for the integration of the sciences.

While the heart of every person functions in each modality, each person has a special talent and love for one or more modalities. This special manifestation or preference for a select group of modalities forms the vocation of the person, that is, that special field in which a person wishes to serve his fellow man. This means that each vocation is linked to one of the modalities, the lawyer with the juridical, the biologist with the biotic, the information professional with the informatory. Vocations such as these must be turned into work and this work is governed by skills found in the operational modality. Furthermore, work does not take place in an isolated manner, but within the social context of an operational system[3] where people gather together to realise their vocations as a community of professionals. For example, in the lower part of Figure 3-2 the operational systems of a hospital is illustrated. Doctors and nurses carry out their work (ruled by the operational modality) motivated by the vocation which is focused on the biotic modality. They serve people by biologically healing them.

These social systems interact with each other and also with the natural systems as indicated by the horizontal axis of Figure 1-1. Each one of these systems in particular, as well as their whole aggregate, must be managed by a metasystem (see Figure 3-2) for them to be viable. Viability constitutes the essence of management which is ruled by the economic modality and which provides the link between the metasystem and the operational system, as indicated in Figure 3-2. By economics we do not mean utilitarian economics, but economics (*oikonomia*) in the ancient sense, that is, the management of the old household with the sustenance of life as its essence. We have therefore defined multi-modal systems management as a new economics that aims at sustaining life in each one of the modalities and where systems though distinct, operate nevertheless in an integrated manner. Human life, however, must not only be sustained but developed; multi-modal systems development is the cultural unfolding of human systems in harmony with natural systems that takes place in each one of the modalities. Once more, this process must take place in a balanced manner,

---

[3] Beer (1994a).

without any of the modalities dominating over the development of the others and where every modal level of life is sustained.

Figure 3-2: Operational and Metasystem

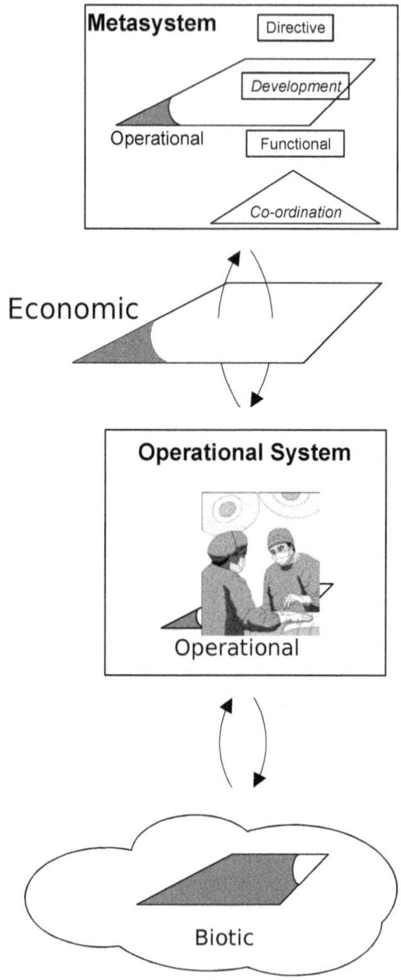

Management is, therefore, the erudition and skill that sustains and develops both human and natural systems as explained by Beer[4]. His theory of management emerges out of his study of regu-

---

[4] (1994a;1995).

lation in biology, especially in the human brain. According to Beer, every living thing, whether plant, animal or man, needs a system to manage its interactions within and with its external environment to sustain its life, or make it viable. This concurs with the modal idea of vitality – life – being the essence of the biotic modality. Human life, however, is not restricted to the biotic: there also is life in the other modalities, such as social life and artistic life. Biological life, then, has homomorphisms in the other modalities and it is these other lives that the economic modality seeks to sustain. Thus the essence and principles of the economic modality, viability, are homomorphic with the essence and principles of the biotic, vitality, but the viability that management seeks is the viability of a social system rather than a biological one as it interacts with its own environment. This viability is defined by the particular mission of the social system and can be attained by the application of managerial cybernetics[5]. The word cybernetics originates from the Greek and signifies steward or governor and when applied to the ancient household, has the same meaning as the word *oikonomia* cited above. Thus the grounds of Beer's managerial cybernetics are in harmony with the ancient idea of economics and in this sense it is most appropriate that he should call it The Viable System Model.

Informatics and Systems Science Programme

The above is, in brief, the intellectual foundation of the department of informatics and systems science inaugurated in Autumn 1995 with the mission to focus its research and teaching programmes on the management of our technological civilisation. The emphasis of our teaching programme is threefold: firstly it is concerned with the development of students as persons by increasing their understanding of life and their mission in it and also by developing a sense of service to their neighbours. Secondly, we aim at developing in them an understanding (epistemic modality) that is critical – in regard to how we should live – managerially and creatively. Education is directed to the whole intellect, which means that our students are not only encouraged to think with rigour in

---

[5] de Raadt (1991).

each one of the departments of knowledge, from mathematics and lingual expression to aesthetics and ethics but also with reference to the whole of life, both cultural and natural. Thirdly, in addition to understanding, education must also be able to provide students with the skill that will allow them to apply their talents in vocational service, specifically management, management information and systems design. While recognising the differences between the many disciplines, we stress in class the essential unity of knowledge. Students are taught how knowledge from the different disciplines can be woven together to understand the world.

Figure 3-3: Multi-Modal Foundation of the Programme

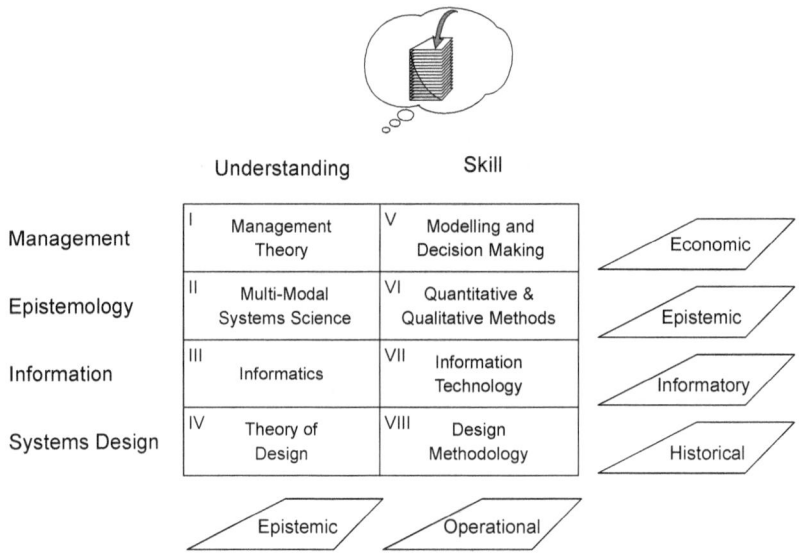

The design of the programme is illustrated in Figure 3-3. The rectangles contain its academic requirements. On the top is placed understanding and skill (involving nature and heart as defined in Figure 3-1); these involve two modalities – epistemic and operational – shown at the bottom. On the left side are the areas in which students are seeking understanding and skill – management, epistemology, information and systems design; these in turn belong to four modalities – economic, epistemic, informatory and historical – listed on the right side. We needed therefore to build a programme of studies that would satisfy these academic requirements. In the centre of the figure are eight boxes containing the curricular domains that were defined by the intersection of the modalities on the right and bottom of the figure. For example, Box III and VII indicate the need for courses in information (informatory). Box III points to course requirements that teach information from a theoretical point of view (epistemic) while Box VII to courses teaching practical (operational) skills such as programming, spreadsheet techniques and so on. These curricular domains were then used to develop the courses that are listed in Figure 3-4. The programme spans four academic years and each year is divided into four terms. The first set of thirty students entered the programme in August 1996 and have recently completed the first year. Therefore it is not possible at this stage to evaluate the programme as a whole. Nevertheless there are some experiences in this first year that are worthwhile noting.

Figure 3-4: Informatics and Systems Science Programme

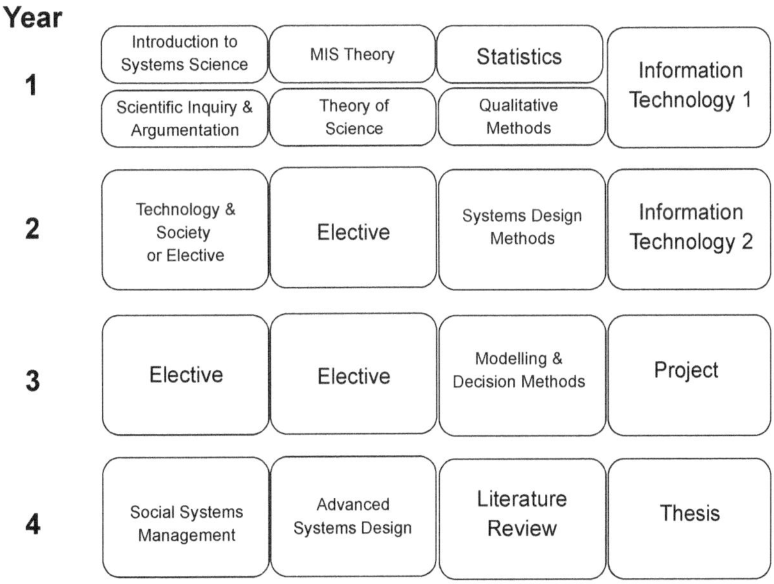

Year				
1	Introduction to Systems Science / Scientific Inquiry & Argumentation	MIS Theory / Theory of Science	Statistics / Qualitative Methods	Information Technology 1
2	Technology & Society or Elective	Elective	Systems Design Methods	Information Technology 2
3	Elective	Elective	Modelling & Decision Methods	Project
4	Social Systems Management	Advanced Systems Design	Literature Review	Thesis

We have concentrated the students' work in the first three terms almost solely in establishing a foundation for thought. Only in the fourth term do they meet with something more practical in Information Technology I. Some students became a little anxious and wondered what they had got into after dealing with so much philosophy and epistemology and were relieved when in term four they finally became involved with computers and software. Yet we believe that it is important to start their studies this way and to give them a sense of priority of what is really important and lasting in their university years. This anxiety I believe will decrease over the next years for the new students will be able to be reassured by their second year colleagues. Students within the different programmes at our university display a strong sense of cohesion across the levels and this facilitates the introduction of a new curricula such as ours.

We have sought to integrate research and teaching, not only by continuously updating our curriculum with the latest outcomes of our research, but also by having undergraduate students share with doctoral students in some research activity of the department. Accordingly in the beginning of March this year, students spent three days on field study in a village south of Luleå. Apart from teaching the practical aspects of qualitative research and exposing the students to doctoral research in a light manner, they were also able to gain first hand experience of threats to the sustainability of village life in Sweden. This made them aware of the community needs beyond the interests of industry and the need to apply managerial and systemic tools – which so far have tended to be monopolised by industry – to help the community as a whole.

Although this programme is somewhat unique, it is possible to make some comparisons with my own experiences in teaching similar multi-modal courses – in management information systems, systems design and management of information systems – to business students in the USA. Most of the responses by students in the USA fell in two opposite poles with very few in between. About 40% of students expressed strong approval of such courses and appreciated an educational experience that challenged their way of looking at life. Most of the rest felt that it was not proper to teach business students material that was of interest to society as a whole but of no specific interest to the business of making money. They felt it was more important to concentrate their studies on skills directly relevant to their employment opportunities.

The experience in Sweden is somewhat different. Most of our students approve the multi-modal systems approach and very few show lack of interest. This may be due to students in Sweden being somewhat more serious, but it may also be that, due to a generous welfare system, they do not feel the harsh employment pressures experienced by their North American counterparts.

Conclusions

We may now draw some conclusions from what has been said. Our world view was firstly a response to the inert, impersonal and static view of the universe held by the classical philosophers and later secularised and mechanised by the Enlightenment and the Industrial Revolution. As such, not only does it ignore the threat to the natural and cultural life of our world, but it is the very cause of this threat. We need a different way of thinking and we have adopted the stance of the prophet. It is upon this that multi-modal systems thinking is built and upon which it integrates the diverse natural and human systems that comprise our world and our different ways of understanding. Multi-modal systems thinking also returns man's heart to its rightful place, for the life of the heart is the essence of civilisation. Sustaining and developing both natural and cultural life is the task of management, but management requires a different perspective than the utilitarian and mechanistic approach that pervades our society today. I propose a multi-modal systems management that also integrates the diverse departments of knowledge, the diverse natural and human systems and the heart of man with his natural side.

We need much research in this area and there is a great need to prepare new leaders among our young people by teaching them a different approach to thinking and managing our technological civilisation. The informatics and systems science programme at Luleå University of Technology is a modest attempt to serve the future generation of leaders and, though still in its early stages, it already shows some promise in what we have done so far. Finally, while I have provided some of the fundamental ideas in which our research and educational programmes are based I would like to conclude by acknowledging the very significant contribution that has been provided by my colleagues at my department and also the Centre for Technology and Social Systems. Right from the beginning this has been a team effort and its success will certainly depend on the continuing effort of this team of committed scholars with whom I have the privilege to work.

4 Vision and Normative Science

J. D. R. de Raadt

Introduction

In a biographical note published some years ago, C. West Churchman wrote about his progress through systems thought as a succession of discoveries made over a period of many years. He had the following to say regarding the first of these:

> ...my earliest speculations... were mainly on the writers of the centuries I admired the most, the seventeenth and the eighteenth. The major writers, from Descartes to Kant, were all systems researchers. Their major problem was not *how* to build systems models, but to address the question of the existence of God. It seemed to them (as it still does to me), that the nature of the human systems depends most of all on whether a perfect being exists.
>
> If it does, then our main attention as systems researchers should be how planning relates to its existence. If it does not, then we not only have a lot of explaining to do in terms of our values, but we also have to find a whole set of god-less values to guide us.[1]

The existence of God has been a topic of much debate throughout the centuries. It includes the extensive work of apologetics, ancient and modern, such as Lewis[2] and Swinburne[3]. Our concern here will not be with theorising whether God exists or not. We shall leave that to the apologists. We will instead concern ourselves with three different, yet not unrelated, questions.

The first question is this. Many, today and in the past and from all walks of life have experienced God in a personal manner. Among these are some of the most famous scientists, artists and humanitarians. Claiming their inspiration as a gift of God, they have in large volume stated significant scientific theories, written great works of literature, composed beautiful symphonies and painted and sculptured masterpieces. Not the least, they have also gone to the slums or ghettos in modern cities, the slums of Cal-

---

[1] (1987, p. 140).
[2] (1955; 1994).
[3] (1991; 1993).

cutta and to the inclement barrenness of Tierra del Fuego[4] and brought love, care and comfort to the suffering and destitute. If one cannot lightly discard these people as lunatics, how is it that we have been persuaded to think that science and belief in God are incompatible; how is it possible that science, together with Western culture, has become so vastly secularised? The second question refers to the normative consequences when science becomes secularised. As we shall see, the classical scientist's main preoccupation was not with the quality of life in the modern sense, but with the quality of the person. What happens when science becomes secularised and loses its thirst to know what makes a good man and a good woman? The third and final question is: how can we integrate our knowledge of God with science, especially systems science, and how can we scientifically concern ourselves once more with the inquiry into what type of people we ought to be? The finding of our search should be of significance not only to systems science but to science in general. However, systems science is placed in a particularly favourable position to make a contribution along these lines because of its aim to provide a unifying link between the specialised sciences and because of its interest in systems as wholes.

The Classical (Pre-Modern) Period

For the purpose of this discussion, we shall distinguish three periods in the history of Western thought – classical (pre-modern), modern and post-modern – and we will regard the first one as extending from antiquity until the beginning of the 18th century and as being mostly rooted in Hebrew and Greek traditions. People as varied as Moses, Isaiah, Plato, Aristotle, Augustine, Aquinas, Luther, Copernicus and Galileo belonged to this period. Among them there was barely any dispute regarding the existence of God, of truth and the absolute; likewise, it seems that the ultimate goal of people's intellectual pursuit was to become better people: "know thyself" seems to have been the ultimate motto of inquiry. Calvin sums it up like this:

---

[4] Golsdmith (1994).

> Our wisdom, in so far as it ought to be deemed true and
> solid wisdom, consists almost entirely of two parts: the
> knowledge of God and of ourselves. But as these are con-
> nected together by many ties, it is not easy to determine
> which precedes, and gives birth to the other.[5]

Yet, there were conflicting ideas of how one should search one-
self and what role God ought to play in all this. The conflict
mirrored firstly the divergent experience of God and secondly the
different perception of how God related to the cosmos. Israel's
Yahweh was thoroughly personal, in fact personhood was entirely
contained in him. Conversely, while there were some indications of
a personal God in Plato's works[6], the Greek perception of God,
such as Plato's Demiurgos and Aristotle's Prime Mover were essentially rationalistic and impersonal. Yahweh on the other hand,
continuously sustained and ordered the cosmos by his personal
rule. As a result of this, the universe displayed everywhere the personal character of God, e.g. his omnipotence, wisdom and kind-
ness. All things in the universe were dependent upon God, including man and his thought. Even man's understanding was dependent
upon God's revelation being mediated through faith. Revelation
contained every form of knowledge, from things eternal to the
more mundane matters of ploughing a field and sowing caraway. It
was revelation that provided the bridge between the mind and the
object. By contrast, Greek thought was somewhat devoid of such
personal involvement of God and man's dependence upon it.
Plato's account of the origin of the world[7], told us that the world
was moulded from a pre-existent image that was "...the fairest and
most perfect of intelligible beings..." In other words, the world
was reproduced, it was not a complete new design and creation in
the biblical sense.

Attempts to synthesise these two views of God seem to have
often led to the sacrifice of the personal for the benefit of the abstract. One can perceive this, for example, in the efforts of Philo of
Alexandria to synthesise the creation account in Genesis with the

---

[5] (n.d., I: 1).
[6] For example, in *The Last Days of Socrates* (1993).
[7] (2008b, pp. 81).

Platonic idea of creation. In his synthesis, God created the world guided by an "archetypal idea conceived by the intellect" and "only perceptible by the intellect"[8] much in the same way as was described by Socrates. Other thinkers who capitulated to the abstract were Clement of Alexandria and Origen Adamantius[9].

This conflict between a personal world view and an abstract reductionism has played a major role in shaping the history of Western thought. In the midst of this history stand two dominant thinkers Augustine and Aquinas representing the two opposing epistemological positions in the conflict. The former relied on a personal experience of God; the latter depended on a synthesis of personal and impersonal views of God.

Figure 4-1: Augustine's Epistemology

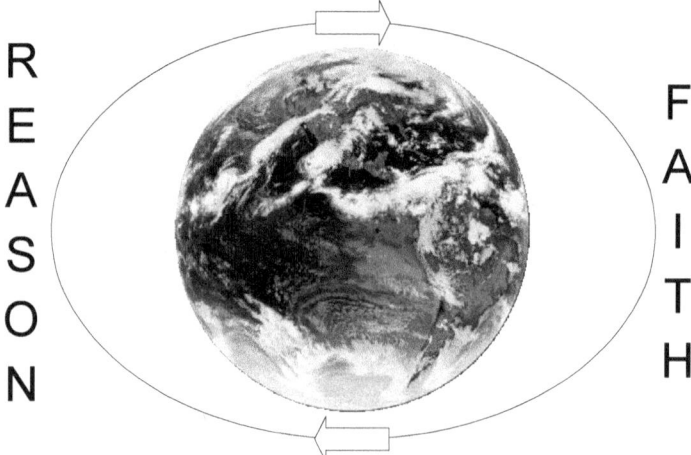

R
E
A
S
O
N

F
A
I
T
H

Augustine was originally influenced by neo-Platonism but, after his conversion to Christianity, adopted a Hebrew epistemology. In his scholarly legacy he left us four main tenets. Firstly, he proposed that reason was not autonomous but dependent upon faith. While every system of thought must start with faith or an intellectual assent to a set of presuppositions, Augustine extended this

---

[8] De Opificio Mundi, IV (1890).
[9] Klapwijk et al (1991).

to a more profound and personal reliance upon a God who revealed Himself and his cosmos to man (see Figure 4-1). Unlike
Plato's or Philo's "eternal model", this revelation personally involved God in leading man into all truth[10]. The intellectual task
was, for him, a fully personal encounter between God and man as
evinced, for example, in his *Confessions* which are written in the
form of a dialogue between God and himself. Secondly, Augustine
promoted an intelligent and educated faith, a faith that dynamically
interacted with reason. While faith provided the foundation for
reason, reason enhanced faith and helped it on its way to maturity.
For Augustine, faith without intellect crumbled into credulity, a
highly unstable state in which man could believe anything without
discernment or reflection. Thirdly, truth exhibited unity. The surety
of this unity was God himself who, Augustine regards as a synonym of truth. Fourthly, Augustine stressed the importance of the
moral character and integrity of the thinker in his scientific task.
This not only meant that the scholar had to give his whole self and
be devoted to the pursuit of truth but, in addition, his life had to be
consistent with his findings.

In contrast to Augustine, Aquinas, living almost eight hundred
years later than Augustine, tried to resolve the conflict between
Hebrew and Greek traditions by finding a middle course. The
philosophy of Aristotle rather than Plato dominated his era, a
factor that may have influenced the type of epistemology that he
eventually was to adopt. Of all Greek philosophers, Plato and his
followers were the closest to the Hebrew tradition, especially by
maintaining that one should seek truth apart from the concrete
reality of this world. It must have been easier for the Neo-Platonist
Augustine, therefore, to have switched to a Hebraic world view.
Aristotle, on the other hand, conceived truth as being located in
concrete reality and capable of being understood by autonomous
reasoning without any aid from God. Aquinas attempted to accommodate this autonomous reasoning with the Hebrew notion of
understanding through faith, by splitting reality into two realms
and establishing a boundary line that kept one epistemology separate from the other. One was the realm of grace which could only

―――――――――――
[10] (1910).

be comprehended by faith and the other was the realm of nature, which could be known by reason. In the realm of grace, Aquinas placed such things as heaven, the soul and the Trinity, while in the realm of nature, he placed the earth and all that resides in it including the human body and, interestingly, also the presence of God. Regarding the knowledge of God, he had the following to say:

> There is a twofold mode of truth in what we profess about God. Some truths about God exceed all the ability of the human reason. Such is the truth that God is triune. But there are some truths which the natural reason also is able to reach. Such are that God exists, that He is one, and the like. In fact, such truths about God have been proven demonstratively by the philosophers, guided by the light of the natural reason.[11]

This division promoted the idea of an objective reality during and after the Middle Ages. In the 18th century the line that divided faith and reason was to take us on a journey leading to the modern and eventually post-modern eras. We shall return to this, but at this stage we must again consider Augustine as we introduce multi-modal systems thinking.

Multi-Modal Systems Thinking

Augustine exerted a forceful influence during the Reformation. This was not limited to the theological arguments of reformers such as Calvin and Luther; it had an impact on the rise of modern science that followed the Reformation. A great number of the post-reformation scientists subscribed to Augustinian epistemology. For many of those living in the 16th and 17th centuries, such as Brunfelds, Bock, Fuchs, Celsius, Lobelius, Kepler and the 18th century's Linnaeus and Boerhaave, making science was a communion and dialogue with God[12]. Multi-modal systems thinking grows out of sharing with Augustine and those who followed him – as well as those who preceded him – the same personal experience of God and the universe and of wishing to integrate this experience with our thought. Figure 4-2 represents this experience with God at the centre, not only caring and governing us and the

---

[11] Aquinas (1955, I, 3, ii).
[12] Hooykaas (1972).

universe, but also speaking and responding to us and offering guidance to our thought.

Figure 4-2: Context of Thought

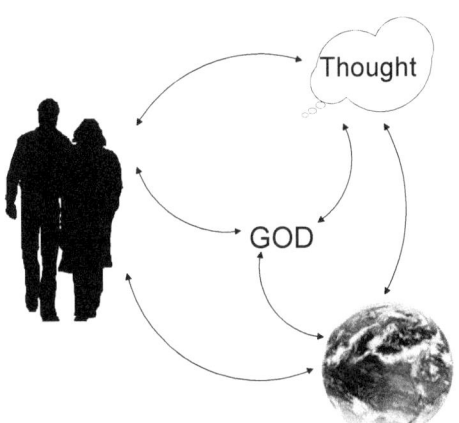

We can think of God's government as reaching us in two intertwined forms. The first is determinative, that is, it always exerts its own fulfilment. To this belong laws such as gravity. Gravity is always obeyed: if a man jumps off the twentieth floor of a high rise building one may be assured that he will go down and is not likely to be seen around again. All the cosmos, including man, is subject to the determinative order. Only man, however, is subject to the second form of order, the normative. This is because this order addresses the human will and only humanity has will. It is what distinguishes us from other creatures and makes us persons. For example, traffic regulations stipulate maximum speed limits on roads, yet the fulfilment of these limits is contingent upon the will of the people to obey or disobey them. One can expect that the majority of citizens will obey such laws, but this is only an expectation.

We can also think that both the normative and determinative orders appear in diverse modalities[13]; Dooyeweerd, who developed an elaborate theory of modalities, identified fifteen: numeric, spa-

---

[13] The idea of modalities is an ancient one as well as a contemporary one. In our times, it has been referred to by various authors such as von Bertalanffy (1971), Bunge (1959) and Dooyeweerd (1958; 1975).

tial, kinetic, physical, biotic, sensitive, logical, historic, informatory, social, economic, aesthetic, juridical, ethical and credal. To these, I have added an epistemic modality between the informatory and social. The order given by Dooyeweerd to these modalities – exhibited in Figure 4-3 – is not accidental. Modalities are increasingly normative (blank area) as one moves upwards from numerical to credal. In addition, each modality has the prior modalities as its foundation. For example, the biotic modality is founded upon the physical, kinetic, spatial and numeric modalities. Note that the line separating the two types of orders – normative and determinative – only represents the intensity of each type of order in each modality and does not represent a separation between the types. As indicated earlier, both types of orders are closely intertwined with each other. Note also that the highest modality is the credal modality, the realm of faith. We will discuss the epistemological significance of this modality later.

Each of these modalities is unique and each is governed by its own modal order. Each modal order is also irreducible, that is, one cannot totally understand one modal order in terms of another and it requires a distinct intellectual discipline to study each modal order. For instance, economics, jurisprudence, theology and mathematics are dedicated to studying the economic, juridical, credal and numeric modal laws respectively. While unique, each modal order weaves itself with the others into a rich multi-modal thread in the cosmic order.

Let us consider, as an illustration, the order that is displayed at each modal level in the tree illustrated in Figure 4-3. The tree has eight apples, two have fallen, the numerical modality would rule that now there are only six apples on the tree. The tree takes space to live, as determined by the spatial modality and the kinetic modality governs the movement of the falling apples as they travel down to the ground. The physical modality determines the velocity with which the apples hit the ground, which can be measured in metres per square seconds.

Figure 4-3: Modalities in an Apple Tree

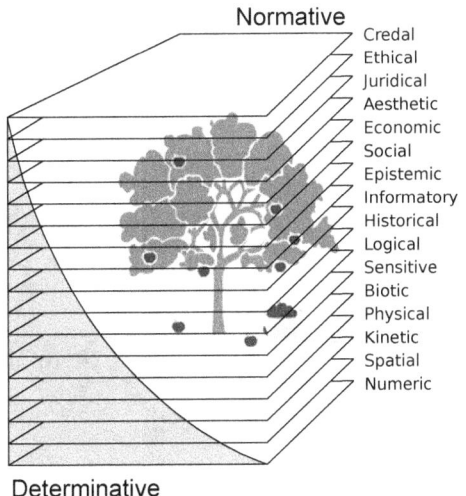

The tree requires nourishment, the nature and quantity of which is controlled by the biotic modality. A person approaching the tree can see, feel and taste an apple, all of which is controlled by the sensitive modality. The tree may be planted in an orchard with other apple trees, ordered in a rational manner to facilitate care and harvesting activities, reflecting the logical modality. The different varieties of apples with their distinctive appearance and flavours, have changed through time because of the influence of tastes and uses; this is governed by the historical modality. Each variety of apple has a name and there are also botanical names for the trees. All these names are governed by the informatory modality. Growing apple trees requires a specialised knowledge, this is governed by the epistemic modality. When the harvest time arrives, the orchardist hires fruit pickers; the manner in which they organise their work and their interaction with each other is shaped by the social modality. The resources needed to run an orchard, such as labour and capital are governed by the economic modality. Apple trees bloom in spring and are beautiful to behold, the appreciation of this beauty belongs to the aesthetic modality. The tree is legally owned by the orchardist and he also enters into contractual obligations with the people who help him with the care of the tree.

Ownership and contractual employment are ruled by the juridical modality. Growing apples may not mean just economics and observance of the law. The orchardist may love his trade and the trees inherited from his ancestors. Likewise, in addition to his economic and contractual obligations, the orchardist may have a special attachment and loyalty to the people who work for him. These are expressions of love functioning in the ethical modality. Finally, after a good harvest, the orchardist may acknowledge that the harvest is not only the product of his and his colleagues' labour, but he may also thank God for the harvest. This belongs to the credal modality.

The modalities and the sciences to study them allow us to look at ourselves, the universe and our relationship to God in a disciplined and ordered manner. There are a few aspects we need to consider briefly. Firstly, the modalities, or their sum, do not represent in their entirety the universe or our humanity or our relationship to God. That is: man, or the universe is not the addition of each modality. Rather, the modalities indicate the rich variety in human life and the universe, flowing as it were, through channels which, though diverse, maintain an essential integrity. Secondly, multi-modal thought, or any type of thought for that matter, is not autonomous, nor able to replace personal knowledge. Any scientific statement is ultimately a personal statement. The arrows that connect thought in Figure 4-2 cannot be disconnected, for thought remains dependant at all times upon our person and our experience of God and the universe. Thirdly, despite the great benefit that can flow out of the experience of God, there are nevertheless people who under the guise of being guided by God, inflict a great deal of suffering on others through oppression, abuse and even violence. Sadly, people are apt to corrupt anything including religion, science and other worthy things. There is no safeguard against this, but among people who attest to a sincere relationship to God and who make a positive contribution to society one can observe that this relationship is often guided by three things: faith, hope and love.

Faith has four main properties. One, it implies certainty or conviction. Two, though their faith is "...the conviction of things not seen..."[14], it is not blind. Faith does not preclude rigorous thinking about the things that one believes. We have already indicated earlier that this was captured in Augustine's integration of faith and reason. Three, faith is the bridge between the person and all reality that surrounds him, including thought. People live by faith. Trust is the essential element in relationships, whether to God, spouse, children, friends or others. Four, faith implies commitment. People who believe with certainty, diligently endeavour to shape their lives by what they believe. Yet, even those who exercise a sincere faith and who make a positive contribution to society would admit that they are far from perfect. They also must struggle to stifle a drive within themselves which in some people, and sometimes in whole societies, becomes unleashed leaving a string of deceit, injustice, cruelty and other crimes against our fellow man. The verdict of history seems to be that our ability to constrain this drive totally has not shown much advance; on the contrary, the power of science and technology have successively handed us the tools to eliminate our fellow man, the whole tribe, the village, the city, the nation and ultimately the whole of life on earth. We seem to be far too clever for our own good.

This does not leave much space for optimism about man being able to pull himself out of his predicament. We seem to be presented with only two choices: an existentialist type of pessimism[15] or hope in God's intervention. The latter does not mean that we take a passive attitude, but on the contrary, if we look at people like Mother Theresa, it appears that those who live by hope often labour with extraordinary self-sacrifice in situations that are utterly miserable. For Lewis and other Christians:

> Hope... means that a continual looking forward to the eternal world is not (as some modern people think) a form of escapism or wishful thinking...It does not mean that we are to leave the present world as it is. If you read history you will find that the Christians who did most for the present world were just those who thought most of the next...It is since Christians have largely ceased to think of

---

[14] Hebrews 11:1.
[15] Evans (1971).

the other world that they have become so ineffective in this. Aim at Heaven and you will get earth "thrown in": aim at earth and you will get neither.[16]

Self-sacrifice is an ingredient of love. Unfortunately, the English language has only one word to cater for a large number of meanings of love. What we are talking about is what the Greek language attributes to *agape* in contrast to *eros*, which means sensual love. Richardson gives the following distinction between these two: "...the latter is brought into action by the attractiveness of the object loved, whereas [*agape*] loves even the unlovable, the repellent and those who have nothing to offer in return."[17] Out of a genuine relationship with God there flows this type of love: a love that goes beyond the boundaries of duty or justice and that comprises self-sacrifice as an essential element and brings comfort and alleviation for those who receive it.

We shall return to consider this further when we discuss the normative order in the modalities but at this stage we shall apply multi-modal thinking to analyse the progress – or regress – of mankind through modernity and post-modernity.

Modernity and Post-Modernity

Modernity was shaped by the emergence of determinism, which in turn was an outcome of 17th century rationalism. Determinism strove to explain the universe by employing two major notions: mechanistic and economic reductionism. These eventually drove society into the modern and post-modern eras. Mechanistic thought became popular during the 18th and 19th centuries and was first promoted by such people as d'Holbach[18] and de La Mettrie[19]. In this perspective (see Figure 4-4), the universe was a closed machine. Thought was reduced to a science preoccupied only with the deterministic side of reality and which pretended to be autonomous from the person.

---

[16] (1955, p. 116).
[17] (1969, p. 269).
[18] (2005).
[19] (2009).

Figure 4-4: Modernity

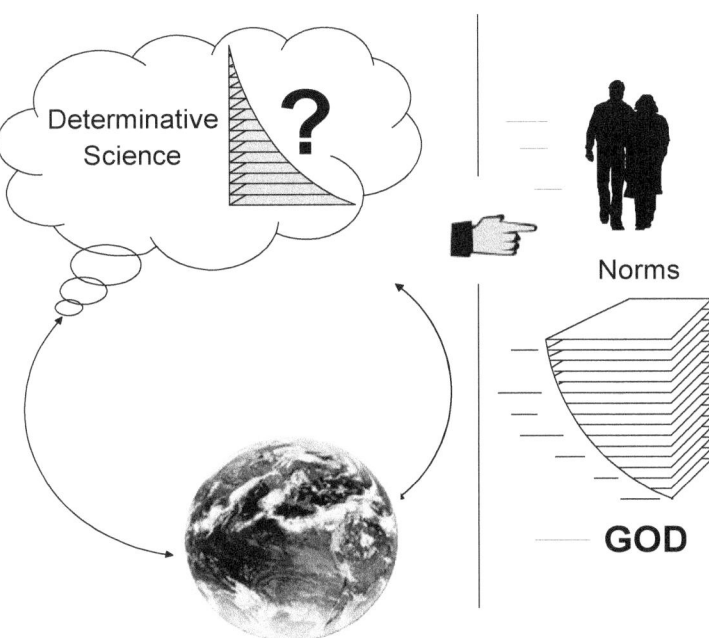

This thought could then objectively study the reality in the mech-anical universe[20]. Since God, the person and normative order had no place in a deterministic (positivistic) science, they were pushed out of science (see Figure 4-4) and replaced by de La Mettrie's "l'homme machine". This mechanical man's morality and con-science did not issue from his soul, but from glandular secretions in his body. Having been banished from science, the ancient pursuit of God, the knowledge of ourselves and of norms meant its intel-lectual decline; and without God or faith – the classical warrantors of the unity of truth – the secularised sciences began their frag-mentation. Here may be found the foundations of the rigid walls that separate today's university departments.

When all phenomena, including human behaviour, was con-sidered determined, a great emptiness appeared concerning the destiny of humanity. Determinism, as Figure 4-4 shows, erased a

---

[20] Clark (1974).

good part of our human image. How should we live? Is there any place for individual and social conscience? What are the rights and wrongs in life? What is the end of man? Determinism sought to fill the void with its second notion: economic reductionism. Laws of economics replaced the normative order and became a sort of catechism for industrial society. Two versions of this economic reductionism exist. The earliest, laissez-faire economics and utilitarianism, was related to the work of people such as Adam Smith and Jeremy Bentham in the 18th century and provided us with capitalism. The second, Marx's economic determinism, is a product of the 19th century and of the disenchantment with capitalism. It supplied socialism. Despite the conflict between these two versions, they share the same deterministic foundation, although they have trodden along different historical paths and met with different fortunes.

Though the rise of modernity in the 18th century expelled God and the normative order from science, it did not displace them from society and from the belief of ordinary people. While industry patterned their work life, their personal life still held to the norms that existed in the pre-modern era: they continued to worship, marry and conduct their affairs guided by the old norms. The intellectual fragmentation of the educational system itself helped them divide off their personal lives from their working or intellectual lives. Within the latter, determinism reigned supreme, but Aquinas' division between grace and nature restrained its reign and kept religion and morals sheltered from the pronouncements of science and industry. It acted like a dam that retained the waters of modernity from flooding the personal lives of an otherwise modernised and industrialised people. This damn burst in the 60s, sweeping away the normative order and ushering in the era in which we now live: post-modernity. Lyon[21] identifies three elements in this era. The first is nihilism or the abandonment of all conception of absolute truth, either normative or determinative. The second is an overwhelming consumerism in a market that trades everything: electronic education, entertainment, sex, truth and religion. The

---

[21] (1994).

third is technology and especially information technology. We shall briefly review each of these with the assistance of Figure 4-5.

Figure 4-5: Post-Modernity

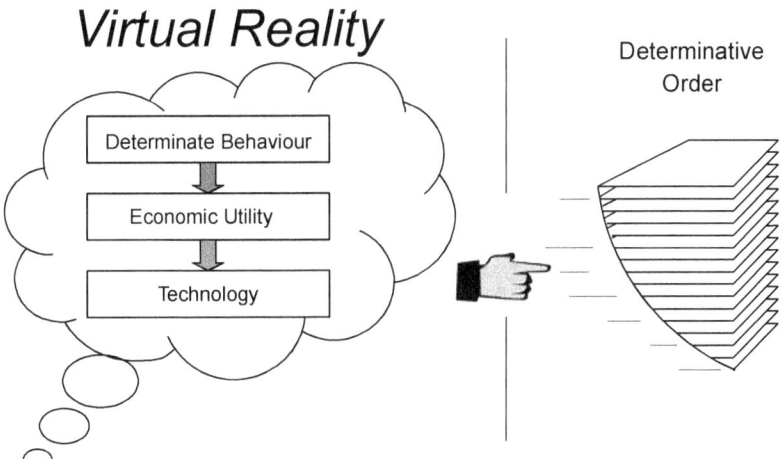

Despite modernists' claims to the contrary, all the sciences have their foundations firmly rooted in the normative order, even when focused purely on the determinative phenomena. This not only manifests itself in the many presuppositions that undergird each science, but also in the personal commitment of scientists to carry out their investigations with honesty and diligence. Without these norms, science could not function. The removal of the normative order in the 18th century started a process of erosion in science; it eventually drove the determinative order itself out of nature and into the limbo where modernity had first relegated the normative order. All that today remains on the left side of this line is an intellectual void; for according to Lyon, post-modernity denies any scientific legitimacy to thought or action.

Post-modernity suggests that the final removal of all notion of order emancipates man. Yet the opposite is the case: when man disdains the idea of order, he surrenders his free will and permits the determinative order to rule completely his behaviour. Free will implies that we can consciously make some choices, but if we dismiss the normative order, there is no criterion left for choice. We are left to the whim of our determinative impulses and in a condition not unlike that of animals. Animal behaviour is purely determinate; it lacks self-consciousness and will. An animal's impulses can only be satisfied by its environment. For example, squirrels who lack shelter cannot trade their excess food with others who lack food but have spare shelter. We, however, besides having our provisions from the environment, can satisfy our impulses through the market mechanism by converting these impulses into economic utility. We can trade this utility with others to increase the level of satisfaction above the one offered by our environment. Without a normative order, the market will inevitably seek to satisfy every appetite (consumer preference). If for some reason appetites are not matched, the market will take care of inciting a new appetite by releasing an 'appetiser' in the form of persuasive advertising and marketing.

The interconnections of an animal to its environment and the limited amount of information that it has constrains its impulses. This has some very salutary effects. For instance, the difficulty of catching its prey prevents an eagle from becoming obese and from exterminating the species on which it feeds. The bird's inability to alter the determinative arrangement that constrains its own behavioural impulses endows it with a good measure of 'civility'. Man on the other hand, can call on the gigantic power of technology to satisfy his appetite through the mediation of the market. Therefore, post-modernity has handed over to technology the place that modernity had previously accorded to deterministic science. This is evident in the privileged position that technology, and especially information technology, occupies in the post-modern world, especially in the technological university and in research funding. Information technology has not only bolstered production, but has also forged the necessary consumerism by reshaping the dissemination and promotion of products in the market. It has also blended television, telephones and computers to fill in the emptiness that has been left in people's minds and lives and to supply a new type of reality – a *virtual reality* – that shapes itself interactively to the whims of post-modern man.

Even on their own, consumerism and technological domination over every sphere of life offer a rather frightening prospect to mankind, but the addition of virtual reality is even more disturbing. Under the guise of virtual reality, it was possible for Baudrillard to declare in 1991 that the "Gulf War had not happened"[22]. Can we also declare that the suffering of people in Rwanda, Somalia and Bosnia has not happened either? This leaves us with nothing to prick our consciences, nothing to move us to compassion; for these things have no reality whatsoever. There is yet one more disturbing message that post-modernity has for us: by its own definition post-modernity marks the end of the road for human history. Society is crumbling into a condition where all is chaos, all relativity and incoherence and beyond which it is not possible to advance[23]. This completes the process through which the personal experience of God has been progressively eliminated from intellectual life.

Systems Science

We now turn to examine the position of systems science in this maelstrom of culture and thought. Von Bertalanffy[24] and the co-founders of systems science seek, in their new science, a departure from the mechanistic world view that rose in the Enlightenment. They also acknowledge the multi-modal nature of order, reject the closed system view of the universe and propose an open view instead. This once more makes space for the existence of God and religion. Yet, systems scientists – in various degrees – remain constrained by the influences of modernity and by the idea of the autonomy of scientific thought. For example, von Bertalanffy[25] deals with religion as a positive force in humanity, but also as phenomena which he can only observe objectively from the outside. For him religion is something experienced by "the esoteric few" and he seems to assume himself free from it as he analyses it scientifically. His view of man, is similar. It is, as if it were, a view of

---

[22] Lyon (1994, p. 52).
[23] Jameson (1991).
[24] (1971).
[25] (1981).

man under the microscope with no explicit link to the man who is looking through the microscope.

Another systems thinker who has included religious thought in his science is Beer[26]. Beer prefers syncretism: he blends teachings from various religions – such as Christianity, Buddhism and Hinduism – within the systems framework he has constructed. There are many instances where Beer alludes to a personal conviction to religious and ethical principles and we owe him much for introducing them into management science as badly needed humanising factors. Yet, when moving from personal conviction to scientific conception, the personal seems to be lost in an autonomous cybernetics to which religious principles are only added as supporting pieces of evidence.

One of the systems scientists who has written most extensively on the issue of religion is Boulding[27]. His work seems to be divided along Aquinas' line; part of it has a modernist detachment while the other reflects an Augustinian inclination to speak out from his faith. At times, he seems to accept the principle of the autonomy of science without question, such as when he affirms that "...[t]he love of God escapes both the test tube and the formula"[28], while at other times he "...long[s] for a new and greater Aquinas, to bring together once again Grace and Truth, Wisdom and Power, Faith and Knowledge in blessed union."[29]. One may speculate whether it was not his longing for an Aquinas rather than an Augustine that may have hindered his efforts to fully integrate his thoughts to his religious experience. Nevertheless, we are indebted to him for his labour in bringing a humanitarian touch not only to systems science but also to economics.

One of the first major departures from the autonomy of thought made by systems science comes out of the work of Checkland[30]. His concern over the vast limitations in *hard systems* design approaches derived from engineering when applied to designing social systems, led him to develop a *soft systems* approach that re-

---

[26] (1994b); see also Harnden and Leonard (1994).
[27] (1956b; 1970; 1987).
[28] (1970, p. 179).
[29] (1970, p. 195).
[30] (1981).

cognises the personal aspect of design. To attain this Checkland adopts a Kantian type of subjectivism, where the normative and the religious aspects fall into a noumenal or *fuzzy* world. Here, rigorous or hard thought appears to be of little use and so this is reached by pooling together subjective interpretations of this "fuzzy world into the systems design process. The danger in this approach is that it succumbs to a relativism where it is no longer possible to judge the content of such interpretations even if some of them should be detrimental to people, a fact that is acknowledged by Checkland himself. Thus soft systems design turns out to be systems science's own post-modern version.

This problem of relativism has preoccupied various systems scientists. For example, critical systems thinkers such as Jackson[31], have dismissed the modern objectivity in systems thinking and recognise the subjective nature of thought while at the same time avoiding relativism. Critical systems thinkers endorse a number of commitments: "critical and social awareness, emancipation and complementarism in theory and practice..." by accepting that "out there are some hard factual conditions that do not exist in the mind only."[32] Here we have a self-reflective struggle for a via media between modernity and post-modernity, objectivity and subjectivity and between optimism and pessimism[33].

There are however two main problems with critical systems thinking. The first is that this may appear as an intellectual formula to have one's cake and eat it at the same time. One can be subjective, but at the same time one may be objective by reaching out "toward the system's epistemological ideal"[34]. This may resemble the Augustinian/multi-modal epistemology, but the difference is this: there seems to be very little to be grasped in the systems epistemological ideal, especially to the non-academic manager or systems designer who knows nothing about epistemology. Conversely, what can be grasped from God seems to be rather significant, if we are to judge by what people have produced out of this. In addition

---

[31] (1991).
[32] Flood and Ulrich (1990, p. 26).
[33] Flood and Romm (1995).
[34] Flood and Ulrich (1990, p. 256).

to this, while theology can be as abstract as epistemology to the common person, it is not a requisite to reaching God. An abundance of religious practices, including prayer and worship are practised by many with most fruitful results, including intellectual.

The second problem is closely linked to the first. While the commitments of critical systems thinking are worthy and necessary as part of a normative starting point, they are by themselves not sufficient. There are a large number of other commitments that are required if systems practice is going to make a significant impact on the industrialised society in which we live and in the management that leads it. The list must be far longer and would include such things as love, patience, forgiveness, perseverance, dedication and so on. All these are essential for human existence and activity and yet they have been effectively deleted from the dictionary of modern industry and management. Once more, reaching out for God may prove a more fruitful endeavour for commitment as is attested, for example in the fact that, long before systems science was even thought of, prophets brought to oppressed people their message of emancipation, something that was utterly foreign to the ancient world. When asked by the oppressors whence they had acquired such a bizarre idea, their answer was: "from God".

Reduction and Expansion in Thought

Let us once more return to Dooyeweerd's modal theory: though each modality has its unique order, there is a certain degree of correspondence or homomorphism with the order in other modalities. Thanks to this homomorphism, it is possible for us to use one modality as the symbolic representation or idiom of another to generate information and enhance our knowledge[35]. For example, one can use numbers (numerical modality) to express economic behaviour (economic modality). This homomorphism provides the key to the symbolic representation of order, which in turn is ruled by the informatory modality. That is, there is a modal order of information that tells us – both in a normative and determinative way – how information can be generated and commu-

---

[35] de Raadt, J. D. R. (1991).

nicated. This order is studied by sciences such as linguistics, information theory, communication theory, quantitative and qualitative methods.

Information, however, is not the same as knowledge. The interpretation and evaluation of symbols, according to the order of the modality that has been selected as an idiom, is regulated by the epistemic modality, which is studied by disciplines such as epistemology and philosophy of science. It is this modality that contains the laws of knowledge that suggest two approaches to knowing: reductive and expansive. If one desires to understand the determinative order, then one selects a reductive method. One isolates the variables in one modality and translates them into another that has a greater proportion of determinative order and, therefore, greater potential for causal explanation. This second modality becomes a scientific idiom that enables the manipulation of the variables in a symbolic manner and according to its own laws.

Let us consider, for example, the following question: how do carpenters determine the price of their work for doing home renovations? This question pertains to the economic modality. To explain the determinative forces that shape prices, economists, in common with other scientists such as physicists, often translate the variables under study (see Figure 4-6) to a modality with a greater determinative order. They usually select the numeric modality, for it best clarifies the cause and effect relations between the variables. Consequently, the relation between the variables appears in the form of a mathematical formula, such as the one shown in Figure 4-6. This is a simple model of the demand function stating that:

$P = a + b\,D$
where P = price
D = demand for this type of work
a and b = constants.

Figure 4-6: Reductive Method

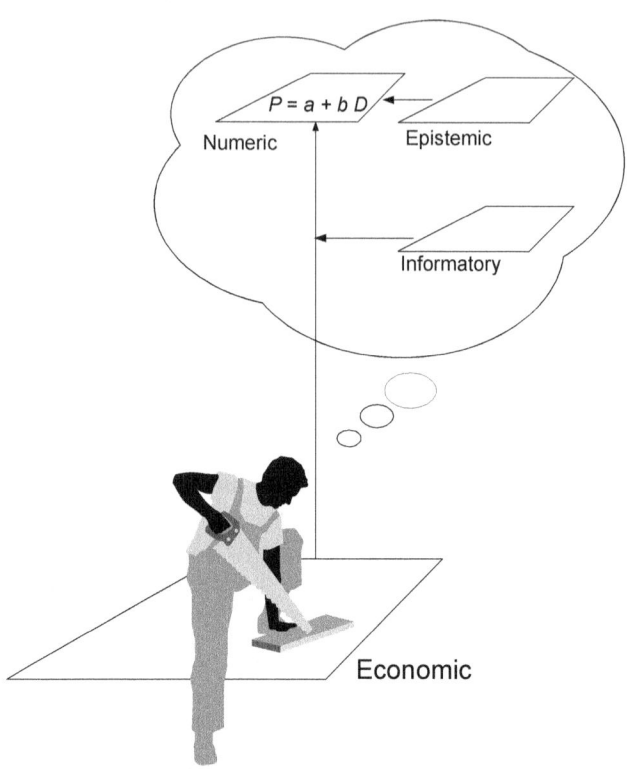

This equation isolates the phenomenon by representing the economic variables as numbers. Figure 4-6 shows the informatory modality regulating the representation of the price and the demand for the carpenter's work in terms of P and D. Given that the greatest degree of determinative order is found in the numerical modality and the ease with which numbers can be manipulated, mathematics is bound to be a favourite among most scientific methodologies, including economics.

Yet P and D are only numbers; we need to refer to the epistemic modality to realise that these numbers and the equation cannot exhaustively specify the economic dimension of a carpenter's work, for the economic modality is highly normative. The carpenter also needs to understand the normative order that is involved in the economics of carpentry. It may be that a large demand combined with a tight supply of carpenters has led to a price that only those with a high income can afford. Others, such as young couples with modest incomes and growing families, may not be able to pay, regardless of their needs. The carpenter ought to set a price not only according to the economics of cost, supply and demand, but also considering the tight economic circumstances of his customers. In employing the word *ought*, we have shifted our discussion to the normative side of this business. Here one needs a different epistemological approach; one must move upwards, from the more simple modalities to the more complex ones, as the carpenter is doing in Figure 4-7. His thought now becomes encircled by the juridical, ethical and credal modalities.

Norms are highly interconnected. They do not become evident by scrutinising them in isolation but, on the contrary, by observing them as they affect other things: eating an apple is not wrong in itself, it is only wrong if the apple has been stolen from someone else's tree. However, taking the apple may not be wrong if a person is starving and the owner cannot be found. To understand the normative significance of an action, one must search for its implication upon other things. This is almost exactly the reverse process of isolating variables to understand the determinative order. To understand the normative implication of charging a price, the carpenter needs to move upwards to another modality that is more normative than the economic, such as the juridical. This modality provides a fuller picture of how his actions affect other people. It shows him that he must balance his own needs with the needs of his customers and that a just price should reflect this. A just price may still be beyond the reach of his customers and he may have to go further into the realm of ethics to find how he should act. The ethical modality is the realm of love and as love often demands self-sacrifice, one needs a deep motivation to enter it.

Figure 4-7: Expansive Method

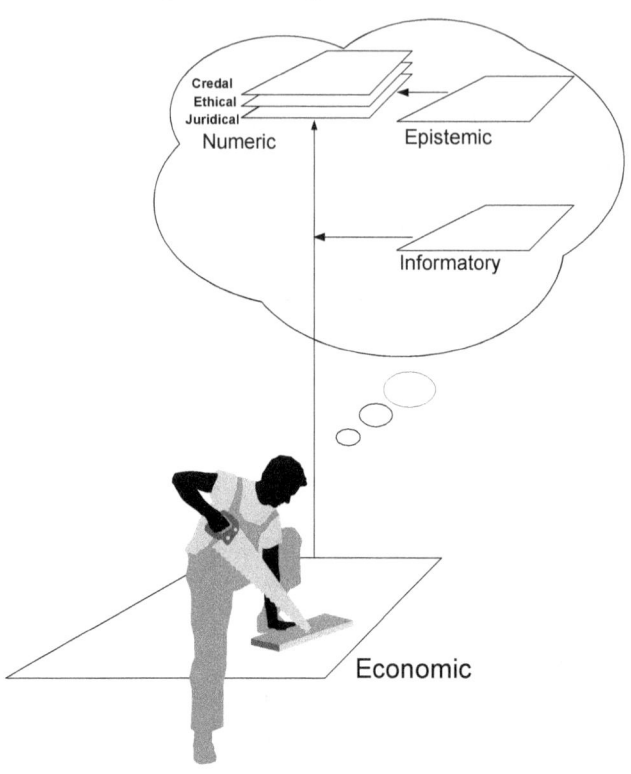

Such encouragement is found in God's own love. God's love is – as we have already argued – a matter of personal experience, but that does not exclude the fact that our understanding of such an experience cannot be enhanced by the study of theology. It focuses on the credal modality, the most normative of all modalities and the one that provides the most ample stage upon which we can scrutinise the consequences of our actions. Hence, it is the ultimate modality in which we can resolve normative issues. This often shows in our discussion about norms; we usually preface them by words such as "I believe that..."

This makes theology's relationship to the normative order somewhat analogous to the one between mathematics and the determinative order. Like mathematics in the determinative order, theology is pivotal for understanding the normative order. However, theology should not replace our personal dialogue with God. Its task is to expand its scope and make it more mature and profound, so that we do not limit in our minds God's sphere of interests to the Sunday school picnic and the health of the parishioners. On the contrary, theology makes us appreciate the breadth of God's involvement with humanity and the universe including the composing of symphonies and the test tube in the laboratory.

Thought, therefore, always combines these two methods of understanding, expansive and reductive. Each method enriches and improves the other at every modal level in a manner similar to the interaction between faith and reason promoted by Augustine (see Figure 4-1). One should subject every reduction, as illustrated in Figure 4-6, to a critical evaluation by an expansion such as that depicted in Figure 4-7. Conversely, every new knowledge gained through reduction should polish and enhance our expansive thought. Furthermore, the combined reductive and expansive thought is not autonomous, but takes place within the elements in Figure 4-2. That is, the thought of the carpenter is an integral part of his person and of his experience of the cosmos and of God. Thought, no matter how scientific and abstract, exists within their context and for the deeper human enjoyment of these. If, as Boulding has suggested, "the conceptual framework of economics....and the practical questions on which it impinges are concepts which inhabit a self-sufficient realm of their own, and seem to have nothing to do with the realm of discourse in which we discuss God...",[36] then this is due to our doing. We have, of our own volition, secularised and de-personalised science at our peril. We can only blame ourselves for a somewhat dull and empty science, chained to industrial self-interests and normative chaos.

What about a carpenter who is an atheist? Are norms beyond his reach? Even an atheist carpenter would have to recognise the inescapable religious foundation of his thought and norms. For he is indebted to the rest of humanity for his ability to think. No matter which culture we consider, it has historically linked its thought to its religious experiences. Thought is a part of our person and we almost invariably seek to understand ourselves as the image of

---

[36] (1970, p. 187).

God: "To seek God is to seek man."[37] The atheist carpenter practices his religion by proxy.

The inclusion of an epistemic modality among the modalities
defined by Dooyeweerd reflects the difference between rationality
in a modern sense and rationality in a multi-modal sense. People
often think that reason is purely determined by the logical modality, some even consider them as synonyms. This is a very dull and
narrow minded reason. Perhaps it is due to this that others conceive irrationality as a necessary ingredient to put colour in an otherwise sterile intellectual life. Irrationality, however, puts confusion in people's mind, not knowledge. It may also make people unable to discern between a healthy practice of religion and the
dogma of fanatic fundamentalism as seen in tele-evangelism, sec-
tarian groups and other practices that have rapidly spread with
post-modernity. Multi-modal thought, on the other hand, includes
the logical modality simply as another useful idiom – like the numeric modality – for thought. The laws of thought and science are
not placed in the logical modality but in the epistemic modality.
Here, human reason stands as much more than mere logic. It em-
braces the whole breadth of intellectual activity: a piano concerto
by Mozart's or one of Rembrandt's paintings is as much the work
of reason as Einstein's theory of relativity. The first two rely more
on the aesthetic modality as an idiom, the latter relies more – but
not exclusively – on the logical and numeric modality. Reason
viewed as such will grab hold of the best fitting modality as an
idiom, depending on the object of it's thought and will make this a
rich intellectual experience.

It should also be a personal experience. If we maintain that
reasoning is not autonomous, but is bound to our person, this
binding works in both directions. Reason is only useful when it
transforms us. Ethics, for example, is useless unless it guides our
personal lives. Without this, ethics is simply a coded list of nice
things to do that end up not being done. The same applies to any
discipline of knowledge, be it theology or mathematics. For even
mathematics, without a personal commitment, is no more than an

---

[37] Boulding (1970, p. 194).

empty game. Science remains part of personal knowledge[38] and only as such will it enrich and make us better people.

However, multi-modal reasoning is not just about systems thought, it is also about systems practice. Efforts have been made to help us regain control of our post-modern technological civilisation and to manage our lives. Naturally, these efforts are modest not only in size, but also in terms of the predicament of the human race to which we have referred earlier. The distinction between normative and determinative knowledge allows us to add some further detail to this. The pattern of humanity's behaviour through history shows that while we have increased our understanding of the determinative order with time, the same has not been true about our understanding of the normative order. Men and women today live with an enormously greater degree of scientific and technological sophistication than people five hundred years ago. Yet they may display no greater knowledge of love, justice or beauty than their earlier counterparts. One may say the same about science. Scientists in the twentieth century know extensively more than their counterparts five hundred years ago, but they may not be much wiser regarding the normative order. The normative reflections of Plato, Augustine and other ancient scholars are as relevant today as they were in their own age. This is not true, however, about their knowledge of chemistry or the movement of the planets.

This constancy of our normative knowledge is a good thing. It allows the normative order to direct the development of human knowledge and action in the determinative order, in a similar manner to a ship's compass directing the course of the ship. While the ship is in motion, it is important that the compass remains pointing to the north; only thus will it able to guide the ship to its destination. Likewise, we may regard the normative order as mankind's compass piloting it to its destiny. Sadly, while mankind's determinative knowledge has accumulated, its normative knowledge has been rather volatile. The path of human knowledge has been somewhat like a spiral (see Figure 4-8). Along the horizontal axis determinative knowledge moves forward with time, yet along the

---

[38] Polanyi (1973).

vertical axis normative knowledge oscillates like a pendulum. At times, it surges upwards, at others it plunges into decline. We have already alluded in the above that while the technological power of humanity has increased exponentially, there is no evidence that, as people, we have become any better. All we can see is that at times in history we improve, only to recede in the next generation. Thus, any form of systems thought and practice – not matter how sound – should have no grounds for optimism within the span of history. One must move beyond history to gain, not optimism, but hope. For even though hope seems a rather long term affair, it has nevertheless a very salutary effect when mixed with our thoughts.

Figure 4-8: Unfolding of Knowledge

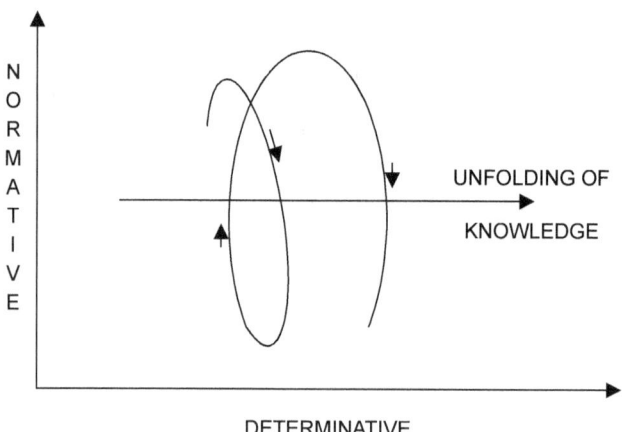

Conclusion

Our investigation having come now to an end, we must sum up our findings and address the questions posed at the beginning of this paper. We have found, firstly, that the secularising force that took over science during the Enlightenment had its root not so much in scepticism, but in the autonomy from God and man that much of Greek philosophy conceded to thought and rationality. This autonomy was in conflict with the Hebrew view of thought, a conflict that was carried on in the later history of Western thought. At times, this leaned towards the personal side and at others, to-wards the autonomous side. During the Enlightenment, autonomy become automata, that is, a deterministic and mechanistic view of the universe took hold of science. God, the person and normative thinking were exiled from science.

Secondly, the normative void that was left by Enlightenment science was filled by economic utilitarianism that arose about the same time. From then on norms within economics and industry became closely linked to money. The progressive expansion of modernity beyond the walls of industry and academia and into our private lives has reached consummation in the age of post-modernity. This is an age of crisis: both the foundations of normative and determinative knowledge are now foundering, tossing our society into normative chaos and intellectual confusion. Meanwhile industry and technology have fully moved into the driver's seat of our private and working lives and lead our world.

Thirdly, we have exposed the fraudulent nature of autonomous thought and rationality and the unwarranted optimism that this injects in us. We have advocated for a recognition that thought is linked to our person and to our experience of God and of the universe and proposed a broad multi-modal rationality instead of a narrow, purely logical one. Science must also recognise the tragic predicament of humanity in history: while our determinative knowledge and power seems to have progressively increased, our normative knowledge and behaviour has tended to oscillate. This dismisses any optimism for the future of mankind that is based on an autonomous rationality. Furthermore, if we wish to learn about the determinative order, it is a good idea to read the latest research reports, but if our aim is a normative understanding, it is wise not to neglect the reading of our spiritual and intellectual ancestors, for they in turn, did the same. We end, therefore, by quoting such an ancestor, who in turning to his own ancestors found that:

> ...those who are praised as having most closely followed Plato... and who are said to have manifested the greatest acuteness in understanding him, do entertain such an idea of God as to admit that in Him are to be found the cause of existence, the ultimate reason for the understanding, and the end in reference to which the whole of life is to be regulated.[39]

---

[39] St. Augustine (2014, VIII-4).

5 Ethics for a Civilised Life

J. D. R. de Raadt

Introduction

As I have struggled in the last ten years to direct my work in systems science towards the issues that really matter in life, I have found it progressively harder to do science without reference to God. Without God, science seems to vanish down an alley of trivialities leaving us empty and helpless. This is even more intensely so when one grapples with something like ethics, at least an ethics worth living. Chesterton seems to have felt the same when he wrote:

> Morality did not begin by one man saying to another, "I will not hit you if you do not hit me"; there is no trace of such a transaction. There *is* a trace of both men having said, "we must not hit each other in the holy place." They gained their morality by guarding their religion.[1]

Ethics has entered human civilisation and my life through the experience of God. That is, people gain their knowledge of ethics by receiving it either directly from God or ultimately from another person who has received it from God. God has planted ethics in mankind. Thus, my effort has been directed "...to create a science that deserves a God"[2] and named this endeavour *multi-modal systems thinking*. This type of thinking is based on four tenets. The first is that understanding is not gained from the study of impersonal, inert and static laws (such as the Greek philosopher's *eidos*) but from our encounter with a personal, living and dynamic God who commands the universe. Secondly, our humanity is rooted in this personal, living and dynamic character of God. It can be said – without subtracting from his transcendence – that only God is truly human, ours is only a reflection of his humanity. If we believe this, then an incarnation of God in man should not surprise us[3]. Thirdly, life rather than mere existence, ought to be the first aim of

---

[1] Chesterton (1994, p. 70); italics are in the original.
[2] Churchman (1968, p. 126).

our search for understanding. Fourthly, our life has become a tragedy through our vanity. We all die, for the crimes against humanity have been committed by humanity either through commission or omission. We die in every form: we die as much ethically as aesthetically, socially, biologically and physically. And the universe dies with us.

The four tenets leave us with what Unamuno has called a "tragic sense of life"[4] and it has been my conviction that wisdom and the sciences should first concern themselves with this sense. They should seek to understand God's command as he leads us out of the tragedy. God's command is multi-modal as is evidenced by the variety of sciences that have emerged in the history of human thought. I have dealt with seventeen such modalities, from logical to credal (see Figure 5-1). These modalities not only represent the variety of dimensions found in God's command, but also the multifaceted character of life. Furthermore, God's command of the universe is not only multi-modal, but also universal and vocational. The universal command is addressed to the universe in general (shaded area in Figure 5-1), the vocational command, to man's heart in particular (blank area). By heart, I do not just mean emotions, but the inner totality of our person that exercises will. We are not responsible for the things that happen to us as part of God's universal command, but we are responsible for the actions we will. The universal command represents what we are as humans and what we cannot change. The vocational command represents the type of life that God wishes us to live; it represents the kind of men and women we ought to be. Though the modalities are diverse, they also are unified and held together by the universal and vocational commands as illustrated by the two arrows in Figure 5-1. The universal command moves upwards making each modality the foundation or raw material of the next one above. In this manner, each modality emerges out of the prior one with new properties but at the same time having lost some of the properties of the lower modality.

---

[3] Therefore, it is through his humanity rather than through his transcendence that we come close to God.

[4] (1912).

Figure 5-1: Modalities

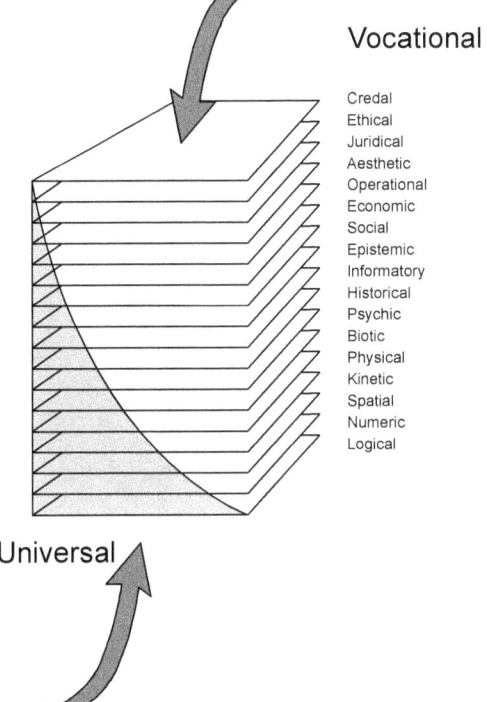

Vocational

Credal
Ethical
Juridical
Aesthetic
Operational
Economic
Social
Epistemic
Informatory
Historical
Psychic
Biotic
Physical
Kinetic
Spatial
Numeric
Logical

Universal

For example, the informatory modality provides the epistemic modality with the necessary information for knowledge. Know-ledge is richer than information but it lacks the close symbolic rep-resentation that characterises information. The vocational com-mand on the other hand, moves downwards. It makes each modal-ity the inspiration or mission of the lower one. For example: we seek information (informatory) in order to understand (epistemic). If we arrange the modalities according to the upward foundation and downward inspiration, then their order will be something like the one shown in Figure 5-2. Moreover, the universal command's presence will be stronger in the lower modalities and weaker in the higher ones as illustrated by the shaded area. The degree of strength of the vocational command will be the reverse. Finally, the highest modality is the credal – the realm of faith – and the lowest is the logical. While the logical modality provides the most basic raw material, that is, all other modalities emerge out of it[5], the credal modality provides the ultimate inspiration for everything. Ultimately, we live by faith in God. That is, life must be anchored outside rather than inside of us.

Figure 5-2: Ethics

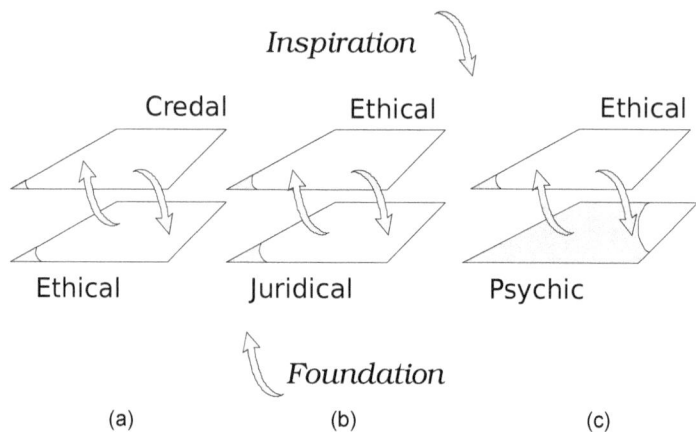

Ethics

Influenced by the impersonality of our philosophy and science, ethics is often regarded as a code of behaviour. While this type of ethics may lend itself to postulation and even logical analysis and justification, it has very little to offer. Such ethics cannot shape our lives and we cannot teach it to our children. For one cannot cast a personal and dynamic life on an impersonal mould. One can only live by an ethics that has a personal and committed love as its essence and is not a mere list of rules. Love is not a constraint, but is a driving and positive force that leads us to do more, rather than less. It is a way of life that marks the character of a person and leads him to care as much for his neighbour as he cares for himself. This is very well pictured in the following passage written by St Paul:

---

[5] This may have led the Greek philosophers to deduce that the universe was governed by pure logic.

Love is patient, love is kind.
It does not envy, it does not boast, it is not proud.
It is not rude, it is not self-seeking, it is not easily angered, it keeps no record of wrongs.
Love does not delight in evil but rejoices with the truth.
It always protects, always trusts, always hopes, always perseveres.
Love never fails.[6]

However, since man has violated all justice due to vanity, love must also entail sacrifice. Sacrifice means paying for the shortcomings – including the injustice – of our neighbour. Therefore, God paid for the shortcomings of humanity by becoming incarnate in a perfectly just man and suffering the treatment Glaucon had anticipated:

...the just man who is thought unjust will be scourged, racked, bound – will have his eyes burnt out; and, at last, after suffering every kind of evil, he will be impaled:...[7]

This sacrificial fulfilment of justice by God must be appropriated by us and made central to our love and ethics. Since there is always someone who draws more than his just share in this world or maliciously causes damage to others, others must compensate with love for society to remain viable. Ethics is, therefore, the art of self-denial whereby we devote our life and work to serve and make up for the shortcomings of our fellow man hoping that someone will make up for our own shortcomings. This is precisely the opposite of the utilitarian ethics that rules our market economies today. But self-interest does not clean the environmental pollution left behind by industry. Greed does not care for the poor and destitute left outside the margin of industrialised wealth. Only self-denial and taking up our cross does.

Foundation and Inspiration of Ethics

There are several connections – both universal and vocational – that exist between the ethical modality and the others. They are of particular interest to systems science for these connections make the various social and natural systems cling together. Love ought

---

[6] 1 Corinthians 13:4-8.
[7] Plato (2008a, II).

to inspire our operation in every modality such as in the arts (aesthetic), in learning (epistemic) and (social) interaction. Love brings its share of sacrifice and suffering, for suffering will be the companion of love in every modality of life. Even our intelligence and understanding cannot be developed without suffering[8]. Figure 5-2 shows the ethical modality as a foundation and inspiration to three other modalities: credal, juridical and psychic. Creed inspires love in two ways (see Figure 5-2a). Firstly, one can only believe in love. Without faith, loving our neighbour, let alone sacrificing our self-interest for his sake, is sheer madness. Secondly, the personal quality of love that St Paul so vividly describes, reflects our experience, again through faith, of the character of God. St Paul taught us the love he saw in Christ whom he believed to be God. Love on the other hand provides the foundation for genuine faith. We may use love as the test of the sincerity of what people believe. God is love. We should be on our guard when people claim to have received direction from God to act in a way that does not show his love. The extreme example of this are holy wars, forcefully imposed moral purges, murder and other acts of so-called martyrdom including suicide. It is a paradox that in industrialised societies that regard themselves as advanced and secular one should find so many cruel religions and such credulity among the people. Perhaps it is an indication that in industrialised societies people do not know much about love to be able to test their religion.

It is common for people to confuse ethics with justice. Many who write about professional ethics, for example, mean justice rather than sacrificial ethics. An action is just if a person has an obligation to act towards another person who has a right. It is a matter of justice that I produce a full day's work for my employer's full day's pay. It is a matter of sacrificial ethics that I decide to do some extra work after closing time to help him without expecting any compensation. Moreover, justice cannot exist without ethics. Ethics is necessary to inspire justice (see Figure 5-2b): justice must be tempered with mercy (love). Justice that is not inspired by ethics will eventually become oppressive and an instrument of repres-

---

[8] A cybernetic homomorphism of this relationship between suffering and learning is expounded in de Raadt, J. D. R. (1991, p. 60f).

sion that will destroy people and society. A judge who severely exercises justice without love will not dispense true justice. Moreover those who thirst for justice without love, turn it into vengeance and this often leads to their destruction, as well as to those whom they seek to avenge. On the other hand, love without the foundation of justice is like mothers who pick up the dirty socks of their sons without disciplining them. This kind of indulging love is not real love, for it is detrimental to youth. It omits teaching them their duty towards others, especially those who love them and provide for them. Likewise, the increasingly popular practice of men and women entering a de facto relationship without a civil marriage ignores that true love recognises the just obligation of spouses to each other. The dissolution of marriage often leads to great injustices to the more vulnerable members of a family, especially the children and without justice and a civil commitment between spouses there is no way to protect their rights.

It is also common for people to confuse committed love in the ethical modality with falling in love in the psychic modality. There is of course an important relationship between love and falling in love: the psychic modality provides the raw material in sensual affection through which ethical love can be expressed (see Figure 5-2c). We can thus feel the ethical love that another person has for us. However, this sensual affection should not be confused with ethical love. Romantically falling in love with someone is not the same as developing a committed love for that person. One may fall out of love as quickly as one has fallen into it, but the commitment of ethical love remains regardless of what our feelings may be at any particular time. Unfortunately, we do not have in the English language appropriate words to differentiate between these two types of loves. In Greek, two words are available: *agape* and *eros*. Psychic *eros* can be angered and the beloved may be bitterly reproached; sometimes the stronger *eros* is, the bitterer the reproach will be. Some of the most vicious remarks are uttered in a lovers' quarrel. Yet, *agape* holds the two lovers together and prevents them turning a lovers' quarrel into an enemy's quarrel. This long lasting quality of *agape* is not only present in romance. Most work requires similar love and devotion. Scholars, artists and others at times reach a point of saturation and exhaustion in their work and experience anger akin to a lover's quarrel. *Agape* for their work keeps them going despite the temporary revulsion that they may feel towards it.

Ethics in Systems

The channel that communicates ethical love to all kinds of systems is the social modality that governs the different roles and the structure of groups in humanity. Ethical love defines two social roles in man and woman. The masculine role is paternal and centres on leadership and the feminine role is maternal and centres on sustenance. These roles are not arbitrary, they reflect the character of God who both leads and sustains and who has created man and woman in his image and has delegated his leadership to man and his sustenance to woman. This means that the complete image of humanity is neither present in individual man or woman but in the complement of both. Leadership reflects itself in the multi-modal strength of man; and sustenance in the multi-modal tenderness of woman. It is this strength and tenderness that respectively form the essence of masculinity and femininity. Of these two roles, leadership confronts the greatest danger, for leadership includes protection and this may cost the leader's life. Therefore, a leader's job demands the greatest ethical love. As Lewis puts it:

> Christian writers (notably Milton) have sometimes spoken of the husband's headship with a complacency to make the blood run cold. We must go back to our Bibles. The husband is the head of the wife just in so far as he is to her what Christ is to the Church. He is to love her as Christ loved the Church – read on – and give his life for her (Eph. V, 25). This headship, then, is most fully embodied not in the husband we should all wish to be but in him whose marriage is most like a crucifixion; whose wife receives most and gives least, is most unworthy of him, is – in her own mere nature – least lovable... The chrism of this terrible coronation is to be seen not in the joys of any man's marriage but in its sorrows, in the sickness and sufferings of a good wife or the faults of a bad one, in his unwearying (never

paraded) care or his inexhaustible forgiveness: forgiveness, not acquiescence.[9]

While Lewis speaks specifically of conjugal relationships, there is a wider principle in his statement. It should lead men to treat all "...older women as mothers, and younger women as sisters, with absolute purity..." and with the same sacrificial love[10]. Yet, vanity turns the very strength that allows a man to lead and protect womanly tenderness into a weapon for abuse. Here lies the core of the conflict between men and women. Woman's tenderness requires protection and leadership to fulfil its sustaining role. This very mark of woman's femininity makes her vulnerable to the abuse of him who should be her leader and protector and who should be prepared to lay down his life for her. Feminism has risen as a response to this abuse. It has sought to constrain it by attempting to redistribute power in society, by removing the exclusive exercise of leadership and other traditional roles from men and assigning them equally to men and women. But, the benefits that this redistribution of roles has accrued on women are questionable[11], often they have left women in a more vulnerable situation. For removing man from leadership does not necessarily decrease his abuse of woman, but on the contrary, relieved from the responsibility of protecting her, he is likely to exercise more freely his advantages against her. Furthermore, equality of roles and women's participation in leadership roles has forced women to abandon their tenderness and become like men. This betrays a view that femininity is inferior to masculinity rather than recognising the equal human worth of the feminine talents. The discarding of feminine titles that differentiate between men and women such as manageress, actress and waitress and their replacement with manager, waiter and actor[12] give the impression that there is something demeaning in calling a woman, woman. This is exacerbated by the tragicomic picture of women dressed like men in army fatigues, in executive

---

[9] (1960, p. 148).

[10] 1 Timothy 5:2.

[11] For a critique of feminism see Bloom (1987), Held (1997), Lewis (1994) and Tar (1985).

[12] This happens in the English language. In other languages, such as Spanish, such linguistics artifices would be regarded as laughable.

business suits or priestly garb. Womanhood is demeaned even more so by some extreme cases of post-modern feminism that recommend the bordello queen style of rock star Madonna as a role model for the empowered woman[13]. Feminism has destroyed the mutual love and distinctive vocation of man and woman, for sacrificial love means giving to the other what the other does not have. Complete equality leaves nothing – either strength or tenderness – to be offered to each other. Moreover, we only have a complete humanity when the male and female character are displayed to the full and their differences exposed the most, just as the fan is most effective when it is widely opened. Only a complete humanity generates the necessary variety[14] to ensure the sustainability of our social systems. Without the strength of its men and tenderness of its women, a society becomes cowardly, uncaring and ultimately unsustainable.

We have seen so far how love relates to faith, justice and the psychic and to masculinity and femininity. However, love, to be real love, must express itself in action; it must be put to work. Self-denial alone is not sufficient, we must also carry our cross. This is done by love entering any modality, turning it into an action in the operational modality and then transmitting this to the social modality. For example, in the ballet company in Figure 5-3, love moves from the ethical modality into the aesthetic modality and induces love of beauty. This love of beauty moves next into the operational modality and turns into dance. It then transfers into the social modality where it becomes a social system: a ballet company with ballerinas, male dancers and orchestra. This social system is termed operational system because it operates. That is, it performs ballet. (If song rather than dance were the speciality of this company, then it would be most appropriately called the opera!) Note also how this operational system materialises ethical love in the male and female roles of the ballet as it gives expression to the tenderness of the ballerina and the strength of the male dancer. There is a perfect balance of the roles. In Swan Lake, Odette is given the central focus of the dance without obliterating the lead

---

[13] Kaplan (1990).
[14] In Ashby's terms, this is requisite variety (1976).

and energy – both physical and in the plot – provided by Siegfried[15]. Classical ballet provides of course, a most elegant and aesthetic representation of tenderness and strength and even of the sacrificial headship alluded to by Lewis in the quote above.

Figure 5-3: Ethics in Action

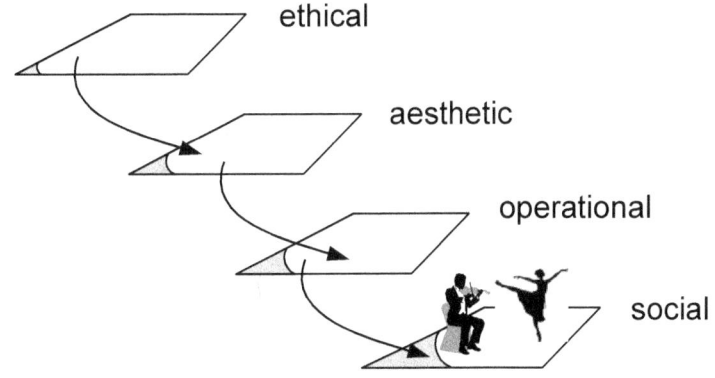

Every social system should inject love into its functioning within the modality that characterises it. Thus the church should nurture faith (credal), the family fulfil conjugal love (ethical), the court dispense justice (juridical), the art company perform works of beauty (aesthetic), the school educate (epistemic) and the hospital heal (biotic). Each of these activities is a blend of the ethical, operational, social and the particular modality that characterises the social system. In addition, as love blends with each of these particular modalities, be it faith, ethics, justice, beauty, knowledge or health it generates the sacrificial ethic of each particular vocation. Unamuno would like to make a religious practice of every form of work but I would go further and make priesthood out of it. For true priesthood is not the performance of symbolic sacrifices in front of altars, but work performed with sacrificial love. True priesthood is the labour, sweat and tears offered by doctors, teachers, nursing sisters, rubbish collectors, professors, physicians and

---

[15] Siegfried's hunting brings him to Odette. Yet, though he drives the plot and she waits, he does not deny her the centre stage of the drama.

many others who not only carry their own cross but also help others lug theirs[16].

Sustaining Ethics

Each of these social systems operating in the particular modality represents a living system exercising life in the particular modality. The artistic company represents the life of beauty. The school gives rise to the life of learning. These lives in each one of the modalities must remain viable; they must be sustained. According to Beer[17] and my own work based on his[18], the social unit that sustains the operational system and that ensures its viability, is the metasystem. This metasystem operates in the economic modality and has as its aim to preserve life in every other modality. A viable and sustainable system comprises therefore both social units: an operational system interacting with its environment and a metasystem managing as in Figure 5-4 which illustrates marriage – the most basic of social structures[19].

Man and woman's love for each other is transferred from the ethical modality to the operational modality where it inspires a number of activities: engendering and bringing up children, offering hospitality to friends and strangers and serving their community. These activities are vital to any society and must also be managed and sustained by a metasystem operating in the economic modality. We have here the most important viable system in society: a viable system that injects love into the community. We shall refer to it as the ethical household, *bayit* or *oikos*[20] to distinguish it from the dysfunctional and fragmented modern family.

---

[16] The New Testament office of pastor, bishop, deacon and elder is to teach, encourage, exhort and lead others in their faith. According to Morris (1964), nowhere are such offices given the title of priest except that they are regarded so in the general sense applicable to every other office such as are mentioned above.

[17] (1994a; 1995).

[18] de Raadt, J. D. R. (1991 and 1998).

[19] Once more, this is different to maximising economic utility as is mostly done in managerial practice today and taught by current managerial theory at management schools.

[20] The respective Hebrew and Greek words for household.

Figure 5-4: The Bayit or Oikos

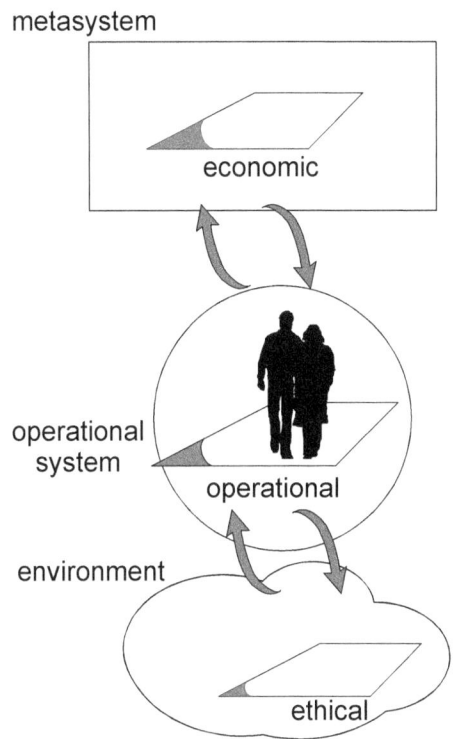

Note that even in the social structure of the viable system we can identify the male and female roles characterising it. The operational system is more masculine, centred on labour and production; the metasystem is more feminine, centring on nurturing and managing in a non-utilitarian manner. Once more, sustainability is dependent on the variety and complement of man and woman's roles.

Recursive versus Global Systems

The final question that we must answer is how can we make the sustainable social structure of marriage – an ethical micro-system – global? This depends, however, in how we are to understand the word global. Much effort seems to be spent in building a global village with a global market economy. It is built by connecting every social system with each other and for this purpose, the Internet has no doubt provided a marvellous tool. The builders of this global village have however ignored a basic systems principle enunciated by Ashby[21]. A system comprised of a large number of richly interconnected sub-systems – such as the global society we are attempting to build – is highly unstable and therefore, un-sustainable. This is because such a global system cannot reach stability until each one of its sub-systems is stable, but none of its sub-systems can be stable until the whole global system is stable. That is, instability in a sub-system proliferates and makes the whole un-sustainable. How can it be made sustainable? Ashby's law specifies two options: the system can become stable by increasing regulatory variety or by eliminating input variety. Since we have limited information and knowledge relative to the vast complexity of a global village, our recourse to regulatory variety is modest. We are therefore left only with the second option. We must standardise. We are forced to take away variety from the system by bringing in standardisation. A global system is only viable if it standardises its sub-systems. The Director in Brave New World perceived it with piercing clarity:

> "My good boy!" The Director wheeled sharply round him. "Can't you see? Can't you see?" He raised a hand; his expression was solemn. "Bokanovsky's Process is one of the major instruments of social stability!"... Standard men and women; in uniform batches. The whole of a small factory staffed with the products of a single bokanovskified egg. "Ninety-six identical twins working ninety-six identical machines!" The voice was almost tremulous with enthusiasm. "You really know where you are. For the first time in history." He quoted the planetary motto. "Community, Identity, Stability." Grand words. "If we could bokanovskify indefinitely the whole problem would be solved."[22]

For us, the Bokanovski's process means uniform "label" clothing, standard cars, standard houses, standard courses, standard textbooks, standard everything. Every attempt is made by our own

---

[21] (1976).
[22] Huxley (1946, p. 4).

world directors to constrain as much variety as possible in the very societies that boast to be democratic and liberal. But love cannot be standardised, decreed or implemented in a policy. It can only be personally transmitted. It can also be implanted in the recursive structure of the diverse social systems. In a recursive structure as defined by Beer (1979), principles of viability appear in each social system without endangering the autonomy of any particular system or level. This is like the genetic code that exists in a seed of an oak tree. The identity of the oak tree is carried by the code within the seed to every trunk, branch, leaf and flower. Through this recursive reproduction, a specific identity is passed from one tree to another without endangering the legitimate extra variety that each particular tree adds to the original code to make itself unique. Thus, while there is a resemblance between one oak and another due to their common genus Quercus, each oak is also different due to the extra variety that is given to every tree. Figure 5-5 illustrates how, like the seed that passes on life to the Oak, the bayit (ethical household) passes on love to social systems at every modal level. There it is transformed into a love for each one of the modalities be it creed, justice, beauty, learning or health. This ethic brings with it the basic social structure of leadership and nurturing which is essential for men and women to realise their vocations in each social system.

Conclusion

We may now summarise our findings as follows. Ethics is not a code of behaviour listing the things we should do and not do. Ethics is a driving force based on personal love and is received from our relationship with God. Because of the vanity of man, ethics must also be sacrificial to compensate for man's injustices. Being personal, ethics is embodied in our full humanity as jointly born by man and woman. Ethics should therefore evince both manly strength and feminine tenderness that should become operational in every field of service and communicated to every social system wherein such services are rendered. Nevertheless, the operation of love must be sustained and this is the task of management. Management should also be an expression of feminine tenderness seeking to ensure the viability of every social system. Finally, the communication of love to all peoples cannot be attained by a centralised global control system, but must be engendered through a recursive structure that carries love like the genetic code of a seed to every social system. And like the seed that must die to be able to transfer its life to the tree, so must ethics incorporate sacrifice to ensure the sustenance of our world.

Figure 5-5: Recursive Ethics

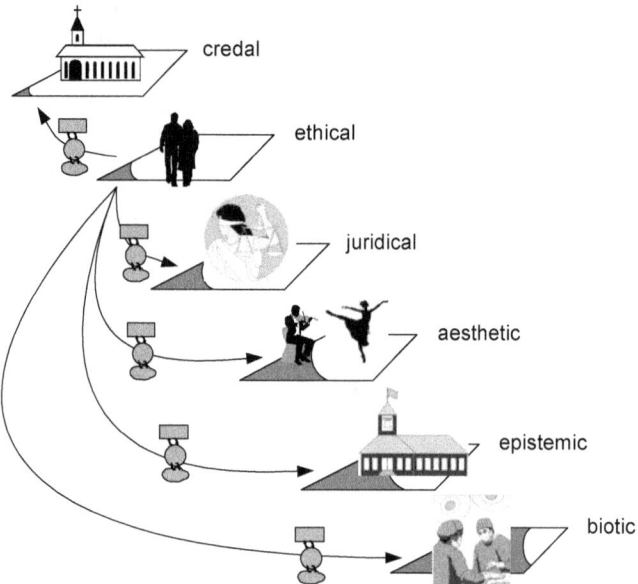

6 Qualitative Operational Research

J. D. R. de Raadt

Introduction

A controversy has recently risen in Sweden around the statements of a well known economist who has metaphorically stated that hunger may drive many people to look for work and thus decrease the rate of unemployment in Europe. The concern of this economist is that excessively generous unemployment benefits act as a disincentive on people to search for work. Some responded to this statement with strong disapproval. They suggested that it was harsh to blame the victims of unemployment for their predicament since it was due to adverse economic circumstances which they could not solve by themselves. It is not my intention to enter here into a debate about the justice or injustice of welfare payments. I will use this as an illustration of the type of problems that face decision-makers today and for which economic modelling of a quantitative nature is of very limited help. I will explain how multi-modal systems thinking can expand the scope of OR modelling and further help decision-makers and leaders in the community to manage the affairs of our society in a more effective and humane way. This particular application of multi-modal systems thinking is based on the epistemology presented in *Vision and Normative Science* (Paper 4) and the philosophical foundation for operational research and its place in social systems discussed in *Humane Operational Research* (Paper 2). A brief overview of the material in these papers follows.

Multi-Modal Framework

Multi-modal systems thinking links three elements together – life, wisdom and management – along two dimensions represented by the axes in Figure 1-1. In the horizontal axis lie a string of interacting systems such as orchards, families, trades, art companies, schools, transportation, courts of justice and hospitals. Within such systems life – both biological and cultural – unfolds. Within them mankind realises its vocation and finds fulfilment. Yet to understand these systems we must also refer to the vertical axis where we find layered a number of modalities that command all these systems. The foundation and character of multi-modal systems thinking – as we have labelled this approach to systems science – is prophetic rather than philosophic. The philosophic approach based on pure logic that we have inherited from the Greeks regards the universe as governed by inert, impersonal and static laws. According to them, the inquiry of philosophy starts with existence. It first asks, what is reality? There being no satisfactory answer to this, philosophy gets bogged down and it is as such that medieval scholasticism and modernism pass it on to us. Modernism has added to this formula its own secularisation and mechanisation. There is no hope, therefore, that an understanding, being built upon such inert, impersonal and static views of the universe can address the predicament of humanity. Post-modernism has attempted to escape out of this condition by regarding reality as the product of our own construction but has left us with no guidance as to how to live. And since life is the essence of our humanity, we do not have any idea of how to make humane decisions. So I have sought to follow the path of the prophet, with its own notion of wisdom and philosophy, rather than the Greek philosopher. In contrast to the Greek philosopher, the prophet regards the world as governed by a living, personal and dynamic God. Life, not existence, is his starting point. The prophet's first question is: how should we live?

Following along the prophet's line of thought, I view God's command of the universe as multi-modal and as both universal and vocational (see Figure 3-1). The universal command is addressed to nature (shaded area in Figure 3-1) in general; the vocational command to man's heart in particular (blank area). By heart, I do not just mean emotions, but the inner centrality of our person that makes us responsible for our actions as being distinct from those things that happen to us as part of nature. Though the universal command extends over all modalities it is greatest in the higher modalities and least in the lower ones. The highest modality is the credal, the realm of faith. Faith is the foundation of all activities that are distinctively human; that is, those for which man is responsible as man. Man therefore lives by faith or by inspiration (represented by the arrow) which means that life must be anchored outside of us, in God, rather than within ourselves as in existentialism or constructivism.

Understanding, in all its forms including scientific, is an integral part of human life and also founded on inspiration. All understanding is governed by the epistemic modality and its final goal is gaining wisdom. This wisdom, though being one, reflects nevertheless all the modalities. This multiplicity is evinced in the variety of specialised sciences that we have for each modality. For example, theology, ethics and sociology respectively study the credal, ethical and social modalities. Yet, to avoid the scientific fragmentation that followed the Enlightenment, multi-modal systems thinking aims to stress the unity of these modalities – without denying their variety – and to provide a bridge for the integration of the sciences.

Modelling Associations

While each of the modalities is unique, they do not exist in isolation nor are they totally different. There is a degree of homomorphism between them which allows one modality to be mapped on to another and this has provided multi-modal systems thinking with a foundation to build models. Let us return to the illustration regarding unemployment. Like most other industrialised countries, Sweden is experiencing a high level of unemployment. According to some, the generous welfare system discourages many unemployed people to look for work. Years of generous welfare has undermined the motivation of people to work and even lessened their esteem of it in a country that in the past was known for its highly developed work ethic. Now many people abuse unemployment benefits. This reflects the timeless dilemma of balancing generosity towards those experiencing hardship with avoidance of abuse of such generosity. Can operations research assist decision makers in managing this situation?

If we apply conventional operational research methods, we could develop a quantitative methods model that relates the number of people at work with fear of destitution as suggested by our economist. A simplified version of such a model could be quantitatively expressed as follows:

W = a + b F

Where: F = fear
W = number of people at work

Figure 6-1: Quantitative Model

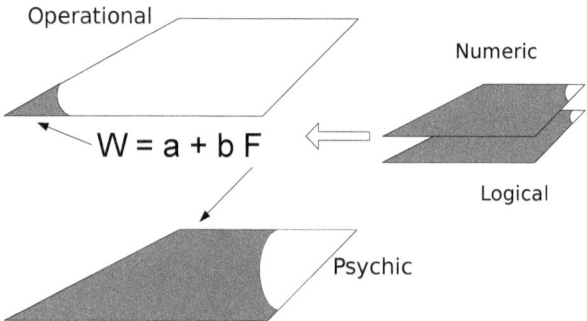

The epistemological assemblage of this model is illustrated in Figure 6-1. On the left side are the two modalities within which are found the variables we are modelling. Employment is located in the operational modality and fear in the psychic modality. According to economics, there is a relationship between these variables: as fear F increases, the number of people at work W will also increase. On the right side of the figure are found the two modalities that provide the idioms for the quantitative model. The two variables – work and fear – have been represented by numeric symbols and manipulated according to the numeric modality. At the same time they have been assembled into an equation – represented by the equal sign – that is governed by the logical modality. If decision-makers were to use such a model, they would manipulate fear to control the number of people at work. The same relationship between employment and destitution can be expressed in a model that employs different idioms. Consider for instance the following quote from a novel by Eliot:

> There's many a one who would be idle if hunger didn't pinch him; but the stomach sets us to work.
>
> George Eliot, *Felix Holt*

Figure 6-2: Qualitative Model

Operational

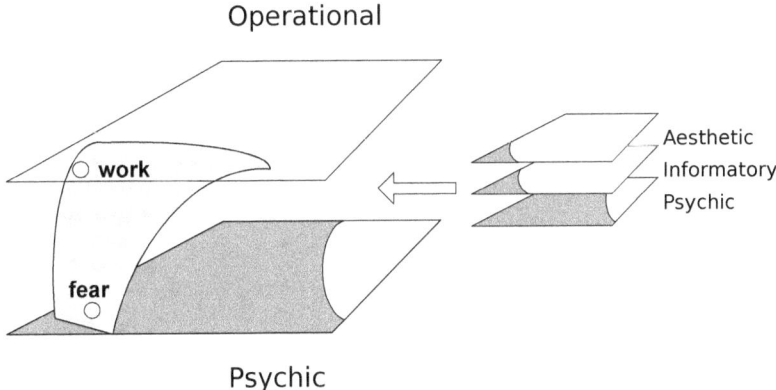

Psychic

This quote constitutes a type of model that states more or less the same as the above equation. However, rather than using numbers and logic as idioms, this quote – and the complete novel of which it is a part – employs beauty, language and the senses to put across its message. These three idioms respectively operate in the aesthetic, informatory and psychic modalities (see Figure 6-2). On the left hand we now find a surface arching over the operational and psychic modalities and representing Eliot's text. Rather than dealing with two isolated variables, we have a text – represented by the surface – that interlaces several words such as *man, stomach, idle, pinch* and *hunger*. Together these words convey a far richer meaning about work and fear of destitution than was found in the letters W and F in the prior quantitative model. The text draws out the personal nature of the situation in a manner that is not possible in quantitative models. This personal character is conveyed by the different modal idioms employed – aesthetic, informatory and psychic (see the right hand side in Figure 6-2). To convey the message to the reader, the aesthetic idiom employs the beauty of the text; the informatory idiom employs the English words and grammar and the psychic idiom, the emotional appeal of the text. Because these idioms – especially the aesthetic and the informatory – are more normative than the idioms employed by the quantitative model, they supply a more distinctively human character to our deliberation. They are able to convey to us a far more personal landscape than is possible when one only employs the numeric and logic idioms of quantitative models. Although a quantitative model can be manipulated more easily, a multi-modal model is far more powerful in conveying to the decision-makers the human content of a situation. If they value humanity, then they should also value such models.

These models do not have variables, but we can identify some key words – represented as *factors* in Figure 6-2 – that allow us to identify in a general manner their contents and to link one text with another through the association of ideas. We have identified two such factors in Eliot's text, *work* and *fear*. They are the same names we used in the quantitative model, but here they cannot be regarded as variables; they are simply key words. Yet, despite the more personal nature of the model in Figure 6-2, its link between *work* and *fear* is still of a universal nature and suggests, like the earlier quantitative method, that a person can be manipulated to work by increasing his fear of destitution. Manipulation of humans can sometimes be acceptable. Many local governments manipulate people to keep their environment clean by offering a small refund for each used container they return to a disposal centre. It is hoped that the long term effect of such manipulation will make people appreciate cleaner surroundings and that they will make it their responsibility to collect containers not for the sake of refunds, but for the sake of the environment. However, to rely exclusively on manipulation is to regard man as an irresponsible machine. What we are endeavouring here is to regard man as man, that is, as a responsible being who can be addressed as such and who can learn some new forms of behaviour, not through manipulation, but through persuasion. Searching for items that address the vocational part of human behaviour can enable this type of learning. The search starts by selecting items that contain the factors that interest us, that is, *work* and *fear*. Below are listed three such texts by Lowell, Gibran and the book of Deuteronomy:

> No man is born into the world, whose work
> Is not born with him; there is always work,
> And tools to work withal, for those who will:
> and blèssed are the horny hands of toil!
> > James Russell Lowell, *A Glance Behind the Curtain*

> Work is love made visible. And if you cannot work with love but only with distaste, it is better that you should leave your work and sit at the gate of the temple and take alms of those who work with joy.
> > Kahlil Gibran, *The Prophet*

> When you are harvesting in your field and you overlook a sheaf, do not go back to get it. Leave it for the alien, the fatherless and the widow, so that the Lord your God may bless you in all the work of your hands.
> > *Deuteronomy 24:19*

Each of these texts provides an insight into the nature of work. By saying that work is born with us, Lowell draws in the historical perspective of work. He attests to the abundance of tools for work – especially true in our technological society – and thereby allows no excuse for idleness. The marks of work in the horny hands are vouchers of blessings that are hoped for in the credal dimensions of work. Gibran provides an insight into work as an expression of love; love is so essential that without it work is worthless. Finally, Deuteronomy links work with concern for the destitute and also as a voucher of blessings. These texts are listed in Table 6-1. Also listed are the names of the various factors (as headings) and the modalities where each factor is found (at the foot). A dark factor signifies that it is shared by two or more texts while a white factor indicates that it is found in only one text. Dark factors provide a path to search for additional texts that are related to the theme under investigation. The arrows in Table 6-1 indicate two alternative paths that are available in a search that starts with Eliot's text. The first path would search texts through the factor *work* in the following sequence: Eliot-Lowell-Gibran-Deutero-nomy. An alternative path would first search through the factor *fear* and reach the factor *blessing*. In this instance the sequence would be: Eliot-Gibran-Deuteronomy-Lowell.

Table 6-1: Texts with Factors and Modalities

	birth	tools	work	fear	blessing	love	joy	God
Eliot			●	●				
Lowell	○	○	●		●			
Gibran			●	●		○	○	
Deute.			●	● → ●				○
	historical	operational	operational	psychic	credal	ethical	ethical	credal

The same is presented graphically on the left side of Figure 6-3. Each of the texts is represented by a surface spanning the modalities that are addressed in the text. Also shown are the three factors that are found in common in each of the texts: *fear, blessing* and *work*. These texts may be combined to produce a single store of information or surface as shown on the right side of Figure 6-3 (the figure also includes the white factors that are not shared between texts). This combined knowledge contributes in two ways to our understanding. Firstly, it provides us with a convergence of thought: the fact that the four texts written by four different authors agree on certain aspects about work and its benefits lends a certain strength and consistency to the conclusion that we may derive from them. It provides a solid base for our reflections and a persuasive power to our argument. Secondly, the surface extends our knowledge beyond the shared (shaded) factors by associating them with another set of non-shared factors (white) which represent new areas of reflection about work in the historical (birth), operational (tools), ethical (love and joy) and credal (God) modalities. The understanding of our responsibilities is enriched because most of the texts' material lies in the vocational region of the modalities. They tell us what we *ought* to do.

Figure 6-3: Combined Texts

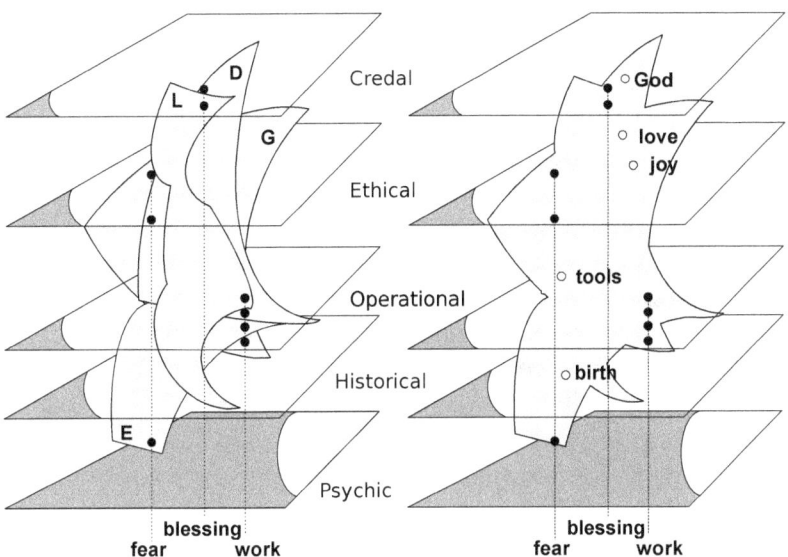

Items that can be included in this type of analyses need not be limited to literature, but can also include knowledge from interviews, anecdotes and descriptions of human experience and also knowledge that is expressed in other idioms such as music[1] and painting. Nevertheless the largest source is likely to be literature for this has historically been the favourite form of encoding human wisdom. The search and storage of these items can be helped by a computerised system. There are many software tools that can be employed. There are also specialised packages designed for this kind of work, but they lack a theoretical base to help organise the data into a structure that is meaningful for analysis. Therefore some time ago, I began developing a software package, SmCube[2], that provides all the operations and searches necessary to apply

---

[1] In an interview, the French sociologist Jacques Ellul said that when writing a book, he associated it with a particular piece of music which he listened to while writing it.

[2] de Raadt, J. D. R. (2001). This software, originally based on FileMaker, is now built on LibreOffice <http://www.libreoffice.org>. Further information is found in www.melbourneccd.com.

the method we have described. It provides an easy method to load this type of text into a database and to link it to factors and their modalities according to a predefined model that can then be iteratively improved. Once this has been done, the decision-maker can easily navigate through the database by selecting factors and identifying texts, diagrams and even sound recordings that are linked to these factors. This does not mean, however, that the database can replace the knowledge of the decision-maker, in the same way that one cannot acquire a solid knowledge of literature by reading the Oxford Dictionary of Quotations. Good reading is still essential for understanding the vocational issues in decision making. It cannot be replaced by the scanning of databases. This makes the distinction between information and knowledge and between the informatory and the epistemic modality most important. For though an information system such as this can assist the decision-maker with vocational information, it cannot provide the vocational knowledge and commitment that only exist within the person and which make him a professional decision-maker. Nevertheless this method, which has proven a useful method of research in scientific research, should also prove helpful to Operational Research and open the doors of modelling to issues that are closely connected with the interests of humanity and that are at present neglected.

7 Normative Factors and Viable Community

Veronica D. de Raadt

Introduction

This is the first paper describing a long-term research project examining factors important for village viability. The paper examines the methods aspects of using the multi-modal systems method in analysing factors affecting viability. As space is limited, the usefulness of applying multi-modal systems theory to small community viability, and a modelling technique developed to redesign the small community, will come later.

We firstly describe the village of Rosvik, the instabilities it is facing and why it was chosen for the study. Secondly we describe the collection of data and the different ways information was sought using interviews and panels of villagers. Thirdly, we describe the qualitative method applied (using SmCube) to identify the normative factors important for the viability of Rosvik. Fourthly, we introduce a matrix that presents relationships between the factors selected. The relationships are also presented in graphic form and shows the collected data being organised according to multi-modal systems theory. The paper concludes and summarises the relationships between normative factors, various modalities and community groups that promote or threaten viability.

Choosing Rosvik as a Case Study

Rosvik is a coastal village of just under 2,000 inhabitants near Luleå, capital city of Sweden's northern-most county. Its problems began in the 1970's when the steel plant in Luleå, a large employer of people in the region, expanded and many people from other parts of the country moved north. From that time until the early part of the 1980's, Rosvik grew more rapidly than ever before. Young couples bought houses that were a great deal more affordable than in the larger towns nearby. However rather than signifying growth and expansion, this marked the beginning of a downward trend. The steel plant grew to a fraction of the size anticipated and some people who bought houses found themselves without a long-term working future. Consequently there was a high rate of marital breakdown and other social problems. Rosvik youth were considered troublemakers and there were fights between them and other groups at the central high school in Piteå, a larger town near-by. From the early 1980's families began to move away from Rosvik and were not replaced. Houses were difficult to sell and sometimes remained on the market for years. Some home owners who managed to sell, got half of the value of their houses. Population loss culminated in a 20% loss from 1997-1999. Such problems make up a pattern of shrinkage and depopulation that has gone on in recent decades in many small villages and towns in northern Sweden. Unemployment in northern, inland communities has risen over the last decade to 25%. It was partly because of unemployment in inland communities that the population of Rosvik grew so rapidly in the first place. There had been a steady drift of population from remote areas towards coastal cities, towns and small communities. It is concerning that the same pattern is now being repeated on the coast and Rosvik and other small coastal communities along with it, are also losing population and unemployment is increasing.

In 1996 the declining number of families in Rosvik brought the village school, the only school option available, under threat. The municipality decided to close grade 6 and bus the children to a nearby village where Rosvik children already attend grades 7-9. Other government funded services, besides the school, were also threatened, including Rosvik's postal, banking, library, youth leisure centre and health services. Concerned parents who felt their children too young to be bussed away from the village, formed a group and exerted enough pressure on school officials to shelve their plans for the time being. They felt politicians were making decisions defined principally by economic pragmatism without concern for the children or the village. This was a negation of what people believed their village ought to be. The parents were so well organised, they not only asked for a reversal in the municipality's grade 6 decision, they got an architect to draw up plans to extend the school to grade 9.

It was at this point that I became aware of Rosvik's problems and was invited by the parent's group in the school to assist. They represented an educated group of people in the village and thought that the problems Rosvik was experiencing were profound problems and would not be fixed up with short-term solutions or more government spending. They talked about social problems among Rosvik's youth, losing youngsters to larger communities, government ineptitude and the need for new initiatives. They saw these culminating together in the long-term survival of Rosvik. It appeared to me that applying multi-modal systems theory could significantly contribute to understanding Rosvik's problems. In the first place their problems, especially the village's survival, indicated the necessity of understanding normative aspects – the focus of the theory. In the second place I was interested in future collaboration and the chance to implement some of my ideas, test and improve them. As villagers had approached me, I hoped we could collaborate some time in the future. Finally, I thought a systems study would be appropriate for Rosvik. It has numerous, interacting systems made up of families, the school, churches, sports clubs, a branch of a political party and businesses. I was also wanting to examine the impact of it being managed by a municipality, the product of a political merger of various villages. In the past each village had been managed locally by village leaders.

Reference has already been made to families and the school in Rosvik and it is helpful now to describe briefly the other village systems or groups. There are two churches in Rosvik. One is a small, combined congregation of the Swedish state church/EFS (Evangeliska Fosterlands Stiftelsen), the latter being a missionary branch of the state church. The other is Betel church, a free church, which means that it is free from state control. Betel belongs to Interact, an amalgamation of free churches in which every church is independent but has a relation with the parent group. Betel has a growing congregation and several families have moved to Rosvik because of the church.

There are two sports clubs; a small one with mostly Finnish members and the other, the Rosvik sports club to which about a third of the village belongs, including nearly every child. It is not only strong in numbers and a social meeting point but, for some villagers, as influential in village decisions as the local branch of the social democratic party.

Politically, Rosvik typifies many communities in the north of Sweden, also known as the red north. The branch of the social democratic party in Rosvik has been strong in the past, although the mood has changed and people are discontent with the party. Despite this however, 84% of Rosvik voted for the social democrats at the last national election. The high vote may indicate that people vote out of habit. Many say they would like change but there is a lack of new ideas and little real debate over the issues at hand. Politically speaking, municipalities are powerful. They control the economic purse strings and manage most of village life in Sweden including education, health and social services, roads, transport, sanitation and business support. Concerning the latter however, small business growth is not well established because large industries predominate in the north. Belief in small business and private entrepreneurship is modest and up until now, discouraged. As a result, although there are about 60 businesses in Rosvik, only one-third provide people with their livelihood. Of the other two-thirds, the owners work in other jobs, mostly in either of the two larger towns nearby.

Collecting the Data

I collected information in a diversity of ways so that different sets of data from different types of sources would compliment each other. The first data was collected in 1997 using semi-structured questionnaires; the second data was collected at presentations made by panels of villagers in 1998; and the third set was collected through non-standardised interviews with individuals. These took place between 1997 to 1999. I also continued contact in an informal manner with individuals from Rosvik and attended various meetings organised by the village.

Preliminary Interviews

In the preliminary stage, semi-structured questionnaires were developed and 51 interviews with representatives from village groups and households took place. The interview questions were used in an open-ended way to make people feel comfortable and encourage them to talk freely. This was even more important than usual, as northern people are known for being uncommunicative and shy. It was also felt that a semi-structured way of interviewing was suited to the type of information we wanted to find out. We wanted people to remark, describe and discuss their opinions about Rosvik, retell why they lived there, describe their business operations etc.

The interview team[1] stayed in the village for 3 days and the people interviewed were from households, churches, sports clubs, businesses, the branch of the social democratic party, the school and the municipality. A breakdown of the number of interviews is presented in Table 7-1.

Table 7-1: Interviews of Village Groups

Village groups	No. of interviews
households	22
churches	2
sports clubs	2
businesses	18
party branch	2
school	2
municipality	3
Total	51

A different questionnaire was developed for each village group although some questions were repeated amongst some groups. Similar questions were used for households, churches, political party branch and sports clubs but different questions were developed for the municipality, school and businesses.

Because the preliminary stage was exploratory, the questions asked were comprehensive and incorporated two specific lines of

---

[1] The research team consisted of members of staff and students from Luleå University of Technology

questioning; some questions asked about management activities[2] and others, to village issues with respect to different modalities, or dimensions of community life. To cover the first, representatives from the municipality and village groups were asked how the village was managed and how they looked at the present state of affairs and the future. For example, questions were asked about how municipal decisions were made, scope of activities offered by the village, what people thought about village services, how good transportation facilities were and sources of information dissemination. They were also asked how the future looked for theirs and Rosvik's other groups.

Questions concerning village issues with respect to the modalities were also asked. The ethical modality included questions about people's level of activity in village groups and how much adults were concerned about teens and their children's future. The operational included questions about how well the businesses, school and municipality were run and the contribution of groups to the life of the village. The economic included questions about decision-making procedures in the municipality, allocation of resources and business development in Rosvik. The social included questions about the community, how individuals and groups liked the village and if they could see themselves staying there. The epistemic included questions about the school, its recent reverses and educational standards; the historical included questions about householders' roots and why they lived in Rosvik; the credal included questions about adult and children's religious activity and how important the church is to Rosvik.

Panels

The second stage of data collection involved organising two panels of village leaders who spoke to an audience of villagers, students and staff from the university. One panel spoke at Rosvik school and consisted of the principal, a representative from the teaching staff and a representative from the parent's group of the school. A member of the municipal school department was invited but was not able to attend. The second panel consisted of

---

[2] These refer to management activities identified by Stafford Beer (1994a; 1995).

leaders from various village groups including the business development group, social democratic branch, sports club, Swedish church, Betel church and a group developing a folk museum for Rosvik.

The discussions were focused on viability and the panels were asked to present what their village groups contributed to Rosvik's viability now and how they saw their contribution in the future. To this end they were asked to present why their group was important to Rosvik, what they did, how they did it and what they saw as their role in Rosvik's future. I tape recorded panel members' presentations and their responses to questions from the audience.

Interviews with individuals

The third stage of data collection consisted of five in-depth interviews with various individuals associated with Rosvik. These interviews were organised to fill in for the information I did not already have. The information collected in the preliminary interviews was diverse and extensive and I felt it necessary to interview people on a deeper level and spend more time exploring their perceptions of Rosvik and their role there. Those interviewed included the leader of the municipal school department, a member of the village development group, a member of the parent's group from the school, a business owner and pastor of the free church. During these interviews I asked non-standardised questions in an open-ended, conversational way and recorded them.

Using the Data Base

The material collected from the interviews, panels, literature and theory was organised and processed with SmCube, a database developed for MMSM. The data was organised into two types of sources differentiating survey and literature data. Examples of survey sources include interviews, panels and annual reports and examples of literature sources include books, journal articles and conference papers. Each source was then organised into items. Items form the building blocks of the data base and are excerpts of a document and a way for the researcher to break sources such as books or transcripts of recorded interviews into smaller, manageable pieces, usually about a paragraph long. Each item represents an idea and any other ideas connected with it and in the process of selecting items, it is important for the researcher to maintain the integrity of the item. For example, the main idea in the following item is that people are making decisions they have little or no competence to make.

> Question: Are decisions regarding the school made by professional educators or by administrators?
>
> Answer: I doubt very much that educators are making educational decisions. For example, the person who has the most influence in the school department is not an educator but an administrator. She knows the municipality well and has worked in other areas of the municipality besides education.

This is a fragment of an interview with a village leader discussing how the decision to take grade 6 away from Rosvik school was made and by whom. His reply indicates that pedagogical decisions affecting educational matters in Rosvik are made by people who are not qualified in education but rather by people who know how the municipality works.

All the material from the survey data and from the literature, were treated in the same way and broken down into items. This meant using only those excerpts from the documents that were salient to the research and disregarding those which were not. After the material from the interviews, panels, literature and theory was itemised, initial factors important to viability were selected. The selection of factors changed several times as the research progressed, as it was necessary to consider many different options. However seven factors were finally selected including *ethics*, which addresses the need for ethical concern; *competence*, or the ability to get involved in the issues facing individuals and communities; *statism* because many village groups are state supported and controlled; *sense of community* and the need for healthy community structures to which people belong; *education* and the crisis in the school and education in general; *heritage* and the role that heritage has in strengthening community identity; and finally *religion* and the need for a source such as religion, to inspire and give vision.

After the factors were selected, the multi-modal theoretical framework was merged with the factors and each factor considered with respect to a modality. For example, because statism is concerned with the provision and distribution of resources by the municipality and state, it belongs to the economic modality. Likewise, because sense of community is about having healthy community structures in which people participate and become familiar with each other, sense of community belongs to the social modality. In the same way, this was repeated for the other five factors. Each of the 1420 items in my database was then associated with any of the seven factors to which it referred. Therefore each item was associated with at least one factor or more. For example, the item quoted from the interview referred to above, was associated with the factors, "competence" and "education", because the item refers to the lack of competence of people making pedagogical decisions.

Building the Matrix

After associating all the items with factors, a matrix was built to examine relationships between factors. We said before that factors can be considered with respect to modalities, and according to our theory, the modalities relate to each other. This suggests that factors also relate to each other and the matrix is a way of summarising these relationships. The matrix in Table 7-2 displays all possible pairs of factors and numbers of items that link the factors together. The left hand columns in the matrix list all possible pairs of factors beginning with "ethics" and "competence" and continuing in the same manner for the rest. The next two columns "literature" and "survey" differentiate the number of items from literature sources as opposed to survey sources that link each pair of factors. The last column tallies up the total number of items irrespective of their type of source. Therefore the first row of the matrix shows that 1 item from literature sources and 0 items from survey sources link "ethics" and "competence" together. These numbers do not indicate strength of relationship but the need to find more support if the linkage is important to our understanding.

Therefore if the linkage between "ethics" and "competence" were important, the low figures show it is necessary to increase the numbers of both literature and empirical supports.

Table 7-2: Number of Items Linking Two Factors

			Literature	Survey	Total
Ethics		Competence	1	0	1
		Statism	11	1	12
		Community Sense	6	3	9
	←→	Education	27	13	40
		Heritage	1	0	1
	←→	Religion	20	22	42
Competence		Statism	5	5	10
		Community Sense	0	2	2
	←→	Education	8	12	20
		Heritage	1	0	1
		Religion	1	0	1
Statism	←→	Community Sense	15	18	33
	←→	Education	58	37	95
		Heritage	1	0	1
		Religion	20	8	28
Community Sense	←→	Education	17	13	30
		Heritage	1	0	1
		Religion	8	6	14
Education	←→	Heritage	4	0	4
		Religion	50	12	62
Heritage		Religion	1	0	1

After considering all possible linkages and weighing them up with our understanding, we can now select some of the links for analysis. We could select all twenty-one linkages but must give priority to those we think can help us most to understand what is contributing to, or taking away, from viability in Rosvik. Here we are guided by the items the factors are made up of. We selected seven linkages that people who were interviewed stressed and that the literature identified as key to understanding viability. The linkages selected are between education and five other factors including ethics, competence, statism, sense of community and heritage. In addition to these, linkages between statism and sense of community and between religion and ethics, are also included. All linkages are shown in the matrix with an arrow linking two factors together. They are also visually represented in Figure 7-1 (below) which merges the linkages with the modalities. This figure shows how the factors link with each other and forms the basis on which we can proceed to analyse the effect that each factor and the linking arrows, have on Rosvik's viability.

Analysis

Figure 7-2 summarises the analysis of each item and identifies with a white arrowhead a linkage that strengthens a factor, and thus the viability of the village, and with a black arrowhead a linkage that threatens it. No arrowhead indicates that the effect of the linkage is neutral in that particular direction. For example, the white arrow from heritage to education indicates that the activities aimed at promoting heritage are having a strengthening effect on education and thus contributes to the viability of the village. The reverse, with no arrow in the other direction, shows that education is having no effect on the historical awareness of the village. We can split the modalities in three domains and these include character, civic and intellect which have been added to Figure 7-2. The overall results indicate that linkages within the character and intellectual domains promote more viability, as shown by the number of white arrows, than linkages between factors within the civic domain, as shown by the number of black arrows. This is because the municipal government and its economic management pose the most significant threats to the community. The following sections look at this more closely.

Figure 7-1: Links Between Factors Selected

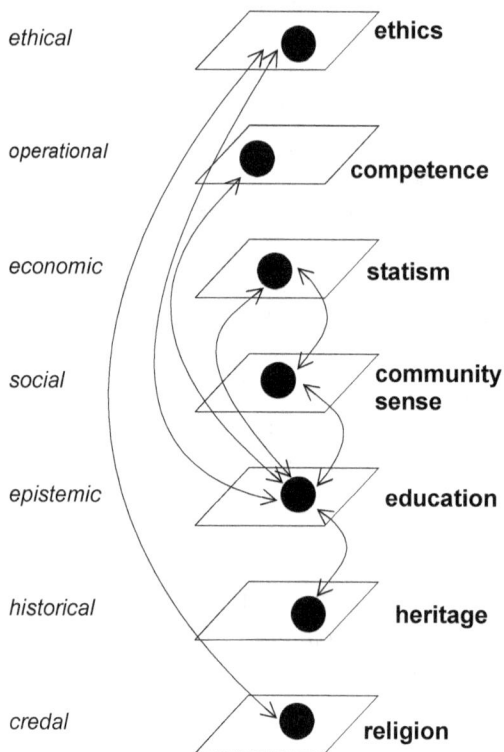

Character and Intellect Factors

The figure shows that heritage strengthens education in Rosvik although education has no effect on heritage. Heritage strengthens education in the plans to build a folk museum and engage the young people from the community to work there. This is considered an educational experience for the youth and many adults expressed a desire for their children to be aware of Rosvik's heritage. On the other hand, education has no effect on heritage. The school does not seem to have contributed much to an historical awareness and parents would like the school to educate the children about Rosvik's heritage by formalising it in the curriculum.

Figure 7-2: Links Between Factors After Analysis

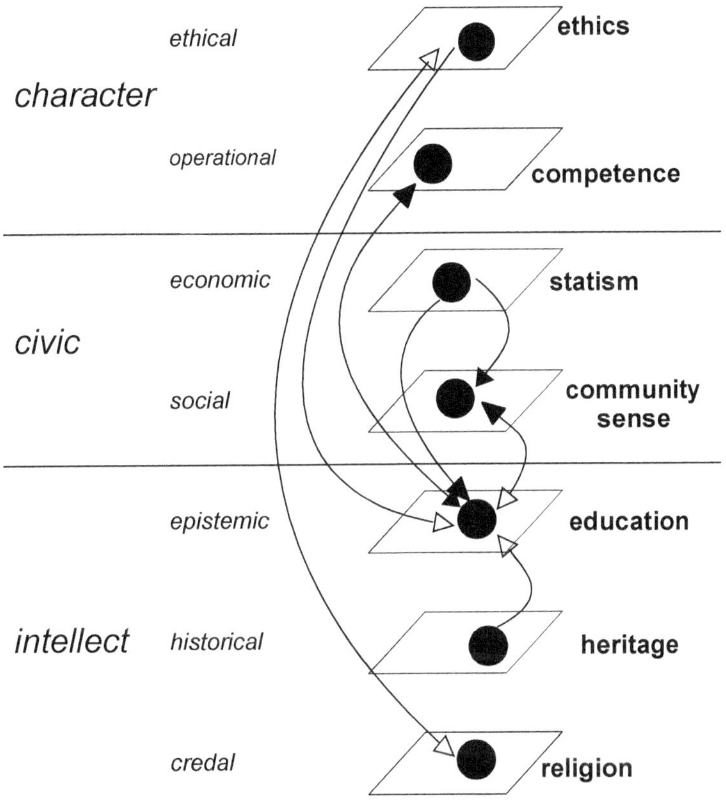

Ethics strengthen education in Rosvik and this was seen in many ways, especially the parents' action over the threats to grade 6. They organised themselves to not only mount a protest which often got in the local press but were prepared to act by getting an architect to draw up new building plans to expand the school building. However there is no clear connection between education and ethics as the school seems to neither strengthen nor weaken ethics. The school staff did not mention ethics or values much in the interviews; it was the parents who did and thought the school should reinforce the family and teach values. Religion strengthens ethics in Rosvik and the church is more active than the school in strengthening ethical care. This is especially evident in the ways the church contributes to Rosvik by offering music education to school pupils; youth work through a club for kids; culture, art and business initiatives because church people work in these fields. Conversely, ethics strengthens religion in Rosvik. People in Rosvik have developed a high degree of community-mindedness and ethical concern, at the same time the church is growing in the village and there is new interest in religion.

Civic Factors

The strengthening effect of factors in the character and intellect domains have not been matched in the same way by factors in the civic domain. Competence, statism and sense of community do not, as the figure shows, strengthen other factors and promote viability to any marked degree. Except for the positive effect that the sense of community has on education, it is all the opposite, as most associations weaken each other and impair viability. Statism weakens sense of community because controlling, statist[3] management contributes to disintegration and fragmentation within small community structures such as families, schools and other small groups. The end result in Rosvik is dependency on the state for education, child-care, health, retirement, initiating business and leisure. Conversely, the linkage between sense of community and statism is neutral. This is to be expected as it is difficult for small communities to have any significant effect on changing statist management, although there are attempts to return to a degree of autonomous village management in Rosvik. Statism also weakens education, for the people who make decisions are bureaucrats and not educators and in Rosvik this was evinced in the crisis that the school was thrown into by a municipal decision to remove a grade. In turn the figure shows that education has no effect on statism. Education has less chance to have an impact on statism for educa-

---

[3]*Statist* management is the means by which the state exercises its power by controlling or interfering in nearly every sphere of life. In Sweden this reached its peak under the social democratic party which was in power at the time of this study.

tion in Rosvik and Sweden in general, is almost exclusively controlled by the state and there is a lack of other, private educational alternatives, especially in the north of Sweden.

The figure shows that competence and education have a mutually weakening effect on each other. This is to be expected as competence and education naturally go hand in hand. Incompetence in school bureaucracy, school leaders, teachers and parents has contributed much to the crisis in Rosvik and in education in general. In turn, former standards of excellence in the school have declined resulting in incompetence and parents complain of falling standards, poor curricula and lower class performance. As already mentioned, the only exception among the civic factors that strengthens viability is the impact of sense of community on education. Community influence on the school is strong in Rosvik and the community has a group of competent people opposing decisions made by the municipality. In the reverse however, the figure shows that education weakens sense of community. A statist education impairs developing curricula and teaching to strengthen sense of community and build up community groups like families. Instead the school has weakened family and other community groups by taking on socialising roles inherent in these traditional community structures. This, evidently, has not been very successful.

Summary and Conclusions

MMSM is a useful tool to handle a large body of data from diverse sources, to construct normative factors often overlooked in community viability and to provide descriptive tools to explore relationships. It analyses relationships between factors, modalities and groups in the small community. Initially, it is effective in isolating factors for analysis: the key issues of viability being studied. The method constructs factors out of items, which are fragments of empirical and theoretical data sources. Items represent ideas taken from interviews, books etc. and form the building blocks of the database. Secondly the method is effective in establishing how factors affect each other by strengthening, weakening or having no affect on each other. The findings indicate many factors converging with education and indeed, in the minds of villagers, education and school issues in Rosvik have become central to the village's long term future. Awareness of, and planning for, the future survival of the village rose at the time the threats to the school began. Behind the concerns about education and factors weakening viability, is state control. The state controls education in Rosvik, as elsewhere in Sweden and tight regulation and lack of choice has lowered educational standards and competence. The state also controls much of community life and weakened community groups and social belonging.

On the other hand, factors outside the scope of the state strengthen viability in Rosvik and individual and personal factors encompassing ethical concern, visionary religion and an appreciation for heritage are proving important for the community through various groups. There is a vacuum in vitality and spirit in small communities in Sweden and project leaders working in community development say people need to care about the future of their communities and to create new ideas. Although Rosvik may at least in part be spared, filling the normative vacuum left by dependency and shrinkage of the welfare state, is an urgent need as small communities face an uncertain future.

8 Evaluation of Community Projects

J. D. R. de Raadt and Veronica D. de Raadt

Introduction

In a recent call for project proposals from the European Commission, "monitoring, evaluation and benchmarking" were identified as one of the "measures" that should be adopted to attain a local commitment (that is, in municipalities all over Europe) to its employment strategy. The document went on to specify:

> Adequate monitoring of strategic approaches depends on effective measurement of progress against targets. The quantitative and qualitative impacts of strategies should be identified and measured *ex ante* and *ex post*… If evaluation can provide answers to the question of what works or does not work, then benchmarking offers a complementary tool to promote collective learning by comparing achievements against the performance of other actors in different local areas.[1]

The above approach betrays a mechanical view of human behaviour that pervades much of public and private administration. According to this view, if one wants to change some pattern of behaviour in an individual or in a society, one must set up a process. This process takes the existing behaviour as input ("ex ante") and submits it to a transformation aimed at a desired behavioural outcome ("ex post"). Evaluation in this context compares the actual and the real outcomes of the process and determines which are the elements in the transformation that lead to success or failure. Likewise, benchmarking, a technique normally used to compare the performance of mechanical devices such as computers is also included in the tool kit for successful behavioural change.

Such "measures" do not address real people but abstract people, conceived within a bureaucratic environment that has lost contact with humanity and specifically ignores two things. Firstly, it ignores the fact that human life is normative, that is, that there is a realm of human responsibility beyond "what works or does not work". This realm corresponds to what we ought to do and what we ought not to do. Unfortunately, ignoring the normative realm

---

[1] European Commission (2001).

due to a mechanistic perspective is common in most of modern human science, especially in such disciplines as management, economics and operational research. We should not be surprised, therefore, if these have influenced public administration. Secondly, man's economic problems, such as unemployment, do not exist in isolation from his other problems: social, ethical, historical and religious. They are all linked together and vast technological and economic resources will not dispel them if we attempt to deal with them separately.

Therefore, we need a method of evaluation and design that addresses the normative realm as well as including aspects other than economics and technology. With this in mind, the rest of this paper will deal with an evaluation method based on a systems science that has been used in various European Community supported projects.

A Case

We will illustrate the evaluation method by referring to TRANS[2], a European Union sponsored project. The aim of this project is to build a mart for the exchange of good practices between different regions in the European Union. In a general manner, a good practice has been defined as an activity that has successfully helped attain an objective in a community, such as a training programme for helping women start their own small businesses. The mart will be a place where people can search and evaluate existing good practices and purchase them in order to transfer and adapt them to the needs in their region. The development of good practices is an expensive exercise and requires substantial subsidies from the European Union. Purchasing good practices through the mart would therefore result in substantial savings for the buyer as well as become a source of revenue for the seller. In addition to these economic incentives, exchanging good practices allows people a greater degree of flexibility and freedom to choose what they believe will contribute most to their communities. By

---

[2] The names TRANS, Nornet, St Jean and Villars are fictitious names and are used to preserve the anonymity of the participants in this project.

contrast, if they wish to develop a good practice by obtaining European Union funding, they must follow the directives and timing specified in each call for proposal.

To build the mart, a pilot project has been set up involving six partners from six different European countries (Germany, Austria, France, Italy, Spain and Sweden); each partner simultaneously acts as a buyer and a seller of a good practice. This means that they will exchange at least twelve good practices. However, apart from its formal objective, the project can deliver further important contributions. In a globalised world, much of the uncertainties and complexities that we face arise from the interactions of many communities with different cultures. To cope with this, we need social systems to generate understanding about these interactions; TRANS provides a unique laboratory to learn about them. Groups from different countries will often collaborate to solve a single problem. Rarely, however, does one find a group of six different nationalities trying to help each other solve their unemployment problems in six different cultural settings. Through this daunting, yet necessary exercise, TRANS offers us an excellent scenario to refine the tools of social systems analysis, design and management to deal with a globalised environment. We illustrate TRANS with the potential transfer of a good practice, Nornet, originating in Norrbotten (northern Sweden) to St. Jean, an administrative department in southern France.

Criteria for Evaluation

Our criterion for evaluation is the long-term viability of the community. By viability, we do not merely mean economic viability, but a multi-modal viability that encompasses the whole life of the community. We identify four domains in life: natural, intellectual, communal and character. While the whole universe operates in the natural domain, only mankind operates in the other three domains. Within each of these domains are the following modalities:

- Character: *ethical, aesthetic* and *juridical*
- Community: *operational, economic* and *social*

- Intellect: *epistemic, informatory, historical* and *credal*
- Nature: *psychic, biotic, regulatory, physical, kinetic, spatial, numeric* and *logical*

The sequential order of these domains, their modalities and the links between them is organised by two forces represented by the arrows in Figure 8-1. The first arrow is determinative; people cannot change it. It runs upwards and determines or sets each foundation of each domain or modality above it, just as a foundation is set before a house is built on top of it. The second arrow, running downwards, is normative; it addresses our responsibility as humans and tells us how things ought to be. Here again, this arrow links all the modalities. Each modality or domain provides an inspiration or objective to the modality or domain below it, just as one must first be inspired by the idea of building a house before building its foundation.

Lack of space forbids a full methodological discussion of this framework. Yet, an explanation regarding the ethical modality (at the top of Figure 8-1) is needed here. We live in an era dominated by modernism and its beliefs. People believe, despite the overwhelming empirical evidence to the contrary, that we live in a world that works; that mankind continuously progresses towards a global world order of peace and prosperity built with technology and economic development. Within this setting, people believe in a utilitarian ethic; goodness is what works for their own self-interest and evil is what works against it. Combined together, these creeds sanction the exercise of greed and pride in every realm of culture. This principle drives our economies and marketing and ensures mankind remains divided into rich and poor by allocating the pleasure to the rich and the pain to the poor. The multi-modal systems approach takes exactly the opposite stance. It recognises that this world does not work and that its non-viable state is getting worse, especially for those who are victims of the unprecedented globalisation of poverty[3]. Due to this predicament, the ethic that should govern our actions is not self-interest but self-sacrifice for others. Sacrifice is essential to compensate for the injustices that

---

[3] Chossudovsky (1998).

will always be present with us. The greater the degree of self-sacri-fice in a community, the greater will be its prospect for viability.

Figure 8-1: Multi-Modal Systems Framework

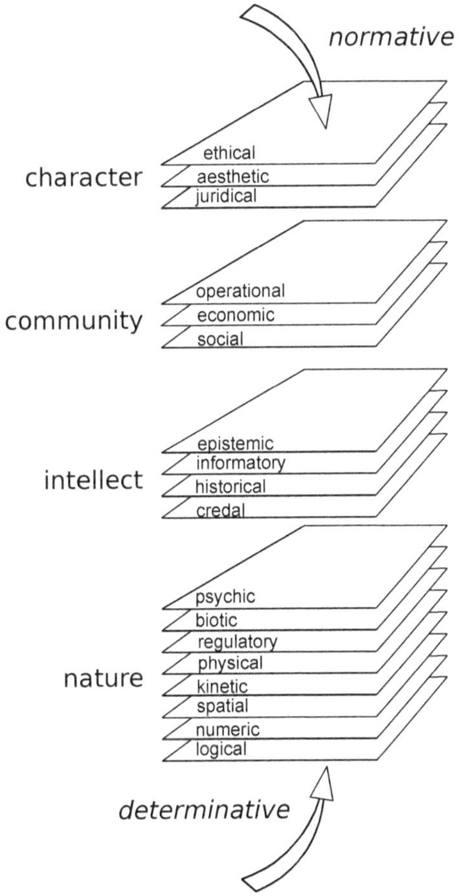

Viability

If the criterion for the evaluation of a project is the long-term viability of the community, then the transfer and implementation of a good practice requires the evaluation of two things. Firstly, one must evaluate the needs of the community (St. Jean) to attain viab-ility. Secondly, one must evaluate the potential of the good prac-tice (Nornet) to contribute to these needs. This requires in turn the identification of the factors in a community that are critical to its viability and that are under threat. Prior research indicates that there is a set of common factors among communities in diverse regions of the world that are essential for their viability and which at the same time represent trouble spots that threaten them. It does not make much of a difference whether the community is a tribal village in Africa, a suburb of Berlin or a rural town in Sweden. Due to their strong normative quality, these factors depend more on the common humanity of their citizens than on the diversity of their economic and technological development or geographical location. The application of this evaluation method includes six of these factors – ethics, work, management, social structure, education and belief – although sometimes as an evaluation progresses, these factors may be changed or abandoned and new ones added. Each of these factors operates in a different modality and interacts with the others in a normative and, to a lesser extent, in a determinative manner. Even a relatively small number of factors generate a very large number of potential interactions, running in both normative and determinative directions. For example, six factors can generate up to 21 interactions. Naturally, the higher the number of interactions, the more complex their analysis becomes. Therefore, in addition to selecting the relevant factors, one must select a subset of interactions small enough to allow for analysis and at the same time large enough to represent the most important threats to viability.

Once the factors are selected, we must collect information to establish how they are relevant to the community being studied. We have stored this information on the database using SmCube, a special software package developed for this method. This database stores both theoretical knowledge and empirical data. By theoretical we do not only mean standard theory and prior research, but every available intellectual work that addresses the factors under discussion. Even fiction such as great literary masterpieces may be included, if they effectively argue a point relevant to our analysis. By empirical data, we mean the content from relevant administrative and descriptive documents, published statistics and interviews with people who actively participate in the everyday life of their community. For example, in the TRANS project, we have interviewed administrative officials in each community and people in touch with the community such as policemen, nurses, teachers and trade union officials. We also have attended discussion meetings, presentations about the regions and visited several local business sites. Transcripts of these interviews and documentary data have then been loaded onto the database.

Next follows the analysis of this data in building a qualitative model of the vital factors in the community. The model consists of two parts; the first part describes each of the factors, as they are experienced in the community; the second describes the links between the factors and the threats they represent for the community's viability. We will review each of the parts below; however, we must once more state that we are focusing on what threatens the sustainability of the community. This does not mean that there are no positive factors in the community –in this case St. Jean – but that we are interested in identifying what is negative in order to decide what must be done to address it.

Factors

Ethics

In an interview, a councillor told us that the ethics motto among St. Jean's officialdom is: "Solidarity not charity, respect not love." This means that the Good Samaritan's personal intervention to help our neighbour in need is regarded as improper. Instead, we must help him through political support of the social structures – such as unions and public institutions – that have become our modern brother's keeper. In a later discussion, it was pointed out to us that this attitude springs from France being a secular state. The result of it, we were told, is not only the loss of charity and love but also a restricted type of solidarity and respect; a "solidarity-for-some" approach that leaves the outsiders to look after themselves. This affects businesses as well as the community at large. People are closed socially and it is difficult to be invited into homes. Similarly, while close-knit groups such as small villages and farming communities have a high degree of solidarity, it is not open but rather confined to the village. Consequently, there is little support from churches, businesses and groups outside motivated by a sense of ethical concern for those in need.

Work

St. Jean's rate of unemployment given to us at the time of our visit was 11.5%. In terms of numbers, this represented 35,093 persons. These are the official figures, but research about hidden unemployment in official unemployment figures[4] as well as admissions in official reports[5] lead us to suspect that the real number of unemployed in St. Jean could be far higher than that officially acknowledged. However, regardless of the definition of unemployment, even the official figures dwarf the results of projects to avert unemployment. Unemployment projects in St. Jean, such as retraining and job creation schemes, have, at the most, an impact on around 200 people. In some cases, the impact is as low as fifteen to twenty people. Of particular concern is high youth unemployment (see Table 8-1). In 2002, 16.5% of the total number of people unemployed in St. Jean were below twenty-five years of age. It seems though, this figure should be higher. According to a person at the government-run youth mission, only a fraction of unemployed young people registers with the mission to obtain help. Youngsters believe there is no help available for them or they are ineligible because they have not worked. In addition, the respondent felt that many others do not register because they, and often their parents, see the welfare system as humiliating and an institution from which they would rather remain independent.

Work in St. Jean should be understood in the light of the specific characteristics of the region. St. Jean has a very long agricultural tradition in wine production, but like other agricultural regions, St. Jean has been undergoing a transition in recent years. Modern notions of work, especially in young people's minds, have changed the meaning of work and replaced agricultural work. Agricultural production, such as grape picking, is hard and undervalued work and attracts low pay. Young people think of work as being "clean" and technologically based. This change in attitude in the younger generation is so pervasive there is a shortage of agri-

---

[4] Migulez (2002); Mitchell (2002).
[5] European Employment Observatory (2002).

cultural labour, despite the availability of local unemployed youth. Farmers resort to imported immigrant labour and university students. These changes in St. Jean are following the same pattern of work attitudes as in other regions of Europe.

Table 8-1

St. Jean Youth Unemployment			
	Proportion	Total youth	Total all ages
Male	15%	2001	13342
Female	18%	2282	12679
Combined	16.5%	4284	26021
Source: Regional Director of Employment 31/03/2002			

Management

Government management creates many problems that affect diverse people. Most governments in Europe exercise excessive control over people's lives while at the same time, people are excessively dependent on government structures and aid. Public administration is embedded in archaic structures that do not meet contemporary needs. In France, for example, administrative units stem from post-Napoleonic times when the idea was that the border of each department should be reached by horseback in one day's ride. This has resulted in multiple layers of government, at the bottom of which are thousands of municipalities with inadequate resources to go around. Many are too small to be able to have their own resources and some municipalities group together and share financial resources and taxes. Yet, despite the shortage of resources, it is these small municipalities and their mayors, rather than the department's council (such as St. Jean's), that are highly considered by the people. They value the closeness of the municipality to their community.

We were told that government organises itself in a manner that concentrates political power rather than promotes efficiency and this results in a lack of co-operation between government units throughout the region. These problems often make the task of those who work in these units so difficult that they necessitate the creation of additional informal organisational structures. Thus, people who work for the St. Jean council and employment committee need to go around official channels and create personal contacts to be able to work together. This results in yet more problems as these informal organisations lack adequate resources to operate efficiently and effectively. There is also a lack of long-term planning. Planning can only be done for one year at a time, as the funding for each employment committee is for only a year. A six-year regional plan also exists but it is already obsolete when implemented, as changes in employment needs occur rapidly.

Social Structure

St. Jean was described to us as being fragmented and this seems to apply to other social groups as well, including families, communities and government organisations. Class divisions segregate communities and the region has both very wealthy and poor agricultural sectors. The people in the higher classes live in the outer suburbs while the lower classes live in the middle of the towns and cities of the region. One of the wealthy and exclusive sectors is Villars, which has many resident artists. It attracts thousands of tourists who visit the area for its unique natural beauty. Unfortunately though, privilege means that those in similar socio-economic brackets co-operate with each other but not with other communities. This results in the wealthier communities being seen by the outsiders as keeping the privileges for themselves. This privileged mentality has a conservative effect on the youth and there is a tendency in the young population to stay in the region. For example, unlike other places, most youth in St. Jean do not take advantage of the European Union's Erasmus programme that promotes student exchange. One of the respondents felt that this regional outlook applied across the socio-economic brackets and that parents influence these patterns of behaviour.

Immigration and breakdown in the family also create social fragmentation. St. Jean has a large number of migrants and there is a high degree of mobility of people within the region. A respondent felt that the region has an identity problem and this may partly explain why St. Jean was a strong supporter of the extreme right nationalist party in recent national elections. In addition, there is breakdown in the family and single parenthood is frequent with 40% of children being born out-of-wedlock. There are indications, however, of an upward trend for the young generation to marry. Added to these socially induced differences, there is a widening gap between population groups in St. Jean. Although the proportion of youth is high at present, growth rates for the younger population are much lower than for older people (see Table 8-2). If these rates continue, the population will become older with time, especially as the region's mild weather attracts the retired and elderly. This has important implications for employment and the economic future of the region.

Table 8-2: Population Growth 1990 – 1999

Age	1990	1999	Growth 90/99
0-19 years	121 928	125 960 25%	3,2%
20-39 years	134 602	130 728 26%	-2,96%
40-59 years	112 409	131 491 26%	14,51%
60-74 years	63 827	71 264 14%	10,44%
75 years and over	34 457	40 222 8%	14,33%

Finally, government units are fragmented and the community is not actively involved in decision-making processes. The fragmentation between the general council and municipalities has already been mentioned. In addition, pacts are built on partnerships between the unions, employers' federation and government. This excludes grass-roots community groups from the decision-making processes and limits their participation to an advisory rather than voting capacity. This problem and the lack of focus on small community groups are now recognised at the national level. Thus the French Prime Minister, who wishes to reverse this, talks about "France from below" or the idea of looking out for the people at the grass-roots.

Education

Despite the statistically high number of people in France completing secondary education when compared with other European countries, we were told that the quality of education in St. Jean is low. The problem stems, according to one respondent, from the "big machinery" of national education, from which many of the young people from St. Jean are left out. In her work with high school drop-outs, she observes that the public education system helps the achievers while it tends to abandon the non-achievers. In a wider sense though, it seems high school drop-outs are not the only ones being left behind in the modern educational system. This region, with its traditional focus on agriculture, is also being left out of the technologically driven educational system. Although the region has a lyceum (high school) for agricultural studies and there is a university-level agricultural college, we were told that the modern educational system undervalues agricultural studies. These issues and the proper focus of education are receiving national attention and there is a philosophical debate going on in educational and government sectors. The question being debated is: are schools a training ground for a job, or for life?

Belief

Belief is important because it centres on the driving forces and assumptions on which people base their actions. Like any other European nation, France has absorbed modernism with the intention of liberating people from the former oppression of church and aristocracy. Public life has replaced faith with the ideologies that emerged with the French revolution. Although the powers of the medieval church and aristocracy have been long left behind, there is still a climate of suspicion about the church and religion in general. This suspicion has allowed modernist ideologies to embody themselves, with almost no challenge, in the large institutions of government and industry. These have brought about their own kind of oppression on people. However, despite these beliefs, the state is succumbing to new post modernist beliefs preached by the media and the peer group. An interviewee working with young unemployed people confirmed that the peer group exerts the strongest pressure on youth in the region.

Links between Factors (Arrows)

These brief descriptions represent a static picture of the selected factors at the time of our visit to St. Jean. Our next step is to develop a dynamic model describing what may happen in the future due to the interactions or links between these factors. The arrows in Figure 8-2 represent these links.

Figure 8-2: Black Arrows

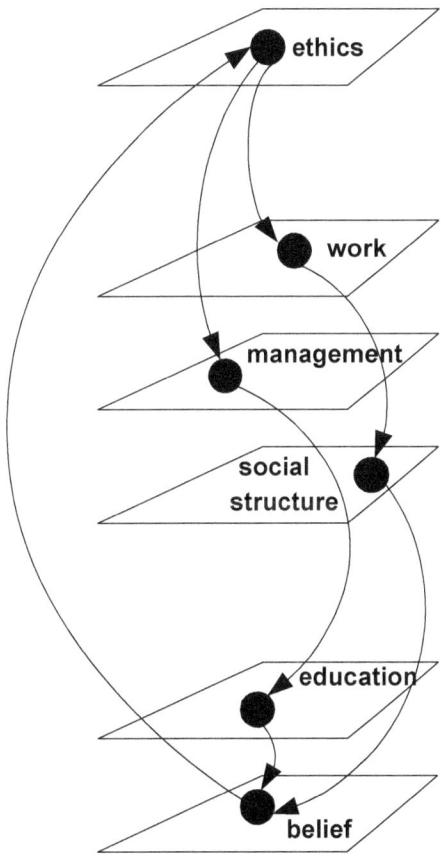

Again, it has been necessary to make a selection of the most relevant from all possible arrows. Each arrow indicates how one factor has an impact on the other, a black arrowhead indicates that this impact threatens the viability of the community, while a white arrow indicates that the impact strengthens the viability. Since at this particular stage of our analysis we are still interested in seeing how the community's sustainability is threatened, the model focuses on black rather than white arrows. Furthermore, given that we are attempting to establish what may happen in the future, the selection and analysis of the arrows draw heavily upon theory and application of prior research. This is in contrast to the description of the factors, which relies mostly upon the collected empirical data. We have selected the seven arrows described below.

ethics ➔ *work*

The first arrow refers to the reduction of work opportunities that result from the self-serving attitudes espoused by some in the community. One of our interviewees told us that "in many cases all that young people need is motivation" to be able to find work. What kind of motivation should we look for? Before the rise of utilitarianism, motivation to work used to be based on the ethics of service. Service to our neighbour was the first aim, monetary reward followed from service. In a world where there is much work to be done, such an ethic could be an effective job creator, but our modern ethic has reversed these priorities. People are first motivated by what they can get out of their work rather than what they put in for others. In St. Jean, where there is plenty of agricultural work available, young people will not engage in this type of work, for they do not regard it as well paid. Immigrant workers have to be brought in to the region to do it. Moreover, moved by a spirit of self-interest, small businesses do not collaborate with each other and do not help new entrepreneurs start their own business. They do not realise that helping newcomers stimulates the economy and in the end, all businesses benefit by this and create more opportunities for work.

work ➔ *social structure*

A large proportion of the unemployed are young and there is a pattern for the young unemployed to remain in the region while those who are more qualified move away. Therefore, we can expect that in the long term the sector of society that responds to a "welfare culture" will increase. This is especially alarming when one considers that the population in St. Jean is ageing rapidly. Should this pattern continue in the future, St. Jean will have a large sector of "welfare-oriented" seniors with very few young people to sustain them.

social structure ➜ *belief*

Many children who grow up in a welfare family tend to inherit their parents' welfare-oriented belief system. Such parents, we were told, "educate their children to think: why bother to work when you can receive from the welfare state?" In addition to their parent's influence, youngsters have their beliefs reinforced by the peer group to which they belong. This generates what Piccone[6] has called the "state dependent personality" evinced, for example, by the large group of women in St. Jean who choose to become single parents because of generous welfare support. They believe that this support enables them to live "a comfortable life". Paradoxically, the state dependent personality, while happy to live at the expense of the government, has its pride when it comes to seeking private help. We were told that parents, who cannot afford to pay for their children to attend a summer camp, would rather forfeit such an opportunity to their children than experience the humiliation of asking for private financial assistance.

ethics ➜ *management*

Utilitarian ethics has three major effects on management. Firstly, utilitarianism gives legitimacy to self-preservation and self-interest in private and public organisations to the point of breaking the law, if necessary. Evidence of this is the recent collapse in both Europe and the USA, of several giant corporations (and their auditors) due to fraud. We have seen similar breakdowns in our public institutions including corruption charges against the president of France. Secondly, self-preservation in state and corporate managers leads them to dominate nearly every aspect society. Using the media and public policy, they tell people how they should live their lives. Thirdly, the desire to dominate society has led to a disproportionately large number of corporations and state institutions

---

[6] (1998).

that are not only difficult to lead and manage but, therefore, inefficient and ineffective.

management ➜ education

Utilitarian management aims at controlling not only how we live, but also how we are educated. This type of management has subjugated the educational system to industrial and state control and established a gap between the classroom and the local community. Piccone states it thus:

> The deployment of public education is part and parcel of this dialectic of modernity. While providing some immediate results and solving some important problems, the government's gradual take-over of mass education has contributed considerably to the marginalization of local, particularistic cultures and the disempowerment of local communities.[7]

As we have indicated, the French national education system is regarded as "a big machine" where many "young people from St. Jean are left out of the system". The achievers are able to adapt to the system, but the non-achievers are left behind and eventually drop out. Furthermore, knowledge is presented in a fragmented, compartmentalised manner[8], because it suits the short term, specialised needs of industry. The outcome of this control over the system of education is not only poor and fragmented education, but also a growing proportion of uneducated people. This is not only a problem in France, but also a problem all over Europe (and the industrialised world). Recent reports indicate that education is in an acute crisis in European countries which claim the most educated population such as Germany[9], Great Britain[10] and Sweden[11].

education ➜ belief

The secularisation and fragmentation of education has split believing from understanding in the mind of the student. This split has undermined the critical examination of beliefs and encouraged gullibility, especially among youth. Many youngsters do not know

---

[7] Piccone (1998).
[8] Eagle (2002).
[9] BBC (2002).
[10] Chrisafis (2002); Wintour et al (2002).
[11] Scherman (2002).

how or what to believe and believe anything promoted by their peer group or peddled by the media, a state of affairs that the philosopher Ortega y Gasset[12] predicted 70 years ago. This has led to the suspicion of religion except when circumscribed to the private realm of life. Exclusion of religion and belief from the intellectual realm and in social dialogue encourages the spread of extremist beliefs, for there are few avenues to openly challenge and discuss them.

belief ➔ *ethics*

The vacuum in beliefs has impeded challenging worn-out statist ideologies that date back to the same time when one day's horse ride was used as a measure to create administrative departments. The promotion of political solidarity based on the exclusion of mercy will naturally result in the citizens' neglect of their personal responsibility to help the neighbour in need, of whom there are plenty. Likewise, promoting respect without love ignores the close interdependence between them and results in a society where not only is love in short supply, but also human respect. A more extreme syndrome may be the people's confusion between love and pornography, recognised by French MP Charles de Courson. It is this confusion which has been blamed for the 23% increase in violent crime in France during 2001[13] and the recent incidents of sexual attacks by schoolchildren on other school children.[14]

Black Loops

A closer examination of the above seven arrows as drawn in Figure 8-2 reveals that they form two reinforcing loops.

1) ethics ➔ work ➔ social structure ➔ belief ➔ ethics
2) ethics ➔ management ➔ education ➔ belief ➔ ethics

The peculiarity of these two loops is that each feeds on itself. That is, the effect of the arrows on the factors becomes stronger with

---

[12] (1992).
[13] Kirby (2002).
[14] Coomarasamy (2002).

time[15]. We refer to loops that are composed of black arrows as *black loops*. The presence of such loops creates an increasing deterioration in the community that follows the pattern shown in Figure 8-3. It shows that due to their mutual negative impact, all factors decline with time. Like any social change, this decline is slow. Its unit of measurement is not a month or a year, but at least a generation (around twenty years). Three periods can be observed in this decline. In the first period, although the loop is active, its effects are too small to distinguish it from the random fluctuations of the factors. Detection is possible in the second period; this is the time to act and to implement good practices. Since people do not like bad news, often leaders in the community and in organisations will ignore these signals and hope that things will improve by themselves in better times to follow. They seldom do. The third period is when the full effect of the black loop is felt; now no one doubts that the situation is calamitous, but unfortunately, it may be rather late to act.[16]

Figure 8-3: Black Loop

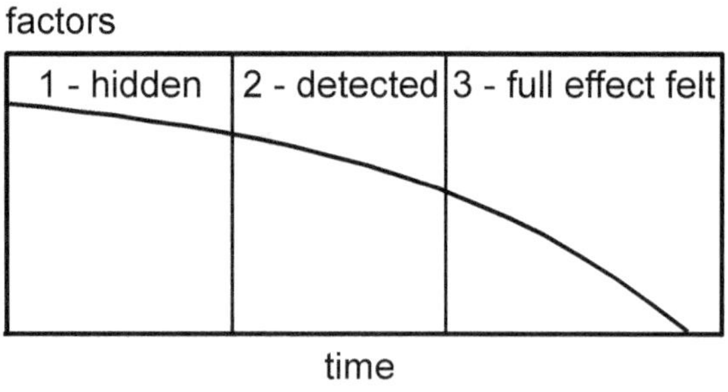

factors

| 1 - hidden | 2 - detected | 3 - full effect felt |

time

Evaluation Criteria for a Good Practice

It is important, therefore, to respond to a black loop at the earliest time with a good practice. However, to be effective against

---

[15] The systems term for this is "positive feedback". Positive refers to the growing magnitude of the effect of this type of loop upon the system. It does not imply that it is beneficial to the system.

[16] This pattern is as applicable to the natural environment as it is to the cultural. At the recent 2002 Earth Summit in South Africa scientists warned that we were at a late stage of the second period.

a black loop and given what we have discussed above, a good practice should meet the following requirements:

1. Since the factors belong to the realm of human responsibility, individuals must decide by themselves how to act on threats to them and their communities. To help people as human beings and not abstracts, the most legitimate and influential instrument of change for a good practice is education, information, persuasion and not manipulation.

2. It is not sufficient for a good practice to act upon one single factor and to ignore other factors linked to it. For example, it is ineffective to help underprivileged families (social structure) without ensuring at the same time, that there is work for them. A good practice should address at least two factors, that is, providing more work as well as helping underprivileged families. By handling two factors at any one time, a good practice can generate a *white arrow* where one factor (work) will reinforce the other factor (social structure) in a positive manner.

3. A good practice should be combined with other good practices to form a *white loop*. That is, it should be possible to incorporate it into an ensemble of good practices that together generate a set of white arrows. Moreover, these white arrows should also reinforce each other and generate a white loop to counteract the effect of the black loop.

4. An ensemble of good practices will require the involvement of good practitioners who represent the diverse sectors of the community such as project managers, community workers and educators. This is in contrast to the narrow definition of partnership of the European Union veiled under the misleading terms of "social partnership" and "social dialogue". Full participation in this partnership is limited to government agencies, unions and employer federations while other sectors of the community are excluded or at best relegated to an advisory and non-voting role[17].

---

[17] European Commission (1998).

Evaluation of Nornet

We will apply these criteria to Nornet, a project identified by the representatives from St. Jean as showing potential for a successful application in their region. Nornet is a network of twenty entrepreneurs operating in the coastal region of the Pite river in northern Sweden. In the past, most entrepreneurs in this region had a history of competition rather than collegiality. The entrepreneurs saw individualism, different levels of competence and experience, and lack of a platform for co-operation, as obstacles to progress in their businesses. Therefore, the Nornet network was established in February, 2002 to create the necessary conditions for trust, respect and commitment. Its method of work is flexible and established along several lines: network-based measures and practices, raising competence through workshops and displays, informal mentoring, independent thematic working groups, close dialogue between project management and network on a daily basis. The activities performed are closely related to the needs of entrepreneurs. Planning and selection of activities are approved by the group before accomplishment. The network is made up of small-sized companies and associations, including the local parish church. These associations are proud of their history, traditions and rural identity and are active in art, crafts, experience-based tourism, traditional foodstuff processing and accommodation. These small-scale actors value the tradition of production and direct selling being performed in their own studio or gallery in the countryside. Culture and nature are often reflected in the profile of their business. Members regard their network as being very successful and many activities have been carried out or are planned in the near future.

Our evaluation of this network aims to go beyond its economic and business aspects and examine the special human qualities that have contributed to its success. In our prior analysis, we aimed to draw out the negative aspects in St. Jean. In this analysis, we aim to identify the positive aspects of Nornet that may contribute to the difficulties in St. Jean. This does not mean that a good practice such as Nornet is free of problems, it only means that we are trying to evaluate to see what Nornet can contribute to St. Jean. An analysis of Nornet shows it as a multi-modal system. It possesses the inter-linked qualities we should seek in a good practice. This is illustrated in Figure 8-4. Nornet has an impact on six factors vital to the community: ethics, aesthetics, work, management, tradition and belief. This impact is delivered through a set of white arrows whereby a good quality in one of the factors positively affects the quality in another factor.

Let us examine the arrows in this figure by starting at the bottom with belief and tradition. Despite the impact of modernism and secularism in Sweden, rural communities still hold to their heritage through the interaction of these two factors. Swedes cherish their traditions (belief ⇨ tradition) and these in turn inspires the beliefs of many in an age of scepticism (tradition ⇨ belief). The connection between belief and a sacrificial ethic, however, is no longer strong in Swedish society. For over half a century, Swedes have been told that it is not necessary to love one's neighbour, for the government will take care of them. But, statism has not been able to erase the connection between belief and aesthetics. Most art in the rural areas has remained largely unaffected by political ideology. This has allowed people to channel their beliefs into music, paintings and other artistic expressions and attain world acclaim in some areas.[18] Piteå has a notable music conservatory that specialises in church music and organ performance. Luleå, 50 km north of Piteå, boasts a renowned organ factory. For Swedes, art has remained a channel of the soul.

It is particularly interesting in Nornet, that the link between belief and ethics has now re-emerged in a new arrow: aesthetics ⇨ ethics. Beauty has led people to care for each other; this becomes quite apparent as one discusses art and partnership with the members of this network. Their work therefore, not only benefits from their pursuit of aesthetics (aesthetics ⇨ work), but also from the mutual support they obtain from their network in doing their job (ethics ⇨ work). They expect, for example, that newcomers to the network will be able to gain from the experience of long-standing members and improve the quality of their work.

---

[18] For example, Swedish choirs are among the best in the world.

Figure 8-4: White Arrows and Loops Generated by Nornet

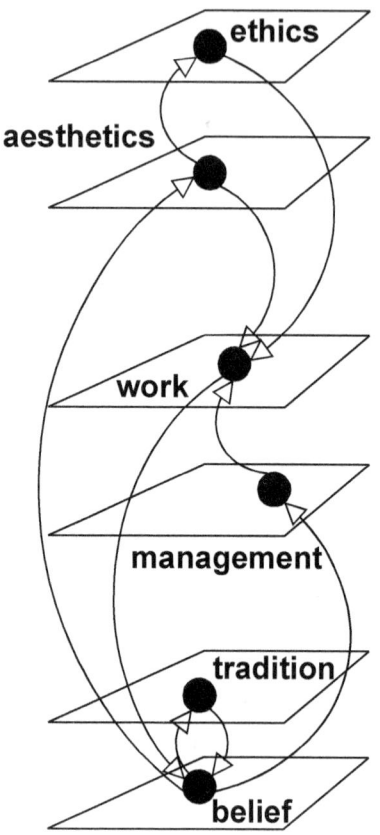

When talking to the participants in the network, one gets the impression that they believe in their work, that what they produce reaffirms and strengthens their beliefs and encourages them to go further (work ⇨ belief). This has an impact also in the way that they manage their businesses. They have made managerial choices that put the quality of their product above the creation of profits and that ensures that their methods of production are sustainable and environmentally friendly even if they are more costly (belief ⇨ management). This style of management contributes further to the enhancement of their products and the benefits they produce to the community (management ⇒ work). We can observe three main white loops that emerge from these links:

1) tradition ⇒ belief ⇒ tradition
2) belief ⇒ aesthetics ⇒ work ⇒ belief; reinforced by aesthetics ⇒ ethics ⇒ work
3) belief ⇒ management ⇒ work ⇒ belief

Although these loops generate the opposite effect of the black loops, we should expect that the pattern of their effect through time would be similar (see Figure 8-5). At the beginning, the effect will be almost undetected but with time, it will become more evident. Once more, we must be reminded of the slowness of social change. This is a fact that is consistently ignored by the modern approach to management, where the time frames of such things as accounting, planning and evaluation are totally out of phase with the historical rhythm of humanity. Consequently, good practices such as Nornet could be discarded because they do not provide quick results. Yet, given a suitable period of time, and with the necessary perseverance, the presence of these three loops should strengthen their network. As it expands, it should benefit new members as well as the community, hopefully encouraging other such networks to be formed in Piteå and other communities. The challenge for St. Jean is to find people who can reproduce the above qualities and who are willing to collaborate in a way similar to Nornet to generate a white loop. This, however, falls outside the present evaluation.

Conclusions

Normative threats to community viability are just as significant, if not more so, than determinative threats. Despite the optimistic picture that most administrators and leaders paint, people in private acknowledge that things such as incompetence, lack of caring and dishonesty plague their communities. To deal with these foibles, we must stop pretending that they do not exist and include them in a normative methodology and method for evaluation. Secondly, a community's decline and the positive contribution that good practices can bring to reverse this decline follow a long time cycle. The evaluation method must be capable, therefore, of incorporating a dynamic model of the community. Moreover, due to the long time span under analysis, the model must include knowledge from other scientific studies and theory to complement the data collected. Therefore, we must alter the way we evaluate a good practice and a project's effectiveness. Evaluation based on what works and what does not work is no longer adequate. Our evaluation must primarily be based on what is right and what is wrong from a normative point of view. Nor is there time for experimenting and finding out what is right and what is wrong. When the outcome of the decisions and actions we make today are fully felt, it would be far too late to correct them. The circumstances demand that we act right now and act rightly. The multi-modal systems methodology and method introduced above has been specifically developed to handle these requirements and to increase the possibility for decision-makers to make the right decisions today.

Figure 8-5: Effect of a White Loop

factors

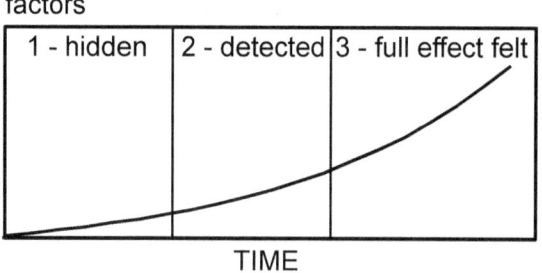

9 Where there is No Vision the People Perish

J. D. R. de Raadt and Veronica D. de Raadt

Introduction

Considerable debate has been raised regarding the preamble to the proposed European Union constitution, which is supposed to contain uplifting words for Europeans, such as the following:

> Drawing inspiration from the cultural, religious and humanist inheritance of Europe, which, nourished first by the civilisations of Greece and Rome, characterised by spiritual impulse always present in its heritage and later by the philosophical currents of the Enlightenment, has embedded within the life of society its perception of the central role of the human person and his inviolable and inalienable rights, and of respect for law...[1]

Some people, the Pope being foremost among them, believe the exclusion of Christianity from the preamble dismisses history and the foundation on which European culture has been built[2]. It ignores for example, that the heritage from the civilisations of Greece and Rome has been preserved in European culture through the agency of Christianity. It disregards the fact that the church was the only official Roman institution that survived the fall of the empire; that it preserved the Latin language and various aspects of Roman law, administration and culture. It does not recognise that the church was the sole social system that retained the pan-European structure after the empire was fragmented into the many medieval states. This structure is what the European Union is now trying to emulate 1600 years later. Furthermore, when the Greek classics were brought back to Europe, their ideas were first incorporated and promoted by the universities that had been created and were part of the Church. The emergence of the Renaissance and its rediscovery of Greco-Roman classicism found some of its greatest advocates and workers among convinced Christians, such

---

[1] BBC News (2003b).
[2] The Scotsman (2003).

as Erasmus of Rotterdam and Fray Luis de León. The University of Alcalá, a church institution, was the most important centre where the old Castilian language was latinised[3]. Thus today, modern Castilian, the second most often spoken European language in the world, is the closest to classical Latin. Likewise, the Enlightenment would not have taken place without some Christian intellectual and moral foundation that encouraged it to reject the abuses of the established Church. Many Enlightenment thinkers such as Pascal and Leibnitz professed Christian beliefs. Nor did the insurrection against the established Church emerge solely from outside its ranks. It also sprang from inside giving rise to the Free Church movement in several northern European countries including Methodism in the UK and pietism in Germany and Scandinavia. Can we justly exclude such a powerful cultural force from the European constitution?

Some have argued that identifying Christianity as the religious inheritance would exclude other religions. Thus according to the Commission's representative to the intergovernmental conference, Stefan de Rynck, "When you start to mention a particular belief or tradition, you exclude traditions you don't want to exclude"[4]. However, de Rynck's argumentation is inconsistent and prejudiced. The civilisations of Rome and Greece and the Enlightenment are included in the preamble while cultures such as the Germanic, Scandinavian, Celtic and Anglo-Saxon, are left out. Naturally, de Rynck does not condemn this exclusion, for if one were to include every culture that has played a role in European history, the list would be too long. One is forced to limit the list to those cultures that have played the greatest role. However, when the issue is the inclusion of Christianity, de Rynck applies a different criterion. That is, to make sure that none — regardless of how insignificant their contribution — should feel excluded, everyone must be excluded regardless of the greatness of their part. Two thousand years of history should make no difference.

Notwithstanding the absurdity of de Rynck's rationalisation, in this paper we add a different argument for including Christianity in

---

[3] García López (1996).
[4] BBC News (2003a)

the constitution. In our research we have found that the Christian vision has a number of systemic properties – its sacrificial ethics being foremost – that have enabled it to sustain European communities over many centuries. Conversely, the abandonment of this vision has been largely responsible for communities becoming increasingly non-viable. Our argument is divided into three parts. Firstly, we describe the systemic properties of the Christian vision that allow it to contribute to viability. Secondly, we incorporate it into a multi-modal systems framework. Thirdly, we apply this framework to a community in south-east Austria to illustrate how the erosion of the vision has made this community un-sustainable in the long-term. Naturally, this debate has wider implications, especially given emergent globalisation and multi-culturalism, but space has limited our discussion to the Christian faith and European culture. It should provide, however, a prelude to deliberation beyond these boundaries at a later stage.

An Ethical Vision

During the last two years, we have been engaged in a broad research project conducted in six different regions of Europe investigating the un-sustainable[5] predicament of their communities. In the process of collecting information, our interviewees, especially those who are leaders, have repeatedly blamed lack of vision as one of the main factors standing in the way of their communities' long-term viability. This is consistent with studies performed by a wide circle of scholars. Some argue that rather than defining sustainability, governments should include it in a vision along with the goals and priorities of the community [6]. Others believe that vision should flow from religious beliefs as expressed in the Sermon of the Mount and the Greek classics[7]. Wray and Hauer[8] argue that "…[k]nowing what is the right thing for a community can only come from a partnership of citizens, elected officials and public

---

[5] We use the term "sustainable" as a synonym of the system's concept "viable", implying therefore that a sustainable community is also self-sustainable.
[6] Geis and Kutzmark (1995).
[7] Buttimer (1990).
[8] Wray and Hauer (1997).

employees working together on the community's vision…". Vision is also regarded as a starting point for leadership development[9] and education in the community[10].

We propose that there are four main systemic requisites that a vision must fulfil to provide a solid foundation for a viable community. Firstly, the vision must conceive viability as comprising both culture and nature bound to each other. Ortega y Gasset warns us that if we allow nature and culture to drift apart, our thought will turn subjective and escape nature or it will embrace positivism and ignore culture. Such intellectual divergence has unfortunate consequences upon society:

> We are governed by two counterbalancing imperatives. The cultural imperative commands that man, the living being, must be good. The vital imperative says that one must be human – a living being – and that therefore goodness must be compatible with life. Life must be cultured, but it must also have vitality. Life without culture is barbarism; culture without vitality is Byzantine decadence[11].

Secondly, a viable vision should not assume a perfect and harmonious world. On the contrary, it must confront a world of conflict, injustice and other evils. In our own particular application, it has to address communities that are facing unemployment, lack of participation in democratic institutions, social fragmentation, low birth rate, population decline and poor standards of education. Moreover, it should perceive that the root of this problem is mostly normative: people's selfishness, lack of solidarity, apathy and materialism. Thirdly, since many people in a community will not assume their responsibilities and contribute towards its viability, others will have to compensate for this by taking on extra obligations without expecting anything in return. Therefore, a vision must incorporate a sacrificial ethic. Fourthly, it is not sufficient for a vision to be believed, it must also be practised. Praxis is what turns belief into vision.

---

[9] Sorensen and Epps (1996).
[10] Nixon et al (1999); Edwards and Brown (1996).
[11] Ortega y Gasset (n.d., p. 51); authors' translation. Ortega's concept of *vital* and *vitality* roughly corresponds to our n*ature.*

To what extent does the Christian faith[12] satisfy these requirements? According to the teachings of Christ and the Old Testament, to which he subscribed, God has created the world through his Spirit[13], the third person of the trinity. In contrast with the mechanical theories of the world's origin held by both ancient and modern world-views, this understanding stresses the personal involvement of the creator Spirit. Personal implies three main things: intellect, craftsmanship and sustenance. The creation of the world is not a magic act of waving some magic wand, but the product of a careful intellectual activity involving wisdom, understanding and prudence all poured into a magnificent design. This design is then implemented through craftsmanship, metaphorically expressed by God using his hands, marking circles, measuring and drawing out boundaries while building the universe[14]. Finally, the universe is not self-sustainable but depends on the constant and personal care of the Spirit.[15]

The universe has two realms, nature and culture. Although they are distinct and only man operates in the cultural realm, they are nevertheless closely linked[16]. Culture cannot exist independently from the natural realm and the natural realm is dependent on culture. Culture is the product of the inspiration of God's Spirit, bestowed on man through a covenant relationship that makes him God's servant, an assistant designer and steward[17]. It also bestows freedom on man; he does not need to be told by others what to do, but receives his direction direct from the Spirit[18]. Due to its being a product of inspiration, cultural life is also referred to as spiritual life. However, since the same Spirit designed, built and now sustains the universe, both nature and culture are spiritual. Therefore,

---

[12] Naturally, there are many interpretations of the Christian faith and we have had to make a choice. However, the interpretation used in this paper represents general beliefs held by most of the Christian traditions and is based on concepts drawn from the Bible.

[13] Genesis 1:1; Psalm 104:30.

[14] Jeremiah 10:12; Proverbs 8:27-30.

[15] Isaiah 32:15.

[16] Psalm 19.

[17] Genesis 1:28-29.

[18] Genesis 2:7.

Christ presents a notion of spiritual life that is tightly bound with the ordinary everyday activities of life. Spiritual gifts include such things as craftsmanship, wisdom, agricultural, zoological and managerial expertise and juridical insight[19]. They are all necessary to provide creativity to culture and sustenance to nature. Furthermore, this link between culture and nature bridged by God's Spirit adds a further benefit. It presents reality, both cultural and natural, as knowable not because of an inherent property in them – as the Greeks supposed – but as an intellectual gift of the Spirit to man[20]. Yet, our ability to be realists, thanks to the Spirit's intervention, also makes us responsible for both our understanding and our actions.

Time plays a central role in Christ's teachings[21]. While not dismissing cause and effect, a far greater stress is made on events happening because their time has been fulfilled. Time has a circular rather linear motion. Just as in nature, events follow a cyclical pattern and take place according to day and night, the seasons and the phases of biological life[22], culture also has this circularity so that "…there is nothing new under the sun."[23] Nevertheless, history is superimposed on time providing us with a deeper meaning and understanding of life. History centres on the drama of mankind; while it confers hope, it dismisses any shallow optimism of progress or future utopia for mankind and squarely focuses on the misery of life and ravages of evil[24]. Moreover, due to the close link between culture and nature, these conditions also affect nature, as it were by proxy[25]. Four historical ages may be discerned: Eden, the past age, our age and the age to come. During Eden, culture and nature are created unspoiled, but this ends abruptly with the fall of man. Ultimately, man's undoing is his ambition to become independent in thought and deed from God[26]. In fact, he aspires to become like

---

[19] Exodus 31:3-6; 1 Kings 3:9-12, 4:29-34.
[20] Isaiah 11:2.
[21] Mark 1:15; Mark 13:26; Luke 5:35.
[22] Ecclesiastes 3:1.
[23] Ecclesiastes 1:9.
[24] Genesis 6:5-6.
[25] Romans 8:20.
[26] Genesis 3:4.

God; but his mistake is to forget that he is a designed and sustained creature and that by design he is incapable of redesigning himself. Man's expulsion from Eden, his separation from God's Spirit and the entrance of evil and death into the world begin the past age. Without inspiration, man loses his freedom; now he cannot be free without becoming a barbarian. He must be told by others what to do, he must be constrained. When he is fortunate enough, "others" are prophets, but most of the time he is told what to do by tyrants and exploiters[27]. Learning and understanding is only available to a few; the ordinary man lives in ignorance and oppression. Slavery becomes the symbol of life. Nature is also dragged down, since it is dependent on a cultured mankind for its sustenance. It is an age marked by oppression.

Given the tragic predicament of man and the world, man's redemption and the restoration of life become the chief theme of history. The Greek philosophers' chief preoccupations are existence and perfection; the prophets' concern is life and emancipation. Thus, the liberation of slaves from Egypt is the first major redemptive event in history. While the Spirit of God is not restored to all Israelites and therefore the ability for everyone to receive direct instruction from God, they are given the law instead, which embodies justice. The Exodus and the law not only characterise the past age, but also foreshadow the crucifixion and the restoration of God's Spirit and life which marks the beginning of the present age and are the centre point of history. Both justice and love play an essential role in this. Justice means that God does not turn a blind eye on the crimes of man; love means that he attains this justice by serving the sentence himself through the death of Christ. By it, man not only receives acquittal, but also his and the world's emancipation[28].

Emancipation and the removal of evil from the world are delivered in two instalments. This is illustrated in Figure 9-1 where the presence of evil is symbolised by the shaded areas and its absence by the white areas. The first instalment belongs to the present age and brings cultural emancipation. God's Spirit is

---

[27] Deuteronomy 15:15; Isaiah 10:1-2.
[28] Isaiah 61:1-4; Luke 4:18-19.

offered to man together with freedom. This allows us to live life to the full, the way God would want us to live. Moreover, this starts today; culturally the present age and the age to come have been merged into one.

Figure 9-1: Ages in History

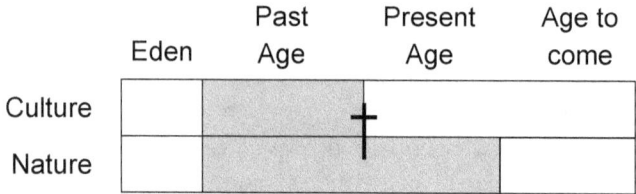

This is what Christ meant when he said, "…the kingdom of God is within you."[29] Culturally, emancipation is a concrete reality that has been experienced by Christ's followers – comprising a vast variety of people – for two thousand years. Despite the difficulty of describing this cultural emancipation – for it is itself varied – for many it is quite an ordinary thing, such as the adjustment of our sight to darkness. Where once nothing could be seen, now silhouettes can be discerned gradually allowing us to make sense of what was previously concealed. We do not see with perfect clarity, for nature has not yet been restored, but we can see in part. Here again, this seeing and understanding, even if it is in part, bestows a corresponding responsibility upon us. We are to turn our newly gained sight to this world and fight against the mess that plagues it. Inspired by an ethic of sacrificial love, we are to serve others even when they cannot repay us: food for the hungry, shelter for the homeless, liberation to the oppressed[30]. We will thus hasten the arrival of the age to come – the second instalment – when nature will be recreated and evil finally and completely eradicated. Thus, from the beginning to end, the redemption of this world is gained through sacrificial ethics which, in contrast to mysticism or contemplative religion, is real and concrete like Christ's suffering: real timber, real nails, real sweat and real blood.

---

[29] Luke 17:21; Colossians 2:7-17; 1 Timothy 6:19.
[30] Isaiah 1:17; Mathew 25:31-46.

Multi-Modal Systems Thinking

Our next step is to incorporate this vision into a systems framework – multi-modal systems thinking – in order to make an empirical application. This framework pays special attention to the interrelationships between the diverse systems in the world, both natural and cultural, as well as the links between their various aspects or modalities within which these systems function. Briefly, the approach identifies four domains in culture; each domain is comprised of a number of modalities, represented by the parallelograms in Figure 9-2. The character domain has three modalities: ethical, aesthetic and juridical; the community domain also has three modalities: operational, economic and social. The intellect domain has four modalities: epistemic, informatory, historical and credal. Likewise, nature has two domains, vitality and matter, each with its own modalities. The vitality domain has three modalities, psychic, biotic and regulatory and the matter domain has five: physical, kinetic, spatial, numeric and logical.

The sequential order of these domains and their modalities and the links between them is brought about by the two arrows symbolising the creative and sustaining power of God's Spirit flowing in two directions. The first arrow is determinative; it represents things – like the weather – that are out of human control. It runs upwards and determines or sets each foundation of each domain or modality above it, just as a foundation is set before a house is built on top of it. The second arrow, running downwards, is normative; it addresses our responsibility as humans and inspires how things ought to be. Here again, this arrow links all the modalities. Each modality or domain provides an inspiration or objective to the modalities or domains below it, just as one must first be inspired by the idea of building a house before building its foundation. Within this framework, a community and its natural environment are regarded as viable if two conditions are fulfilled. Firstly, life extends itself over all the modalities. Secondly, creative development takes place within each of the cultural modalities. That is, life is lived to the full and with ongoing cultural creativity – in contrast to mere technological and economic progress – in the community.

Figure 9-2: Multi-Modal Systems Framework

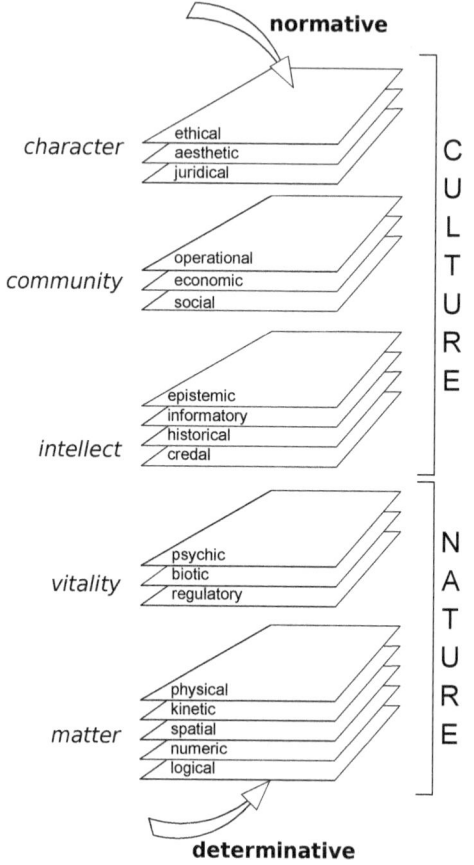

Of special interest are the credal and psychic modalities that simultaneously provide a boundary as well as a link between the cultural and natural realms. On the one hand, they set a boundary that differentiates man from animal; on the other, they provide the link that makes man an integral part of the natural realm. Thus, a dog inevitably behaves the way it feels. Sometimes man behaves the way he feels, but most of the time he will behave in the way he believes he ought to behave.

Application to a Non-Viable Community

In our study of communities in Europe, our aim has been to identify the critical factors that threaten their long-term viability and to design possible responses to these threats. One of these communities is located in Mürztal, a valley along the river Mürz, in Styria, south-east Austria. Our findings in Mürztal are similar to those in the other five communities we have surveyed. However, we prefer to deal here solely with Mürztal in order to preserve the integrity and peculiarities of our observations in this particular community. Mürztal is a region that seems to have everything in its favour. Geographically, it is placed in a most advantageous position in the midst of transport routes that connect Vienna and other major Eastern European cities with Milan and the industrial centres of Italy. In addition to its industrially strategic position, Mürztal is well endowed with natural beauty provided by rivers and quaint villages surrounded by the backdrop of the Alps. It has a long cultural tradition, offers the complete range of educational institutions, including universities and technical colleges and all types of recreation in its beautiful mountains. It is rich. It has the highest ownership of Mercedes Benz cars in Austria and, we were told, "old people have too much money" and "banks have problems lending it". It is near Graz, the capital of Styria and the 2003 Cultural Capital of Europe. Yet despite this cultural and natural endowment, it is a non-viable society, mostly due to loss of people (the population loss is one percent per year) through emigration and a low birth rate. Its population is rapidly ageing and in spite of its present wealth, the region faces a barren future.

In our research in other European regions, we have found a number of common critical factors threatening the viability of diverse regions. Moreover, other studies[31] have also identified similar factors among communities in diverse regions of the world that are essential for their viability and which at the same time represent trouble spots that threaten them. Due to their strong normative quality, these factors depend more on the common humanity

---

[31] Ahlmark (1998); Buttimer (1990, 1998); Dodds (1997); Edwards and Brown (1996); Nixon et al (1999); Ryn (1981, 1990); Råberg (1997); Schutte (2000); Smailes (1995); Sorensen and Epps (1996); Taylor et al (1997).

of their citizens than on the diversity of their economic and technological development or geographical location. In Mürztal, we identified seven of these factors – ethics, work, management, social structure, education, vision and fear. Figure 9-3 shows the factors – represented by the black circles – operating in different modalities and interacting with each other through twelve links – represented by arrows.

In addition to a variety of empirical data, we also conducted in-depth, non-structured interviews with leaders who actively participate in the everyday life of the community. This included several managers dealing with family business and training programmes for youth, the unemployed and disabled people. Also interviewed were two consultants working with a variety of municipal projects, a union leader, a university student, a director of a government educational authority and a mayor of a village. These data were stored on a database using SmCube, a special software package developed for this method. The data was then analysed to build a model of the factors in the community.

Critical Factors

Below is a summary of what we were told about the seven factors selected:

Ethics

Traditional ethics in Mürztal, inherited from Christianity, have been replaced by a utilitarian preoccupation with self-interest. This has meant that individualism and competitive behaviour have overrun the old spirit of unity in the community. It has also led to materialism, where "each one wants his own ideas and his own money and his own car"[32]. People regard less fortunate people as "others". This has hit the family hardest, the institution that is supposed to embody a caring attitude. Parents have neglected duties towards their children by putting "me" in first place and consider work for its monetary benefits rather than for the family. We were told that many fathers and mothers provide only a "short-term par-

---

[32] In this and the next section, text in quotes are statements by our interviewees.

enthood" and "while parents are at work children are alone at home watching television." Parents do not blame themselves for this, but blame the lack of low-price, well-organised child minding facilities available to them. Neglected children mimic their parent's selfishness and "lack respect for them" and in the most extreme cases reproduce the aggression and violence they learn from the television in their own behaviour.

Work

Work in the region has been affected by two major changes. One is the disappearance of large state-owned industries, mostly associated with steel mining and processing; and the other is the migration of industry to other countries that offer lower costs of labour and infrastructure. We were told that "when a company moves out of the region it is difficult to replace it". These changes have hit older people and women the hardest: "if you lose your employment and you are old (more than 50 years) it is difficult to get a job again". Of the 350 women recently retrenched by a company, it is expected that only 50% of them will get a job compared with 75% in the past. Until recently, much hope had been put in the high technology industry but the industry has turned out to be very unstable and generated highly inflated expectations, especially among the young. Many university students chose information technology studies at university expecting to gain high salaries and wide choices in employment. The burst of the information technology bubble has left them both unemployed and with an education that is inadequate for other types of work. This is especially true in Styria where the opportunities for highly technologically trained people are mostly limited to Graz. In addition, the closure of industry has left the region with a large number of unemployed people who do not have mobility due to low skills.

Old ideas about work and employment – linked to large industry and government – have hindered the opening of new possibilities for people. For example, there is a lack of development of small and medium size enterprises and the great opportunities the region offers for tourism have not been utilised. Likewise, we were told that with the closure of traditional industry, the region has been left lacking identity, vision and leadership. Although university studies in the humanities and the social sciences are highly popular with young people, they do not necessarily lead to employment. This is exacerbated by the view of young people that the purpose of work is "to earn a lot of money".

Management

In common with other places, the region has suffered from the emergence of "managerialism"[33], which has been pressed upon Mürztal through the main centres in Vienna, Linz and Brussels. Their control of society and the economy is driven by political motives and by the idea that problems of economy and society can be solved entirely through the application of an impersonal and quantitative oriented management. It can be detected at every level of administration from prime ministers to mayors of municipalities. The role of mayors in villages, for example, has shifted from leadership to management. We were told that "it was the tradition that the mayor was the father of the community but now he is the head of the council". Since vision, ideas and getting people to work together are the province of leadership, its demise and replacement by management has left the region fragmented and without vision or ideas. "The old managers [who also were leaders] went into the factory and made people feel that they [the managers] were aware of their contribution".

Managerialism is also characterised by generating a virtual reality where organisational rituals claim to represent concrete results. Interviewees pointed out that "many organisations are engaged in planning but not necessarily in implementation" and "there are a lot of studies but no action". This leads to people feeling that their communities have no direction. They believe that they are being "manipulated by MBA's" who manage from overseas and "by their knowledge obtained at business schools" but who are out of touch with the people and their circumstances. The split between management and leadership affects especially small to medium size enterprises, for "in a small company the manager must also be a leader". Given that the future of the region will depend heavily on the development of small companies, the emergence of manageri-

---

[33] Protherough and Pick (2002).

alism weakens considerably the ability of the region to respond to its economic difficulties.

Social Structure

People lamented the loss of the old community spirit and its replacement by an uncaring attitude, individualism, an emphasis on self-pursuit, leisure and youth culture. Furthermore, competitive behaviour and greater individualism have fragmented people and "politicians have made mileage of this by dividing one group against the other". There is also fragmentation between one community and the other; towns will not collaborate and, "if there's an event in one town the people in the other towns will not attend". This is exacerbated by the lack of volunteerism in Austria, "whose values are still derived from imperial times and are focused on the bureaucracy". However, the rapid ageing of the population, instigated by the low birth rate, is of greatest concern, especially due to it being spread all over Europe. A drop in the birth rate has cut down the population numbers of young people, that is, it has truncated the future of the region. This is made worse by the fact that young people are being born to families who offer them short-term parenthood and who put material prosperity before them. They are therefore more susceptible to the problems of alcohol, drugs and social handicaps. Furthermore, in Mürztal, a large number of its well-qualified youth – the future leadership so badly needed in the region – are moving into the larger cities. In this they are encouraged by the older generation who say to them, "go to Vienna, go to Graz, don't stay here". This leaves behind those who lack mobility because they are unskilled and the long-term unemployed. To make things worse, immigrants "are not welcome" even if they come from neighbouring Eastern Europe, therefore denying an inflow of talent into the region.

Education

Although the Austrian educational system is committed to the lofty ideals of "truth, beauty and goodness" and has shown greater capacity to adopt these than other countries – such as in Germany and Switzerland – it shares their common weaknesses. A serious problem has been the subordination of education to a politically instigated "managerialism" that aims to control the educational system through the development of centralised policies and a standardised approach. An interviewee said, "we have a very centralised system; our schools and universities are ten years behind other developments in Austria". In addition, efforts have been made to bring education and scientific research closer to the needs of industry. Several studies[34], including the long history of education in Europe, attest that the development of culture, intellect and science thrive on variety rather than standardisation and that variety cannot be dictated through centralised policies. On the contrary, any attempt to centrally control intellect, culture and science stifles them. It acts as a discouragement to creative and intellectual people who, by nature, are inclined to be independent and different. Furthermore, subjugating science and education to the dictates of industry and government, eliminates any possibility of a critical and independent evaluation of their decision and policy making. Such critical and independent evaluation is especially important given the managerial blunders and dishonest practices that have recently plagued industry and government. However, despite the vast influence governments and industry have had over education, education has failed to help either industry or the community and "the gap between society, especially work and education has become wider and wider". Education was also described to us as lacking "life relatedness". We were told that, "if the issue of life relatedness were taught to the young, they would respond positively". Educational institutions have failed to relate technology to society and even "information technology and information have not been brought together".

Developments at the tertiary level have not been successful either. Universities have taken refuge behind their traditional research image and the alternative Fachhochschule[35] system, where the "greater priority is given to developing students, has not been very successful". Success has nevertheless been reached at the vocational level, which has become a fast growing area of education.

---

[34] Graham (2002); Maskell and Robinson (2002); Pelikan (1992).
[35] A tertiary educational system equivalent to the institute or university of technology in the English speaking countries.

Yet, while vocational education and apprenticeships are important, they cannot fill the gap of leadership and highly educated people that Mürztal needs to get out of its predicament.

Vision

Religion is taught at school and many students choose to study it of their own free will, but Catholicism has stopped being a strong influence in Austria. Despite the fact that 86% of Austrians regard themselves as Catholics and pay their contribution to the church, only 10% are active. This split between faith and everyday life seems to run parallel to the split between education and life-relatedness. This has especially left young people without defence against the advances of materialism and intellectual and cultural decline promoted by the media. More than seventy years ago, Ortega y Gasset[36] warned us that the loss of moral influence by the church and the university would place the media as the main shaper of society's values. This has been fulfilled and "ethics and morals are now learnt from the television and the media."

Fear

Adversities in life, such as economic uncertainty, unemployment and social decline such as is at present being experienced in Mürztal, drives people to fear. Fear often turns into aggression. We were told that aggression and violence among the young have increased. Likewise there is "a suspicious attitude towards outsiders in the region" and a negative attitude especially towards "Rumanians, Czechs, Bulgarians and Russians". Due to the fear of losing their jobs people show more "competitive behaviour", less "solidarity and teamwork" and a striving to "advance themselves".

Fear may also turn into lethargy. Some people consider themselves "too old to learn something new". Teachers are "not motivated" and "push the problems of the family and social adaptation out of the school". "People procrastinate when starting small businesses" or reject new opportunities for change offered by tourism with statements such as "we want tourism but not in our mountains" or "we need no new vision". "Disabled people are fearful of learning. They say – I could not handle it in the past, why should I

---

[36] Ortega y Gasset (1992).

be able to handle it now?" Finally, "people who study at university don't like to take risks and start their own businesses" and prefer the safety of jobs in government or large business. These emotions are of course normal, but when vision is eroded, these feelings tend to take control of people's lives with highly detrimental effects.

Links between Factors

The above factors represent the substance of what was described to us in Mürztal at the time of our survey. Some may dismiss it as an overly pessimistic picture constituting problems that have always been present in any community. This denial may partly be motivated by a static paradigm that dominates people's thinking about life while ignoring the dynamic nature of history. However, our next step, in which we examine how these factors are linked together, will expose the rashness of such a dismissal. For even if the negative intensity of the factors were to be exaggerated by our interviewees, the links between these factors – represented by the arrows in Figure 9-3 – assure us that such intensity will undoubtedly be reached in the future. It is just a matter of time for the twelve selected arrows described below to bring this about:

vision ➔ *fear*

Faith should instil trust and hope in people. When beliefs and vision are forfeited, as has happened in Mürztal, people become reliant on their feelings rather than their convictions. In times of adversity, these feelings often turn into fear. Fear is a strong force on people. Thus, the fear of losing the comforts of life is stronger than the desire to increase those comforts.

social structure ⬅ *fear*

Since there is no longer an understanding of suffering in life and a hope to compel people to cope with hardship, fear overtakes them. The fear of economic hardship, of immigrants and their foreign cultures and of emotional and physical suffering, leads people to set up protective barriers around themselves. The community becomes thus divided, not only is there a rise in individualism, but even villages become suspicious of each other. Newcomers are suspected, or even despised and kept at a distance. Families become fragmented and uncaring. The fear of economic adversity drives parents to place their greatest effort on their jobs and neglect the needs of children, youth and elderly in their families. Even disabled people are looked upon with suspicion, for they do not fit the success image that is today promoted as essential in society. People associate suffering with failure and therefore fear suffering and sufferers alike.

Figure 9-3: Factors and Black Arrows

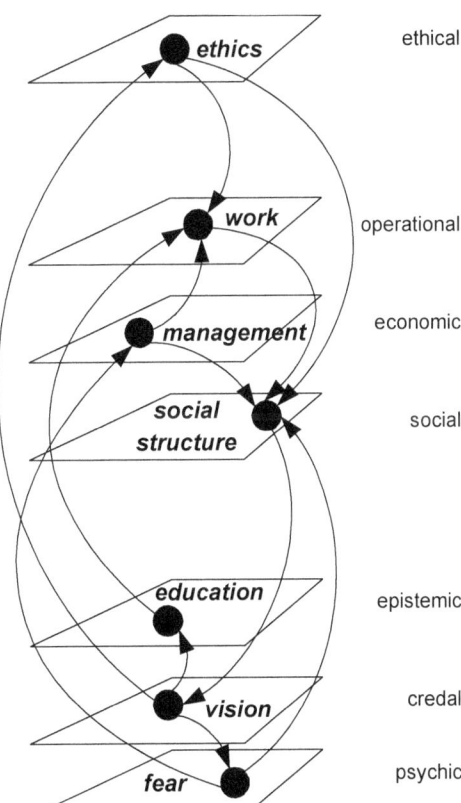

management ← *fear*

The fear of suffering is well embodied in the utilitarian principle that governs management and our western economies. This principle states that managers are driven as much by allure of profit as by fear of loss. However, when adversity strikes, fear tends to be a stronger force than allure. Managers' dread of a loss in the balance sheet becomes stronger than the appeal of a profitable one. This fear often inhibits management taking the right decision or starting a worthwhile venture in terms of their benefits to the community due to the risk of forfeiting monetary gains. This is happening as much in private corporations as in public institutions, such as universities, symphony orchestras and hospitals, which traditionally were meant to seek the public good rather than the increase of material wealth[37].

ethics ← *vision*

The relationship between the ethical and credal modalities resembles the support provided to the light bulb by the base of a standing lamp. While the light bulb is held up by the base, it illuminates everything under it, even its base; but if the base is removed, the light bulb falls and darkness follows. Likewise, the ethical modality illuminates every modality under it, but if ethics is no longer part of our creed or vision, it collapses and people become driven by self-interest. Self-interest takes first place while self-denial and sacrifice for one's neighbour is laid aside.

ethics → *work*

The light of ethics also illuminates the operational modality by displaying the needs of people and thus creating opportunities for work to fulfil these needs. However without this light, work is driven purely by a labour market where people seek work "for better pay and fewer hours" with no regard for the service they provide to the community. The market has no intellectual power to evaluate the needs of humanity, the strength of the region, civility and culture and the long-term viability of the community. For example, at present the market regards work which produces highly technological gadgetry (that is often not needed) as deserving far

---

[37] Protherough and Pick (2002).

higher payment than the parental work to bring up and educate children or caring for the elderly by family members.

ethics ➜ *social structure*

Ethics should be the glue of society that holds people together. Nowhere is this truer than in the family. Without ethical love, as against purely emotional love – operating in the psychic modality – the family fragments and crumbles. We already have made mention of the critical state of the family and the declining birth rate. If the bricks crumble, so does the house that is built with them; fragmentation of the family is tearing apart the community through competitive behaviour and individualism which replace solidarity and collaboration. Thus, on top of a society with few – and largely neglected – youths, we have added the bane of its being divided against itself. All this unfolds without people being quite aware of it. They may not yet experience the full impact of a senile society, but people should be alarmed at the harsh prospects of life in a couple of decades if this trend is not arrested. The recent death of many elderly people in France due to a heat wave has been blamed on the government and hospitals. Not much mention has been made of the families, friends and care providers who abandoned the elderly in the hot cities while they took vacations on the cooler coast[38]. This may be the future old age that awaits today's youth.

work ⬅ *management*

Contemporary management regards the worker as a human resource necessary to process its products; as such, it signifies a cost in the utilitarian equation that must be minimised. Therefore, the aim of industry is to decrease employment and, as corollary, increase unemployment rather than reduce it. As the number of employees has sharply declined, a large proportion of the working population has been left without spirit of enterprise, vision or initiative. An interviewee said, "we do not have an identity and if we ask where we are going there is no answer". This managerial approach adds to the lack of ethics. It generates a myopic work force unable to transcend the boundaries of employment, discern the needs of the community and grasp the opportunity for work.

---

[38] BBC News (2003d).

work ➔ *social structure*

The impact of industrial work and employment has taken place in two phases. The first one incorporated mass employment and the organisation of large numbers of workers in an industrial society that destroyed the important human fabric of family, friends, village and church. With the erosion of these, the social skills necessary to interact in a civic manner were lost. The second phase, marked by the rapid introduction of technology, reversed the trend of mass employment to mass unemployment. Unemployment has hit women and older people the hardest and the social structures that industry destroyed are no longer there to support them. This is exacerbated by the immigration of talented young people to the larger cities, further undermining Mürztal's community by robbing it of its future leadership.

management ➔ *social structure*

In the absence of ethics and beliefs, government and industry is given a free hand to control every aspect of the community's life. It has made people dependent on government and industry to dictate to them: where they ought to live, what they should consume, what they should study and even how they should run their families. Finally, this management is practised from a distance. Thus ordinary people have imposed on them policies and objectives that are concocted in places far removed from the realities where their lives unfold.

work ⬅ *education*

Attempts by the government and universities, including the Fachhochschule, to bridge work and education and thus diminish unemployment have failed. The reason for this is that the educational agenda has been tethered to a failing industrial system. We seem constantly to ignore the gross mismanagement and incompetence that is progressively destroying companies that have operated for more than 100 years. We naively accept the bland excuses that executives give to the press every time they report failures in their companies and justify the retrenching of thousands of workers as a necessary corrective step for their own incompetence. Why should universities, colleges and schools shape their curriculum to match this managerial incompetence? A large proportion of our youth was lured into studying courses in information technology and promised future bliss. In Mürztal it meant that the type of technology that students learnt "is not of much use to small industry in the region because they cannot afford it". The poor intellectual quality of these technological programmes has meant that students have wasted their time learning obsolete software and hardware. Instead they should have learnt how to seek a vision in life, how to think and create the opportunities for realising that vision. Now they sit unemployed, uneducated and betrayed by the system they trusted.

social structure ➔ *vision*

Vision should be inspired and focused on the life of the community. This life includes social interaction between family, friendship and common interests, the work of service to the community and the wise management of the resources available to sustain this work. When social structures are destroyed, the concrete objectives of the vision are also removed and people fall into escapist beliefs. This may be expressed in a "Sunday only" Christianity or in an assortment of experimental spirituality that people seek in Eastern religions, tarot cards and Satanism. The focus of all these is personal self-gratification rather than service to our neighbour. Such beliefs are encouraged by the media, commercialism and academics[39].

education ⬅ *vision*

Formally, the educational system seems to embrace high ideals. It stands for truth, goodness and beauty. It provides ample religious education (quite popular among young people). It stresses important values such as family, civic and social duties and even the integration of the disabled. Why has all this failed? Although these worthy things are included in the educational programme, they are not integrated into it. Students are seldom taught how compassion, family, love, civility and "truth, goodness and beauty" relate to technology, work, science, different branches of industry and even to their family and community lives. This represents a

---

[39] BBC News (2003c).

deep intellectual crisis in the west, which we will have to address if we are to live intelligent and cultured lives.

Projection of the Future

This set of twelve arrows provides a model of the dynamic change that is taking place in Mürztal and, by projecting the links forward into time, they picture what may happen in the future. We can especially appreciate in Figure 9-3 the critical role that decline in vision has played in the community and will play if things remain unchanged. Looking upwards, it has allowed fear to take over control of management and social structure and at the same time undermined ethics. Looking downwards, we note that a weakened ethic no longer exercises a caring inspiration in either work or the social structures of the community. They are now defenceless and can be preyed upon by fear, either directly or through managerial intervention. Since an attack on work, management and social structure strikes each of the modalities that comprise the community, we may now understand why the community as a whole is gradually disintegrating. Furthermore, the model indicates that the arrows form several loops that accelerate this disintegration. Some examples of these loops are:

vision ➜ fear ➜ management ➜ social structure ➜ vision
vision ➜ ethics ➜ social structure ➜ vision
vision ➜ education ➜ work ➜ social structure ➜ vision

The peculiarity of these loops is that they feed on themselves (the cybernetic term for them is "positive feedback"). That is, the detrimental effect of the black arrows on the factors becomes stronger with time. We refer to loops that are composed of black arrows as *black loops*, for they destabilise the community and make it non-viable in the long term. The future of Mürztal – and of many other similar communities – is at the mercy of these black loops.

Conclusions

Our research in Mürztal has confirmed the relevance of the criteria we established for a vision at the beginning of this paper. Firstly, the presence of fear due to lack of vision illustrates the link between nature and culture. Fear belongs to man's nature — psychic modality — while vision pertains to the credal modality in his culture. In Mürztal, the loss of faith has given in to fear and in turn fear has brought detrimental effects upon management and the community's social structure (see Figure 9-3). Secondly, even a community such as Mürztal, which is blessed with almost every conceivable advantage, presents a disharmonious world carrying its particular set of ills — selfishness, unemployment, mismanagement, social fragmentation and inadequate education. Thirdly, since this is not a perfect world and many will fail to pull their weight, a sustainable vision needs to encompass a sacrificial ethic to make up for this shortage. Fourthly, this ethic must be put into practice, not only in terms of work, but also in terms of bringing people together into the social fabric of the community, as is shown in Figure 9-3.

Christ's vision not only addresses all of these criteria but, as we indicated earlier, it has proven its ability to sustain and renew society over a period of 2000 years. If de Rynk and others who hold similar views wish to suppress Christianity from the constitution and yet preserve their moral and intellectual integrity, they must disregard the churches that stand in every village and the cathedrals that adorn European cities. They must disregard Europe's universities, its science, Michelangelo, Rembrandt, Cervantes, Tolstoy and Dickens. They must disregard Bach, Beethoven, Bruckner and Sibelius and the symphony orchestras. They must disregard every Christian ideal of justice, love and compassion that has defended Europeans against tyrants in every institution. In fact, they must disregard almost everything that has made Europe European and admired and imitated by the peoples of other cultures. Furthermore, our research in Mürztal suggests that Europe will encounter an un-sustainable future with a declining population and almost no children: a very sad picture indeed. If de Rynk wants to avoid this, without the help of Christianity, he will have to turn for help from the unnamed and untested traditions he does not wish to exclude. In the short period of time that is left, they will have to attain sustainability and fill the vacuum left by 2000 years of excluded Christian vision.

10 Arresting the Collapse of the City

J. D. R. de Raadt and Veronica D. de Raadt

Introduction

Despite being regarded as the father of education and psychology[1] and being the author who was most read in the sixteenth century after Erasmus[2], the Spanish humanist Vives is, with some exceptions, relatively unknown today. Perhaps this is because he was forced to live most of his life outside Spain to avoid being persecuted by the Inquisition and was thus never able to implement his ideas about education in Spanish universities. Although he certainly deserved it, he was impeded from becoming the "teacher of Spain" like his contemporary, Phillip Melanchthon who became the "teacher of Germany". Nevertheless his ideals influenced the development of the universities transformed by the Renaissance and Reformation, such as Leyden, Groningen, Heidelberg and Uppsala. These universities were built on principles of education that pitted them against their medieval counterparts and which he succinctly put forth as follows:

> We [scholars] must transfer our solicitude to the people. This also did Christ, with Whom a Prince is not valued more highly than anyone of the people...Certainly there can be nothing more pleasant to Him, than that we offer our erudition and whatsoever of His gifts we possess to the use of our fellow men, i.e. of His children, for whom God has imparted those great goods that to whomsoever they allotted, they should be of use to the community at large.[3]

Here are three worthy precepts set before us. Firstly, education was for all people and not just for the privileged classes. Secondly, one was not meant to seek knowledge for knowledge sake, but for the "common good". Thirdly, education was no individualist pursuit, but aimed at service to the "community at large". This educational orientation brought great scientific, cultural and social advances among the communities that embraced it. It provided, for

---

[1] Moreno and Calero (2006).
[2] Marín Ibáñez (1994).
[3] Vives (1971).

example, the thrust that transformed fifteenth century Holland from "...a wretched little country of boatmen and peasants... [that] had no university"[4] into "...a society, and culture, which regularly fascinated contemporary diplomats, scholars, merchants, churchmen, soldiers, tourists, sailors and connoisseurs of art from many lands..."[5] in the seventeenth century and which boasted five of the best universities in Europe.

It has been our concern for many years, to reintroduce this ideal and systemically – according to the methodology described below – link science, education and community together into university education for young people who live in an increasingly chaotic world. Our present work with a community in Melbourne comprised mostly of university students and recent graduates has provided a further opportunity to continue our endeavour. Most of these youths have come from countries such as Malaysia, Singapore and mainland China to study in Melbourne, some of them with plans to return to their country, others intending to settle permanently in Australia. Most of them come from traditional homes and communities and Melbourne is their first experience of Western affluence and alluring "do-as-you-please" life style, which at first inspires delight and excitement in them. As one young man from Kuala Lumpur put it, "there is so much freedom here that we do not know what to do with it". Yet, soon the true nature of this "freedom" is revealed to them. While the watchful eye of parents, grandparents and aunts are no longer close enough to restrain youthful escapades, it is also too far away to provide the love, guidance and support to which they have been accustomed. Before long, many of them will experience a marginalisation similar to the one sustained by the throng of about 10,000 youth (by conservative estimates) aged between twelve and twenty-four years, who live in the central business district of Melbourne. Ninety percent of them are homeless and ninety percent are engaged in substance abuse[6].

---

[4] Huizinga (2007, I).
[5] Israel (1995, p. 1).
[6] Information obtained during an interview with CEO of the Melbourne City Mission.

There are dedicated people who endeavour to meet the needs of these youth and they could indeed do with more support. However, even if all needs are met, we must arrest the inflow of new youth into this pool of homelessness and drug abuse to eradicate the problem. This means that we should not only be responsible for the present but also for the future. To arrest the flow, these young people require several things. They require a vision that shows them the full potential of life and an educational system to enable them to pursue it. They require a community to which they can belong and where they can experience a familial relationship with its members. They need a natural environment that is viable and safe and where natural and cultural life unfold harmoniously and support each other. They need to develop a sense of vocation that leads them to a life of service and they need to manage resources, not in order to exploit natural and cultural life, but to sustain it. Above all these essentials, they need a hunger for justice, beauty and love which they can project into their work and into the interaction they have with their communities and nature. We define "community development" as the process by which we build up a society that fulfils such requisites and with this in mind the Melbourne Centre for Community Development was established to seek the above transformation of the city by operating as a *universitas scholarium*, that is, a community of students with a systemic perspective.

The aim of this paper is to describe how we have integrated community building, research and education guided by Vives' ideals. We start by introducing the particular systems approach for identifying and analysing threats to community viability using Melbourne as a case study. A large proportion of the paper is dedicated to the analysis of these threats, for we wish to establish in a convincing manner, the grave predicament of the city, especially as it affects youth and their education. We then describe the type of responses needed, the role education must play to attain them and the requisites it must fulfil to be effective. We end with an overview of a Master of Arts degree especially designed for this purpose.

Methodological Framework

We emphasize the multi-modal nature of living systems and integrate the humanities with the natural sciences, especially emphasising the normative nature of science. We believe that the humanities, especially as understood by the classical tradition of the Renaissance and the Reformation and which emphasised their interconnections[7], must be included in a theoretical framework if we are to deal with human responsibility and *oughts* and stress the systemic importance of community for human life. Within this framework (see Figure 10-1) we identify three domains in culture – character, community and intellect. Nature also has three domains – vitality, matter and order. Each domain has the number of modalities which are homomorphic with each other, a useful property that not only helps to develop a general systems methodology but also to understand the diverse natural and cultural threats that can disturb a living system's viability. Homomorphic properties furnish a conduit for the two sets of arrows that link domains and modalities with each other; the first set is determinative and runs upwards and the second set is normative — indicating our responsibility — and runs downwards. By horizontally projecting three of the domains (matter, vitality and community), we can identify four axes of living systems. While material systems such as mountains, rivers and seas are not in themselves living, they nevertheless provide the essential habitat for the vital or biological axis — animals and plants — above it. Likewise, the vital axis provides the biological habitat for human culture, which finds its expression in a variety of social groups and institutions — such as school, family and clubs. Neither the intellectual nor character domains have horizontal projections, but they respectively provide the foundation and the ultimate aim of civic life as ought to be embodied in social institutions.

---

[7] Melanchthon (1999).

Figure 10-1: Domains and Modalities of Living Systems

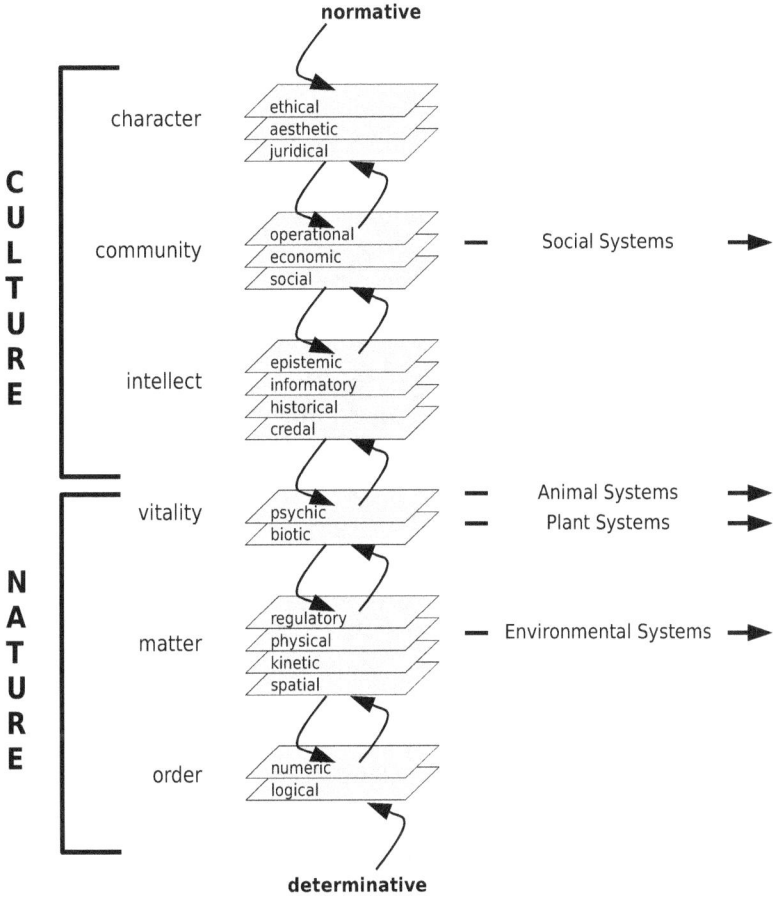

Perhaps this methodology may seem too structured for today's taste, but we regarded it as a necessary tool to find the various states of equilibrium of a non-viable community. Cybernetics has taught us that equilibrium and stability are essential for every living system, including communities and that there will be "...a state of equilibrium if and only if each part [of them] is at a state of equilibrium..."[8]. Our experience has brought us across many young

---

[8] Ashby (1976, p. 83).

people who are victims of the chaos and uncertainties of post-modern society and who crave stability and direction to bring meaning and purpose to their lives. It is for them that we have developed this methodology and a corresponding educational programme in order that they may not only stabilise their lives, but also the communities to which they seek to belong.

A Model of Melbourne

Since equilibrium and stability are essential for living systems, either natural or cultural, we have developed a method to model the threats to the equilibrium of communities in a variety of modalities. Based on past work in several countries in Europe, we have identified a number of factors operating in different modalities, that are essential to a community's life but which are often out of equilibrium. This work was part of projects sponsored by the European Social Fund and directed towards regions in Europe that were losing population, especially young people. It was believed that the main factor behind emigration from these regions was unemployment. However, our studies revealed that unemployment was not an isolated factor in a community, but that it was systemically interconnected with other factors that had also changed with the rise of unemployment, such as education, ethics and social structure. This meant that solely addressing unemployment, in isolation from these other factors, was not a solution. Therefore, with the assistance of the above methodology we traced the links between these factors to establish the systemic nature of their instability in the community. By following these links we also discovered other factors contributing to instability.

Recently we built such a model of the city of Melbourne – shown in Figure 10-2 – and drawing on our prior research, selected nine factors, each belonging to a different modality, which are critical to the long term viability of Melbourne. They are listed in Table 10-1. As we have pointed out, the impact on the stability of the community depends to a much greater extent on the links between factors than in the factors themselves and therefore these links are also plotted in Figure 10-2.

Table 10-1: Factors and Modalities

Factor	Modality
ethics	ethical
work	operational
management	economic
social structure	social
education	epistemic
media	informatory
vision	credal
mental state	psychic
ecology	regulatory

Figure 10-2: Melbourne Factors and Links

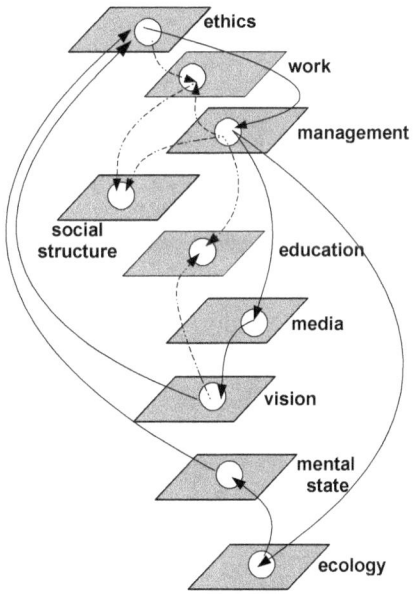

Although all factors have a systemic impact on the others and there is no precise sequence in the arrows in Figure 10-2 – representing the links – there is nevertheless a *primus inter pares* among these factors which we have labelled *vision* representing the beliefs of the community upon which its cultural life is built. We will start by observing its impact on other factors.

Vision ➜ *Education*

Systems scientists are well aware that the closed system's mechanical vision remains dominant in our times and has a powerful impact on all aspects of our culture. With the closed system's vision gaining prominence in the university, the humanities, the sciences that according to Vives restore our humanity[9], are gradually being dragged out and beyond its walls. Monash University closed its department of classics about 10 years ago and the University of Melbourne has recently begun a contraction of its Faculty of Humanities. If our humanities are being pushed out of the university, where will the large number of students that daily parade up and down Swanston Street and who attend the University of Melbourne and the Royal Melbourne Institute of Technology gain an intellectual grasp of what it means to be a good professional, let alone, a good citizen, a good husband, a good wife, a good parent, or a good friend? Yet, these are the essential roles that make up a civilised society.

There is sufficient historical evidence to show that the development of the natural sciences was driven by the erudition of the humanities. This may explain the decline in competence in the natural sciences that has paralleled the demise of the humanities in Australia as much as in Europe.[10] It is now generally acknowledged that the Australian academic system is significantly inferior when compared with the past[11]. A study carried out by the Australian National University and composed of interviews of more than 1,400 scholars from around the nation has produced disturbing findings about the conditions existing in the university classroom. These include lecturers fearing to fail students because of financial

---

[9] Vives (1971).
[10] Scherman (2002); Rood (2007); Tomazin (2008).
[11] Cain and Hewitt (2004).

consequences and work overload. Some think that the award system has taken a complete step down; that is, a master degree is now equivalent to a bachelor degree offered a decade or so ago[12]. Similar conditions prevail in the school system with deteriorating educational standards[13] and buildings, an increase of bullying and a shortage of teachers[14].

Vision → Ethics

A closed systems vision is essentially secular and has brought with it the rejection of classical ethics, whether based on the philosophy of Plato and Aristotle or on the Samaritan ethic built on agape love[15]. These systems of ethics were based on the existence of God with which the closed systems approach became uncomfortable, despite its failing to replace them with a believable and viable ethical alternative. This left the field open for utilitarianism to rule unopposed in our economy and society and to impose its own doctrine described as:

> The creed which accepts, as the foundation of morals, Utility or the Greatest-happiness Principle, holds that actions are right in proportion as they tend to promote happiness, wrong as they tend to produce the reverse of happiness. By happiness is intended pleasure and the absence of pain; by unhappiness, pain and the privation of pleasure.[16]

Mill's ethic is purely behavioural for there is no conviction or conscience behind it. It is therefore wholly inadequate to guide our actions towards a civilised human life. As might be expected, in the beginning, this morality encountered strong resistance from a traditional society. However, thanks to its application to economics and the opportunity it provided to make some people and nations rich at the expense of others, it progressively gained ground in Western society. An economic paganism has got hold of us with Mammon deciding what one ought or ought not to do in almost

---

[12] Anderson (2001); Anderson et al (2002).
[13] Topsfield (2007).
[14] Edwards and Rumble (2006); Rood (2007).
[15] Boulding (1969).
[16] Mill (1969, p. 249).

every issue of life including the goods and services we purchase, work and also romance.

Ethics ➜ *Management*

When the variables of the utilitarian formulae, pain and pleasure, are replaced by money, we have income and expenses, the raw materials of capitalist economics and management. Naturally, the greater the difference between the two, the greater the profit and the more "ethical" the management is supposed to be for, as Friedman preaches, "the social responsibility of business is to increase its profits"[17]. Vast amounts of arguments have been forwarded to defend this approach. Yet, behind this argument lie two profound fallacies. Firstly, it assumes that the resources of the earth are unlimited and that unhindered economic development is possible without detrimental repercussions to people and nature. Development built on this assumption has had a disastrous impact, as Raven, a British environmentalist points out:

> Virtually all graphs of the consumption of resources, the extinction of species, and the destruction of the soils, the seas, and the atmosphere, show exponential growth, mostly growing much faster than the "population explosion". But the most striking single index of the need for radical change is that, for everyone on the planet to live as we live in the West, it would be necessary to have five back-up planets engaged in nothing but agriculture to support us and handle the pollution we produce. Yet vast billions of people in China, India, and elsewhere have embarked on the quest to live as we live. It cannot be done.[18]

Secondly, advocates of capitalism assume society is homogeneous. They ignore the huge chasm that divides rich and poor and sets them at a disadvantage in every modality of life. Consequently, the pursuit of economic pleasure by the rich has devastating effects for the poor, especially when we consider that the poor represent the vast majority of humanity and the rich only a small minority. The relationship between the pleasure of the rich and the pain of the poor is curvilinear, that is, the constant pursuit

---

[17] Friedman (1970).
[18] Raven (2005).

of ever-increasing consumption of the rich produces a disproportionately higher amount of pain for the poor. We are all aware that
our appetite for purchasing an assortment of goods manufactured
in Asia – clothing, mobile telephones, laptop computers, flat TV
screens – is satisfied by the work of people toiling in sweat shops
and barely earning a subsistence income[19]. This exploitation, we
are told, is necessary for their employers to increase their profits
and remain "globally competitive" and thus exercise their own
brand of "social responsibility". This disparity between rich and
poor also occurs within a wealthy nation such as Australia and our
city of Melbourne. We have "one city [but] two Australias": the
average annual income of the top 20% of Australia's households is
$225,000; the bottom 20% is only $22,000.[20] Between 1994 and
2004, the proportion of Australians living in poverty increased
from 7.6% per cent to 9.9%.[21] A recent report studying the distribution of disadvantage in Australia[22] elicited the following response from the local press:

> Australia's' neediest communities are being held hostage by a
> succession of social ills from joblessness to jail time, child ab-
> use, poor health and limited education, according to a study that
> maps disadvantage across the nation. The research reveals a
> startling concentration of social and economic problems in vul-
> nerable neighbourhoods, suggesting disadvantage multiplies
> once a community starts to fall behind.[23]

To this must be added the exorbitant price of housing and inability of young families to purchase their own home, partly due to
investors who horde properties (certainly a limited resource) in order to profit from exorbitantly hight rents, forcing people to a
third-world standard of living and having to forfeit spending on
health and food to meet housing costs[24]. As a result, low income
people who live in areas that are now becoming attractive to the
rich are being forced out of their homes into areas that lie far away

---

[19] McDougall and Doward (2007).
[20] Mackay (2007).
[21] The Melbourne Age (2007c).
[22] Vinson (2007).
[23] Schubert (2007).
[24] Khadem (2007).

from their work or into rural towns that lack the infrastructure to accommodate them[25]. Docklands is an illustration in the very centre of Melbourne. Meant to provide housing for low income people, the price of its apartments can only be afforded by well-to-do couples on a double income and with no dependants[26].

Ethics ➜ Work

Utilitarian ethics also dictates the choice of work. The idea of work as a vocation motivated by service to our neighbour has long been replaced by career ambitions that are supposed to generate a substantial surplus of pleasure in terms of satisfying one's own interests, social status and of course, monetary income. This is evinced by the choice of careers of young people. Our experience with university students indicates that their choice is mostly guided by the opportunities for well paid jobs. The favourites are commerce, marketing, tourism, sports management, a variety of technologies and prestige careers such as medicine and law. All of them offer substantial pecuniary rewards. Vocations that address needs such as teaching, nursing[27] and social work[28] are, as may be expected, at the bottom of the list of preferences. The favoured professions are oriented mostly to produce goods and services for the rich; the poor lose out.

Management ➜ Work

The choice of profession is strongly influenced by management, since we live in a world where, despite there being so much work to do, one cannot work unless a job is "created" by industry. We must emphasise the determinative force management plays in the choice of work of people and which is reflected in the language of corporate executives, politicians and public servants when they speak of "job opportunities" and "increasing jobs"[29]. Citizens and university students are brainwashed into believing, in accordance to the laissez faire creed, that the economic system is ruled, like the weather, by forces beyond our control and that their choice of

---

[25] The Melbourne Age (2002b).
[26] Millar (2003); Millar and Boulton (2005).
[27] Dockery and Barns (2005).
[28] Lonne (2007).
[29] The Melbourne Age (2006); UNINEWS (20 August 2001).

profession must fit accordingly. Young people we have questioned about this matter almost uniformly justify their choice of work by the job opportunities offered to them, as well as by the pressure that their parents exert upon them to study in order to elbow their way "to the top".

Management → *Education*

This deception is reinforced by the educational system which, by numbing young minds, has inculcated a closed system perspective dominated by marketing, accounting, engineering, technology and suchlike careers. This trend in education has not only been determined by the secular vision of our society but by the utilitarian, managerial doctrine that now inspires educational establishments. Universities such as Melbourne and RMIT are no longer led by scholarship but by managerialism[30] exercised by a "chief executive officer" who has replaced the former vice chancellor and principal. University departments are run as businesses that must generate profits even when it is at the expense of the quality of education[31]. A disturbing by-product is the gradual replacement of academic staff who hold a vocational view of their profession by a new generation of pseudo-scholars who feel comfortable with academic commercialisation and the utilitarian ethic that buttresses it and who are satisfied to define their work on the basis of entrepreneurship rather than on the pursuit of truth.

Servility to managerialism has led universities to exploit students from poorer countries who come to study in order to obtain an Australian permanent residence visa rather than to equip themselves to work in their own country. This means that part of the universities' profits are earned not through legitimate educational and scientific activities, but through the abuse of immigration laws and the unhappy economic and social circumstances that drive young people to seek their fortune somewhere else.

A more sombre picture of this is provided by students who find it difficult to meet their living expenses and university fees and who are driven to "...product testing by unscrupulous companies

---

[30] Protherough and Pick (2002).
[31] Morton (2007).

and even turning to prostitution..."[32] A recent survey conducted by The Melbourne Age newspaper reports that 40% of female prostitutes working in city brothels are university students. A disturbing question is raised here: what kind of educational institutions are these that supply almost half the "sex-workers" in Melbourne's brothels from youths supposedly under their intellectual and moral care? Monash University's spokeswoman furnished a chilling answer to this question:

> Obviously these ladies are adults and are free to make their own choices about what work they want to enter into. However, we do have extensive services for those who are suffering money problems. Any student can visit our financial counsellors, who are available on all campuses.[33]

We may conclude that in a society ruled by the utilitarian creed, even the university believes that humanity's moral problems can be solved with money.

Work → *Social Structure*

Originally, the word economics (oikonomos) referred to household management. It meant the arrangement of work and resources in order to sustain a family or small community. The work of women in their homes under this arrangement was always regarded as economic activity. Capitalism reversed this so that the purpose of economics became the use of people and resources in order to accumulate wealth. The technological advances that accompanied this change were directed towards the industrial and economic machinery rather than to the household. After women were displaced from their original economic activity and started to join the workforce of industry and commerce, those who remained behind were the most vulnerable, mainly the elderly and the children. They were left to fend for themselves, or more accurately, they were shifted to child-minding centres and homes for the elderly to be looked after by emerging industries ironically called "caring industries". A visit to an elder care home is a depressing

---

[32] The Senate Employment, Workplace Relations and Education References Committee (2005, p. xv); Lantz (2005); Kostas (2006).
[33] Reilly (2008).

experience, even if it is one of the better places. Elderly people are removed from society and denied the experience of observing the activities of different generations going about their everyday life. They are deprived of the stimulus of being part of a community. If they are well looked after medically and physically, they are lucky. Many elderly are neglected and even mistreated by those who are supposed to take care of them[34] and seldom visited by their "loved ones": "Visit any medical ward, in any hospital, and you will find a large number of elderly people without a toothbrush or toothpaste, their bags of unwashed clothing sitting in wardrobes waiting to be collected, many don't have a shaver, and some, not even a comb."[35]

The other victims are children. Their neglect is creating developmental problems that show up once they arrive at school, such as in social competence, emotional maturity and language skills[36]. Another report indicates that:

> There is a growing body of evidence that children from the "mainstream" of suburban Australia are displaying serious physical, intellectual and emotional problems. We know about the seemingly inexplicable rise in behavioural disorders from attention deficit hyperactivity disorder to mild autism. We know Australian children are fatter than they should be and are getting type 2 diabetes. We know boys are falling further and further behind girls in academic achievement and that an alarming number are killing themselves.[37]

Much of this can be traced to the lack of family experience that today's children and youth enjoy. Parents complain about the conflict that exists between job and family[38], a contest that is usually won by the job. This is even more of a quandary for single parents. Meanwhile, there is a growing number of unemployed men who

---

[34] Medew (2006).
[35] The Melbourne Age (2005).
[36] The Melbourne Age (2003).
[37] Shanahan (2003).
[38] Shaw and Cooke (2007).

have stopped looking for work, have abandoned all hope and dropped out of society[39].

Management ➜ *Social Structure*

Despite the pious claims about social responsibility that corporations usually state in their promotional material, management has remained unmoved by the social hardship of the elderly, of children, of single parents and of the jobless. Their idea of "social responsibility" does not change their goal of maximizing profits and to attain this, they seek to control society; a practice not confined to private corporations but also embraced by government institutions run by the same utilitarian philosophy. We are in the midst of an emerging form of totalitarianism, exercised by the corporate state; that is, a partnership between corporations and the government. The emergence of such a new form of "totalitarianism" has recently been addressed by Naomi Wolf[40]. In a recent visit to Australia, she pointed out that many of the laws and policies emerging in the U.S. resemble the measures taken by fascist regimes in Italy and Germany during the 1930's and that the degree of control exercised in Australia is even greater[41]. Part of this tighter control and people's acquiescence towards it is rooted in Australia's past and the regulated life forced upon its first settlers. It resulted in Lachlan Macquarie, an enlightened Governor, to be ceaselessly harassed for his emancipatory ideals[42].

However, in contrast to the old methods of coercion, the new fascism avails itself of much more subtle tools: manipulation through marketing and the media. For manipulation to be most effective, one needs a society that is the least structured, something like a *Brave New World*[43], where all sense of family and community have been abolished and replaced by a collection of individuals organised into a production-consumer line. In this way, every interdependence between individuals is removed and replaced by sole dependence on the corporate state. The most pliable

---

[39] Colebatch (2006).
[40] Lyons (2007).
[41] The Melbourne Age (2007a); Bachelard (2007).
[42] Ritchie (1986).
[43] Huntford (1971).

target of this type of manipulation is the teenager[44]. As a youth enters into the teen years, a process of changing dependence begins; there is a lessening of dependence on parents and an increase in dependence on people outside the immediate family. When this new dependence is on teachers, mentors, relatives or friends who provide a role model and have the welfare of the youth at heart, this transition process is a healthy one, for it results in the adolescent assuming responsibilities for his own life. Business has exploited this vulnerability in youth using marketing and advertising techniques, impregnated with a considerable amount of sex, to control and induce them to consume uncritically and avidly what they do not need or what is harmful, such as liquor and tobacco[45]. Moreover, to expand the proportion of teenagers in society, management has expanded the span of teen mentality by pressing it backwards into the "tweenies" years and pushing it forwards into the thirties. It explains why so many people in their thirties still live as teenagers. This has not been helped by the concomitant decline of family values[46].

Management ➜ *Media*

In an address to the Federation of University Students in Madrid in 1930, Ortega y Gasset warned of the increasing power that the press would have over people's behaviour by substituting the earlier influence of the church and the university[47]. Modern corporations avail themselves of this power to control people. Just as it has absorbed the university, the corporate machinery has captured all the media's branches, whether they be newspapers, television, radio or the Internet into its fold. Moreover, media corporations, such as the BBC, CNN and Rupert Murdoch's conglomerate have extended their sphere of power beyond national borders and have become commercial empires comparable to other large multinationals[48]. An intellectually neutralised university and a spiritu-

---

[44] Barber (2007).
[45] The Melbourne Age (2007d); Sharp (2007); Stark (2007); Dubecki (2008); Miletic (2008); Rush and La Nauze (2006).
[46] Zwartz (2008); Holroyd (2008).
[47] Ortega y Gasset (1992).
[48] Multinational Monitor (1995).

ally trivialised church have left the field open for the media to manipulate ignorant people at their pleasure. In the words of Carl Bernstein, one of the journalists who uncovered the plot behind the Watergate break-in:

> The reality is that the media are probably the most powerful of all our institutions today and they, or rather we [journalists], too often are squandering our power and ignoring our obligations. The consequence of our abdication of responsibility is the ugly spectacle of idiot culture![49]

Media ➜ *Vision*

Having replaced the church and the university, the media then becomes the oracle, shaping the global culture by dictating what the citizen of the global village should believe. We may accurately depict the vision of the average person on Melbourne's streets as *tele-vision*; it is a new religion with its own prophets and priests. Virtuous heroes of the past have been dethroned and replaced by the anti-heroes of sport, rock music and film. Most of the behaviour of these modern priests stand in open rejection of the values that have held traditional communities together in the past. The media constantly flashes on its headings the bizarre self-indulgence, violence, rape, drugs and even incarceration of football players and starlets[50]. The greatest victims have been the young people who have been brought up in social isolation from family and improperly educated and who flock into the centre of Melbourne because the old suburb culture supported by growing families and gardens has shrunk. For them the new community is comprised of reality-shows, chat-rooms and blogs[51] that have replaced the traditional channels of social interaction with a self-assembled kit of the "idiot culture".

Management ➜ *Ecology*

Almost harmonising with the common root *eco*, systems science[52], has stressed the homomorphism between economics and

---

[49] Bernstein (1992).
[50] Caldwell (2004); Cleary (2004); Hellard (2007); Taylor (2007); The Melbourne Age (2007e); Associated Press (2007).
[51] Hill (2007); The Melbourne Age (2007b).
[52] Beer (1994a; 1995).

ecological regulation. For they are both meant to sustain, on the one hand, culture, and on the other, nature. Both have been disrupted by utilitarian management. In addition to being the chief architect of the environmental disaster that looms over us[53], state and industry have coalesced at international summits to block scientists informing the public about the alarming state of affairs[54] and funded conferences to discredit such scientists with research that is ostensibly biased towards the interests of big businesses[55]. It is not only the natural habitat that is destroyed, but also the habitat of humans. The flow from rural to urban centres such as Melbourne is generated by industrial and financial centralism. This, in turn, has been increased by the drought and fires due to climate change that have struck small towns in Victoria[56]. The city itself is undergoing constant infrastructural development, building more motorways (instead of public transport)[57], demolishing old buildings and dredging Port Philip Bay[58] to allow the passage of bigger container ships loaded with consumer goods we do not need.

Ecology ➜ Mental-state

Despite its wealth and great advancement in medicine, modern society has poor mental health; some of its psychic diseases such as anorexia and obesity were virtually unknown a few generations ago. Much of the increase in depression, fear and the increase of suicide among farmers and aborigines[59] can be traced back to the destruction not only of their physical but also social habitat. Yet, our contemporary individualism seldom spares thought of the human need of community which is almost as intense as the need of a beehive for a bee.

---

[53] Pacala and Socolow et al (2004); Morton (2007); Colebatch and Topsfield (2007); Millennium Ecosystem Assessment Board (2005); Stern (2006).
[54] The Melbourne Age (2002a); Friends of the Earth (2002).
[55] The Melbourne Age (2004).
[56] Millar (2007a and b).
[57] Kleinman (2006; 2007); Birrell and Healy (2008).
[58] Bell (2005).
[59] Stafford (2007); ABC Online (2006).

Mental-state ➔ *Ethics*

A mental state dominated by fear, depression and even despair has driven people in two opposite directions. The first one, mostly associated with adults, leads to a stronger utilitarian ethic focused on greed. Melbourne's sobriety and egalitarianism that character-ised it a few decades ago has given way to a show of extravagance and self-pursuit. It is visible in the transformation of the former family house of the past into pretentious, mansion-like buildings that have sprung up even in what were once considered modest middle-class suburbs. The second direction, being adopted by an increasing number of youth – and most disturbingly, children as young as 12 – is a combination of bizarre violence, drugs and alco-hol, a situation described by Prime Minister Kevin Rudd as "...an epidemic of binge-drinking across the country"[60].

Our leaders have become at last aware that the "city is turning ugly". Victoria's opposition leader has warned us that "Melbourne is in danger of losing its position as one of the world's most live-able cities because of an epidemic of violent crime" after receiving "...figures showing that violent crime and assaults have soared in some parts of Melbourne by more than 75% in the last seven years"[61]. And on releasing a new research paper on alcohol abuse, Dr. John Herron, the Chairman of the Australian National Council on Drugs, confessed: "None of us had any idea that one in five 17-year-olds were getting smashed at least once a week."[62] The word *smashed* is indeed appropriate, for it accurately describes what these youth are doing to their lives.

From the above analysis and with the help of Figure 10-2 we observe that the links generate two self-incrementing loops (links forming a loop are marked with unbroken lines), which will ex-acerbate the situation in the future:

vision ➔ *ethics* ➔ *management* ➔ *media* ➔ *vision*
ethics ➔ *management* ➔ *ecology* ➔ *mental-state* ➔ *ethics*

---

[60] Lunn (2008); Houston et al (2008).
[61] Gordon and Rood (2008).
[62] Frye et al (2008).

In earlier research we have postulated that, due to the exponential nature of these loops, one can discern three stages in their development. The effect in the first stage is almost imperceptible. In the second stage, the impact may be observed if one carefully searches for it, but in the third stage it is plainly evident. The alarm of politicians and community leaders at the predicament of the city is likely to be an indication that we have entered into the third stage and that a systemic collapse will follow unless we speedily intervene.

Intervening through Education

The very complex systemic links between the factors should leave no doubt that an intervention that addresses a single factor will not effectively pull the city out of its predicament. Any solution will have to deal with several factors at the same time and if possible, to generate a loop that is beneficial to the city and which counteracts the destructive loops in Figure 10-2. Our aim here is to generate the loop shown in Figure 10-3, linking the following factors:

$$work \Rightarrow social\ structure \Rightarrow management \Rightarrow work$$

The common approach of politicians and bureaucrats to generate desired social outcomes is to re-engineer people's lives by writing policies. The implementation of these policies must rely on some form of coercion. However, coercion may be legitimately exerted to restore justice, but the imposition of policies beyond justice leads to totalitarianism. Furthermore, social circumstances such as those described in Figure 10-2 require more than people behaving justly; it requires a Samaritan ethic to compensate for injustices that will never be reversed. This will require a belief in such an ethic and an understanding of how it can be intelligently applied in a community to ensure its viability.

Figure 10-3: Planned Loop

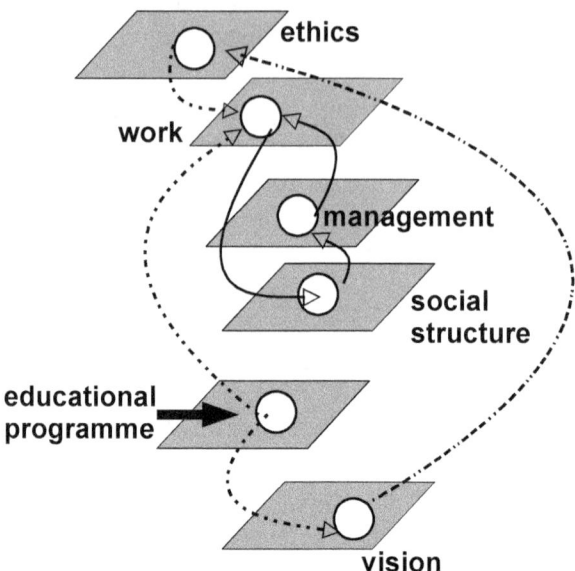

Rather than policy, we rely on education. Having done our research, we have introduced it into an educational programme that should in turn create a set of arrows that are not community action in themselves but that equip students for action in the community, moved by their own convictions and ethical commitment, rather than by acquiescence to policy and coercion. The programme aims at an initial effect on two factors: work and vision (see Figure 10-3). As for work (i.e., education ⇨ work) it helps students to reorient their work towards sustaining and developing the community rather than pursuing a career in the traditionally preferred sectors of big industry and commerce. The programme also seeks to inspire students to view the world (education ⇨ vision), not from the comfort of middle-class suburbs and corporate offices, but from the predicament of more needy people. This vision, if espoused, should make it clear to students of the necessity of a Samaritan ethic (vision ⇨ ethics) if there is to be any hope for our community to be viable in the long term. A Samaritan ethic will encourage students to carry out the work (ethics ⇨ work) for which they have been educated. This work, being directed towards the community, will strengthen its social structure (work $\Rightarrow$ social structure). In turn, a stronger social structure will be more inclined to control and manage its resources for the benefit of the community (social structure $\Rightarrow$ management) and thus economically support those who work for its advancement (management $\Rightarrow$ work). This would close a loop that would help reverse the destructive process that is now in effect in Melbourne.

Educational Programme Design

To achieve this, the programme must fulfil the following requirements:

Disciplinary Integration
The programme must be built upon a methodological systems foundation that integrates the diverse disciplines – both natural sciences and humanities – to facilitate normative analysis.

Common Professional Framework
The programme must offer studies that can be taken by diverse professionals and provide them with a common framework where they can integrate diverse disciplines into their profession and learn how to work together.

Community and Nature Focus
The programme must focus on the needs of communities and their natural environments rather than on the interests of big industry and commerce.

Visionary and Ethical
The programme must equip students to become visionaries in their communities. Their visions must in turn motivate them to set aside their self-pursuit and embrace an ethic of self-sacrifice for the benefit of neighbours and communities without necessarily expecting a lot of money in return.

Intellect
Translating a vision into action requires competence in analysis, design and implementation of ideas; the programme must equip

critical and creative minds as well as provide practical tools to realise the vision.

Research
Given the vast domination of positivism and utilitarianism in the sciences, there is an urgent need to expand systemic knowledge, especially within the humanities. There should be therefore a significant emphasis on methodology, as well as method, in the curriculum. The syllabi should introduce students to systems research and provide a suitable foundation to continue, if they so choose, to a doctoral dissertation.

In summary, the programme should be suitable for a variety of professional people and university graduates — such as teachers, lawyers, social workers, urban planners, engineers, clergy (with the purpose of retraining them into a new role) and physicians. It should equip them to reorient and extend the horizon of their business or professional practices towards the community and open to them at least three alternative paths of professional development. It should either expand the scope of their professional practice or business by making it possible to set up common projects and activities with other professionals and businesses in order to sustain the community in which they operate. In turn, this should also enhance the horizon and opportunities of their own practices and businesses and ensure their long-term viability. Alternatively, it should equip them to move into a leadership and management role in the community such as serving in a municipal council or other political role, or serving in the directorate of an institution such as a hospital or a state-park organisation. Finally, it should also make it possible for some to follow an academic/scientific path by pursuing a doctoral degree that combines systems science and the student's own professional and disciplinary background.

Ideally, one would wish to introduce systemic thinking from the very beginning of a person's schooling. However, given the pressing needs of the city and the vast variety of skills that are needed, we have found that strategically, a masters degree combining course work and research is the most expeditious level to start an educational intervention. By making use of the knowledge that students already have and re-orientating it towards the community, we can reach our objective with modest resources in a relatively short period of time. The design that we here propose is not new, for it borrows from previous work at a Swedish University[63]. It requires two steps. The first step consists of identifying the knowledge that is required for community development (illustrated in Figure 10-4). It is accomplished by cross-associating modalities (set vertically at the left side of the figure) that are most important to address the factors and links we identified above. We have grouped this knowledge into four theoretical blocks: moral theory, social systems theory, systems methodology and cybernetics. The vertical arrows that connect these blocks indicate the normative and determinative interrelationships between these blocks. Moral theory supplies us with an ideal of the kind of society we ought to be, so that social systems theory does not turn into a purely positivist description about how society functions at present, but provides an understanding about how we can change into a responsible and civilised community. This understanding is founded on systems methodology which is, in turn, buttressed by cybernetics focusing on the regulatory and psychosocial principles relevant to social change. Theory must be applied and this requires a body of practical knowledge which is illustrated by the blocks in the rightmost column in Figure 10-4, also linked by normative and determinative arrows. Social systems analysis and design methods is practised with the help of systems modelling tools such as data collection methods and SmCube, a specialised database and modelling software package. Finally, we stress character development as an important component of education. While students in the future will undoubtedly experience great satisfaction in their work, their endeavour to transform their communities will not always be received with appreciation. At times they will encounter outright hostility. This will not be encouraging for people who have sacrificed the high remuneration and other rewards that work in industry, commerce or government would have offered. They will need, therefore, to be motivated by love, grace and justice to press on according to their conviction and vision and this will be de-

---

[63] See Paper 3.

veloped not only through student-teacher interaction in their studies but in their ongoing participation in a *universitas scholarium* that is characterised by these virtues.

The blocks in Figure 10-4 do not represent an educational syllabus, but simply the fields of knowledge that are necessary for community development. We require therefore a second step to furnish a syllabus. Here again we encounter a sharp difference between a systemic education and the current practice of university teaching. In contrast to the fragmented approach to science, a systemic approach presents the sciences in a unified manner but without obliterating their uniqueness. Rather than the large number of compartmentalised subjects (termed "courses" in some countries) and corresponding syllabi in a conventional programme, the core of our programme has only one subject and one syllabus (naturally, extra electives may be added to the core). Students' pattern of learning resembles the spiral path of a glider climbing higher and higher, where learning successively oscillates between the modalities and their corresponding arts. They gradually ascend towards a higher level of understanding with each oscillation until they are ready to undertake their research project.

However, this does not easily fit the government accreditation system. For a democracy, Australia is a rather intellectually repressive society; one may be able to think as one wishes, but there are constraints over publicly expressing such thoughts and certainly over teaching them formally. Many academics happily sit on government boards helping them control science and education rather than defending their autonomy. As can be readily imagined, innovation in education, including systemic thinking, encounters a frustrating barrier of bureaucracy and other obstacles. This, it is claimed, is necessary to safeguard quality, an absurd assertion in the light of the correlation between the sharp increase in regulation and equally sharp decline in Australia's educational standards (a separate paper could be written documenting the emotional agony and frustration that a scientist undergoes when entering into negotiation with the educational bureaucracy). Therefore, we have presented each of the above oscillations as a distinctive subject to satisfy institutional requirements while preserving the systemic integrity of the programme. Each subject title reflects its scientific content, but it may need to be changed to fit the particular conventions of the place where it is taught. This is illustrated in Figure 10-5, where the programme has been sectioned into subjects with names that approximately reflect their content.

Figure 10-4: Learning Blocks

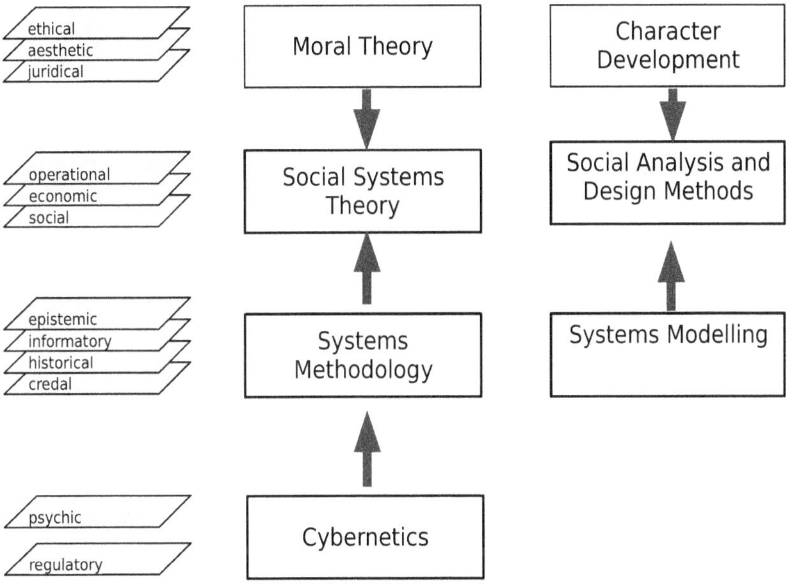

Briefly, the content is as follows:

Philosophy of History

Given that the ultimate purpose of the programme is to equip students for a systemic intervention in their communities that is dynamic and thus part of history, we start our studies by laying out the philosophical presuppositions to justify this intervention. Specifically, we examine human oppression, redemption, Samaritan ethics and cultural restoration as supplying an historical axis upon which to affix a systemic methodology and methods.

Figure 10-5: Educational Programme

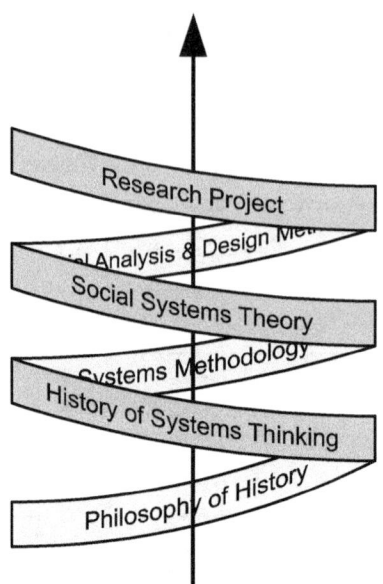

History of Systems Thinking

The 20th century interest in the unification of science, whether it be articulated in von Bertalanffy's General Systems Theory, Dooyeweerd's Cosmonic Idea (Wetsidee) or some other systems of thought is not new but is the rebirth of an idea that was pushed aside by modernism. We trace this idea from the work of Renaissance humanists such as Vives, Erasmus and Melanchthon to more recent scholars such as Ortega y Gasset and Unamuno in order to reintegrate the humanities into systems methodology.

Systems Methodology

Drawing from this humanist heritage, we now build a systems methodology for critical and creative thinking aimed at exercising normative discernment in the times we live. Students learn the role of the various intellectual modalities in shaping thought and add solidity to their thinking. They see the intellectual, social and moral consequences of people's beliefs and evaluate the impact of their own beliefs in these domains. They are exposed to the destructive effect of contemporary utilitarian positivism and are taught how to integrate ethics and a visionary foundation to their thinking.

Social Systems Theory

Next, we explain how community life and its component social systems furnish the scenario of culture. In particular we address the impact that wisdom (or the lack of it) and information (or disinformation) have on a social system. Students will learn to design social structures that assimilate the benefits of wisdom and information to serve their assigned tasks and where the lives of people and nature and their long-term viability as a community is the ultimate aim.

Social Analysis and Design Methods

From theory, the programme moves to practice and introduces tools for systemic application and action. Given the normative nature of community development, the emphasis is on qualitative methods starting with techniques for data collection and organisation. Students learn how to use SmCube to analyse and design social systems. They also learn to identify and define activities and systems to carry them out to counteract the threats to a community.

Research Project

Having completed their coursework, students now undertake a research project where they apply both the theory and the methods previously learnt. The project aims to integrate both specialisation and generalisation by blending the student's professional expertise with the wider needs of the community. The research should advance our understanding of how the various professional perspectives may be incorporated into a systemic intervention with a common language and a common purpose.

The first graduands completed their studies in 2013 and one of them has recently commenced doctoral studies at an Austrian university. In the evaluation of the research work she carried out for our programme, the dean of the faculty of political science and sociology – now her supervisor – praised its quality and ranked it as already meeting a doctoral standard. Part of the programme's material has also been incorporated into Continuing Professional Development workshops, seminars and short courses accredited by the Australian Association of Social Workers. Evaluations from these students have been uniformly positive, showing an appreciation for humanist and systemic thinking in the social work profession. It is well expressed in the list written by a social worker about the things she liked best in our seminar:

> Interdisciplinary approach with arts, theology, ethics, history, systems, social work, sociology, education. Community development which breaks down silos, segmentation, contractions and my own experience. Inspirational and re-visioning for future directions of my work compared to pessimism, despair, frustration and questionable worth.[64]

As systems scholars, we do not endeavour to intervene in society by re-engineering it. Our aim is to introduce change by inspiring its leaders with a new vision and an ethical commitment and to equip them with the intellectual tools to realize them. If we can provide this and through it dispel "pessimism, despair, frustration and questionable worth" even amongst a relatively small group of students, we shall be well satisfied. For, even if there is only a small number of them, humans have the gift to pass on their enthusiasm to others and thus multiply their impact to an extent vastly beyond their teacher's reach.

---

[64] Student evaluation of a seminar delivered in Coraki, New South Wales for the North Coast Area Health Service, February, 2007.

11 Social Work and Community

Veronica D. de Raadt

Social Work and the Need for a New Paradigm

If "a monk when he is cloisterless, is like a fish that is water-less"[1] then it could be said that social work is like the proverbial fish out of water. It is a profession fighting for ideals not upheld by the society surrounding it; a society driven by capitalism and a utilitarian, self-interested ethic. Social work stands for social justice for all, while the utilitarian ethic is determined by self-interest and people seeking their own happiness and pleasure. Social work speaks up for the poor, while capitalism, despite its claims, benefits the rich. Trickle-down economics is supposed to benefit the poor, but there's evidence to the contrary. The situation in Australia is a good example. Since the introduction of neo-liberal ideas, the gap between rich and poor has widened.[2]

Unlike other helping professions, social work is most sensitive to the broad social context. It tackles problems by starting with the fullest understanding of *social* and then adapts itself to a myriad of contexts for practice and engagement defined by culture, geography, demography and need. Contrary to this, most helping professions are being driven by a relentless trend towards narrow specialisation, individualism and behaviourism. In addition to having to deal with these ambiguities, the profession faces increasing proceduralism, standardisation and the effects of rampant managerialism which controls a good part of social work practice and social policy. Managerialism amounts to believing in a creed, the followers of which think that when professional standards are wanting in any profession – be it education, health or social work – improvement can be attained by expanding management tools, such as quality control and targets, rather than by appointing bet-

---

[1] Chaucer (2000, Prologue).
[2] According to the Australian Bureau of Statistics (2013), the wealthiest 20% of Australian households, with an average net worth of A\$2.2 million per household in 2011-12, accounted for 61% of total household net worth. The poorest 20% of households accounted for 1% of total household net worth and had an average net worth of \$31,205 per household.

ter professionals and improving their education and scientific research[3].

In the light of this state of affairs and the dramatically changing ethos of our times, this paper suggests social work needs to shift both from the contemporary vision that government and bureaucracy are imposing upon it, as well as some of the traditional precepts that have governed the profession since its inception. This shift will have to take place in three areas of social work theory and practice. Firstly, while meeting people's immediate needs is necessary, it is not all-sufficient. Social work should go beyond charity and work toward the type of social transformation that aims not just at survival but so that the underprivileged assume full citizenship – the enjoyment of a cultured and dignified life, as well as the responsibility of contributing to the community. Secondly, this social transformation requires knowledge of a variety of disciplines – such as sociology, history, economics and psychology – but this knowledge cannot be compartmentalised. To be useful, knowledge must be integrated into a systemic framework, where its articulation, that is, the link between one discipline and the other, is as important as each discipline's content. Finally, for this knowledge to be implemented, it must be driven by an ethic that is different to that which is commonly understood. At its best, contemporary ethics means justice. However, the ethic we need to bring social transformation must go beyond justice.

In this paper I propose a particular systemic approach – multimodal – that can provide the integrative disciplinary framework social work needs and which makes the ethic that goes beyond justice, an intrinsic part of its articulation. I begin by outlining the contemporary cultural and social environment that faces social work and describe and illustrate the systems framework that should help confront them. I will then describe how this framework has been used in a post-graduate programme in community development which could well serve to train social workers who wish to practise in the wider sphere of social transformation. I

---

[3]From a British study by Protherough and Pick (2002) on the effects of managerialism on the university, school and church and which applies to the human services in Australia.

conclude with a summary perspective of how social work would look if structured by a multi-modal systems thinking (MMST) framework.

Background: Social Work and the Cultural Shift

There is little disagreement that many Australians, despite unprecedented national prosperity, are virtually "dropping off the edge", to use Vinson's description in his 2007 pivotal report on disadvantage in Australia. He points out that the economic boom failed to improve the lives of tens of thousands of Australians. The problem, made even worse since the global financial crisis of 2008, is not only in the increasing numbers of underprivileged but in generations and communities of disadvantage where only long-term intervention can hope to begin addressing the issues. The growing numbers of poor and the stubborn inter-generational problems are, however, the tip of the iceberg as these social issues are part of a much bigger world-wide and global picture. They are the result of an economically-driven, ethical and cultural shift in western societies on a scale not seen before. The shift has been created by the modern individual, described as "homo economicus"[4]. This is the conception of people behaving in a way that is not fully human but characterised by standard economics. Multiply this by millions of individuals and the global net result points to grim, un-sustainable consequences. The quest for economic growth, sought after as much by individuals as nations, is compromising our willingness to share the planet:

> Virtually all graphs of the consumption of resources, the extinction of species and the destruction of the soils, the seas, and the atmosphere, show exponential growth, most growing much faster than the "population explosion". But the most striking single index of the need for radical change is that, for everyone on the planet to live as we live in the West, it would be necessary to have five back-up planets engaged in nothing but agriculture to support us and handle the pollution we produce. Yet vast billions of people in China, India, and elsewhere have embarked on the quest to live as we live. It cannot be done.[5]

[4] Many have utilised this conception including Siebenhuner (2000).
[5] Raven (2005).

Raven is not just another doomsdayer but represents a credible group of scientists who have demonstrated great tenacity, despite their unpopularity, for holding their ground and unreservedly painting the grim picture of the extent of consumption and its implications for human life. Extreme times demand a radical stand and we must address not only the social and physical aspects of un-sustainable life but the underlying ethical reasons for the dramatic shift and subsequent social and cultural breakdown. An inter-disciplinary understanding is needed to address why we are unethical in the first place and to gauge its systemic and inter-related consequences on the sustainability of our society and environment. Let us go on and explore the roots of utilitarian thinking that have contributed to the change in ethos and the social suffering described by Vinson.

Utilitarian thinking, the predominant driver of ethics today, has its roots in eighteenth and nineteenth century social philosophies of Adam Smith, Jeremy Bentham and John Stewart Mill. While it is not possible in this context to analyse their philosophies, we can say that out of their understanding and the rise of new technologies of production during the industrial revolution, a new form of ethics was embraced, motivated by self-interest rather than love for neighbour. It provided an algebraic formula that defined utility, and therefore ethics, as the mathematical difference between pleasure and pain[6]. This ethic of self-interest is behind the capitalist spirit, besides the belief that progress ultimately drives history. It serves the rich, but not the poor. Although it is simplifying things to talk in a historically linear fashion about shifts in mentality, in Australia the utilitarian ethic was limited to commerce and industry up until around World War II and the old values – of community, virtue and sacrifice – acted as a constraint. What we see now, however, is the sweeping aside of the old and a whole-hearted, uncritical acceptance of the utilitarian ethic in nearly every area of life. This not only applies to the private, for-profit sector, but also to government at all levels where policies are driven by a utilitarian perspective of society. In Australia, this especially affects welfare, health and education, sectors formerly protected

---

[6]For a fuller explanation see Paper 12.

from the financial interests of a market economy and whose first and foremost objective was to provide humane service to the community[7].

As a result *service* to the community has turned into *social control*. The result for social work has meant government and NGO's, under the pretext of serving the public, underhandedly impose bureaucratic organisational contexts, practice approaches and programme outcomes upon social work practitioners. Hence the model of social work practice has become individualistic, instrumental, formalised and evidence-based.[8] The 2007 review undertaken by the Australian Association of Social Workers warned of the limitations of working within government-imposed structures and of social workers becoming technicians: apparatchiks with no real role to play regarding the overarching policies, value-base and ethics that drive practice and its relationships.[9] From a cultural perspective, utilitarian economics has altered the national, social landscape and Australia can no longer proudly claim that it is an egalitarian society. Some[10] predict "the eastern seaboard will be pocketed with ghettos that will lock the have-nots out of housing" with not enough material resources to access what is their basic need: to afford a family home, *ever.* For those lucky enough to afford housing, the constraints upon the average income earner is onerous. Others[11] say the Australian family is imploding from within because of the pressures of balancing work with bringing up children or caring for older family members. These extreme pressures on the family led to the quick scrapping of Work Choices almost immediately by Kevin Rudd's leadership of the Australian Labour Party when he became prime minister. Work Choices savagely stripped the most vulnerable of pay and conditions, especially those working in hospitality and retail.

---

[7] Jones (2000).
[8] Evidence-based, like other managerial axioms is a term that feigns administrative and intellectual sophistication while lacking rational, scientific foundation (Protherough & Pick, 2002, p.193).
[9] Lonne (2007).
[10] Gettler (2007).
[11] Shanahan (2003).

Amongst the biggest losers of *homo economicus* and the change in personal ethics are Australian children. Shanahan goes on to say:

> Although most parents are well meaning, the rhetoric of personal liberty has put adult needs and wants at the centre of society at the expense of children. One thing all the experts keep saying is that if the problems of Australian children are not tackled, the future consequences will be terrible.

She concludes that we can no longer ignore the plight by thinking that problem children are confined to the lower strata of society. At all social levels, children need to be treated with dignity, as "the people they are". This means taking marriage and child-rearing seriously, giving children our time and attending their unique needs.

Social Work in a Historical Perspective

These pressures, the removal of Australians' basic rights in housing, work and time to bring up the children, and the standardisation of social work that strips the profession of relationship and limits it to mechanical measures, makes it necessary to review the profession's origins. For we think that its very historical development have stripped it of the capability to resist the mechanical and standardised straitjacket with which bureaucrats have aimed to bind it and thus limit its effectiveness. Space does not allow us a full examination of this historical development, but a comparison between modernity and the era that preceded it will be helpful for the reader – even if it is done in a very general manner – to follow the ideas we propose in the next section. Modernity emerged in 18th Century[12]; the period that preceded was shaped by the Renaissance, the beginning of which is far more difficult to pinpoint. But its beginning is not important for our purpose. Far more important is discerning between two distinct streams of the Renaissance.

The first stream is a secular Renaissance – it is this that people often identify as the Renaissance – and which was mostly centred in Italy and France. The main father of this movement is Francesco

---

[12] Historians regard the French Revolution as its beginning (1789).

Petrarca and its achievement can be associated with the art and splendour of such places as Florence and, in later centuries, became the inspiration of such palaces as Versailles and Schönbrunn and the treasures that adorned them. This was essentially an elitist movement that generated its bounty through the toil and suffering of many, for the enjoyment of a privileged few.

The second stream of the Renaissance is Christian and was centred in Northern Europe and Spain, before the Inquisition annihilated it there. Its main figure is Erasmus of Rotterdam; it had its greatest impact in Switzerland and in the Netherlands of the 17th Century. Instead of the elitism of its southern counterpart, the Christian Renaissance was "socialistic"[13] in character and far more radical in its impact. It was firstly an intellectual movement that rejected medieval theology and substituted it for a Christian philosophy, based on the Bible and studied with the aid of the humanities. These humanists[14] had a high regard for the humanities and the natural sciences which they saw as instruments to transform society and culture as a whole. Out of it sprang great advances in science, education and the fine arts but, in contrast to the elitism of the secular humanists, they directed the benefit of these advances to the whole of the community rather than the privileged. They remained faithful to Christ's concern for the poor and understood his agenda was not limited to charity but to the full restoration of humanity and life to the full. While upholding the dignity of a person as reflecting the image of God, and the importance of the community as being the people of God, they frowned upon extravagance and luxury. A testimony of this still remains for the visitor to cities in Holland and Switzerland, especially when compared with places such as Vienna and Paris. The former are graceful but sober and if there are buildings that are moderately imposing, they were not erected for the pleasure of princes and aristocrats, but to house the business of the people, such as municipal halls,

---

[13] A term used by Kuyper (1950, p. 41) to denote this type of Christianity and to contrast it with state controlled socialism.

[14] It is in this particular sense that Erasmus and his followers should be regarded as humanists. The contemporary meaning of *humanism* and *humanist* is mostly associated with ideology rather than with the study of the human sciences.

churches, universities and welfare-oriented buildings. The following description of these will be of particular interest to social workers:

> Civic pride also contributed to the impulse to build imposing orphanages, hospitals, old people's homes, and workhouses. The towns vied with one another in every sphere and it was natural that in the building of 'God's houses' too a subtle rivalry would prevail, each town wishing to show how caring, responsible, and well-ordered it was and how admirable were its civic institutions.[15]

However, concern for the welfare of the vulnerable was not limited to beautiful buildings. As the statements which follow go on to explain:

> ...few aspects of the Dutch seventeenth and eighteenth centuries were more striking than the elaborate system of civic poor relief and charitable institutions. So exceptional, in European terms, were the conditions which gave rise to this system of civic charity that there was probably never much likelihood of its being emulated elsewhere.[16]

and

> Dutch philanthropy in the seventeenth and eighteenth centuries was legendary. From countries near and far travellers came to admire the alms-houses, orphanages and old people's homes. Modern scholarship agrees with contemporary opinion: nowhere in the Europe of that time, and possibly in the world, was the level of charitable expenditure as great as it was in the Netherlands.[17]

What is even more important is that this philanthropy – in the etymological sense of the word, i.e., love for humanity – and the buildings were not purely the outcome of compassionate feeling. They were also driven by a solid intellectual tradition, inherited from the Christian humanists of the previous century in the shape of the Philosophia Christi[18], a philosophy that was different from both Greek and modern philosophy that are based on abstract thinking. The humanist's philosophy of Christ was strongly empirical and it worked like the trunk of a tree to which were attached the diverse natural sciences and humanities giving them articula-

---

[15] Israel (1995, p. 356).
[16] Israel, (1995, p. 353f).
[17] van Voss and van Leeuwen (2012, p. 176).
[18] Erasmus (2011, p. 7).

tion and integration. This integration of all the disciplines into a central philosophical framework avoided the fragmentation and over-specialisation of knowledge with which we are afflicted today and which impedes one professional from understanding another. The Netherlands of the 17th Century was very much inspired by this all-embracing philosophy and it could be found behind the science of painting, clinical medicine, botany, international law, microscopy and in the organisation of work and welfare.[19]

England never went along with this extent of humanism and accommodated its Anglican Christianity[20] to allow for the privileges of the ruling classes, both in society at large and within the church. As England's empire grew, it overshadowed Dutch influence as a world power[21] and the Anglo-Saxon brand of Christianity it promoted lacked the humanist integration of faith and thought with a systemic articulation of the arts and sciences in an overarching philosophy. England's imperial expansion coincided with the rise of modernity, but its brand of Christianity was devoid of the intellectual muscle to fight the excesses of the industrial revolution and colonialism. It secluded itself behind a firm barrier that separated faith from science, the arts and culture in general. Thus on the one hand, Christian intervention in society was limited to charity which aimed at alleviating the immediate need of the destitute. This meant that it did not engage in the long-term problem of attacking utilitarianism, eliminating poverty and other social ills[22]. It lacked the broad vision of humanism and its pedagogical methodology to take it beyond addressing immediate social ills. On the other hand, science lost its humanity and succumbed to positivism and a mechanical view of the world that helped lubricate the looms of the industrial revolution.

---

[19] For example, see Knoeff (2002), Rookmaaker (1994), Grotius (1901; 1916).

[20] Except for the work of Melanchthon, Lutheranism followed a similar path to Anglicanism after Luther's influence waned.

[21] Interestingly, Holland's decline can be paralleled with its gradual embrace of modernity.

[22] There are some notable exceptions, such as Wilberforce's activism against slavery and authors such as Dickens (1997) and Gaskell (2000) who exposed the absurdity of positivism and utilitarianism and the misery to ordinary people resulting from capitalism.

Out of this era arose a social work practice that, although well intended, was handicapped by these two tenets: charity as a vocation and secular science as the tool to implement it. These two were even combined into a new discipline: the "science of charity"[23]. As expected, charity and modern science turned out to be odd bed-fellows and their joint endeavours were abandoned with time. Yet, they left social work, as much then as now, with some "core values", such as "social justice" and "respect for persons" that, although worthy in themselves, are without an intellectual backbone to carry them beyond pious-sounding statements. On the other hand, social workers have sought to be recognised as a profession which, in the current climate, is bureaucratically defined and views society as a system of production and consumption. In addition, "professions" are mere human resources organised into an assembly line that produces goods such as motorcars and corkscrews as well as services such as tourism, health and welfare.

Thinking Anew

Thus our efforts have been to recapture the spirit of the philosophy of Christ, as elaborated and applied by the humanists prior to the modernist era and give it a new expression as well as a method of application for our times. This expression is philosophical in the etymological sense of the word; that is, it is a search for wisdom. Wisdom implies application, as well as thought. Furthermore, this approach to philosophy (MMST) is systemic[24]; that is, it is an overarching structure that integrates all the disciplines together in order to live well, not solely as individuals, but also most importantly, as a community. This should help to reinstate the *so-*

---

[23] Ruswick (2013).

[24] This philosophy – termed multi-modal systems thinking (MMST) within the systems community – is committed to the basic principles of general systems theory, that is: (1) focus on life rather than mere existence and therefore (2) conception of the world as dynamic rather than static and (3) understanding begins by a general grasp of the totality rather than by the examination of its parts in isolation from each other. Although the origin of these principles is usually attributed to von Bertalanffy (1971), they were already articulated in a very elaborate manner by the humanists in the 15th and 16th centuries.

cial, in the widest, cultural understanding of the term, back into social work. It should put human issues in a community – rather than organisational, administrative and governance – context and draw upon the full scope of the humanities to represent what it is to live a meaningful, human life. Without this wider context, the aspects that make us human may be in danger of vanishing altogether in our economically-driven and subsequently individualist climate. Finally, like the cornerstone of a building, the ethic that goes beyond the demands of justice is the reference point or driving force of this systemic approach.

Some of the main ideas of MMST in relation to community are illustrated in Figure 11-1 which shows a community unfolding along two axes. Different types of community systems lie along the horizontal axis: sports clubs, churches, schools and families are shown but a myriad of other community groups could also be added such as specialist clinics and hospitals; organisations serving welfare, retail and commercial needs; and local or municipal councils. Because the function of community groups is to address the social needs of human life, they intersect at the social modality on the diagram. However, despite being qualified by the social modality, all the modalities operate within each of the systems. Adding them is essential, because, for a system to reach its potential, it must satisfy a wide range of demands. Therefore ethical, juridical, aesthetic, operational, economic and other demands, besides social, must be met for a community to become fully viable[25] and humane. The extent and weight of these demands is represented by the three domains and their ten modalities (represented by parallelograms) in the figure. The character domain is made up of the ethical, aesthetic and juridical modalities; the civic domain of operational, economic and social; and the intellectual domain of epistemic, informatory, historical and credal modalities. Within each parallelogram are factors (drawn as dark circles) which represent essential qualities that determine the likelihood of the community being viable in the long term. Starting at the first modality they include ethics, beauty, justice, work, management, sense of com-

---

[25] I use the term *viable* and *sustainable* interchangeably; they both refer to broad cultural issues of sustainability.

munity, education, information, heritage and vision. Using the multi-modal method, local community leaders would determine the factors that are important to their community.

Figure 11-1: Multi-Modal Systems Framework

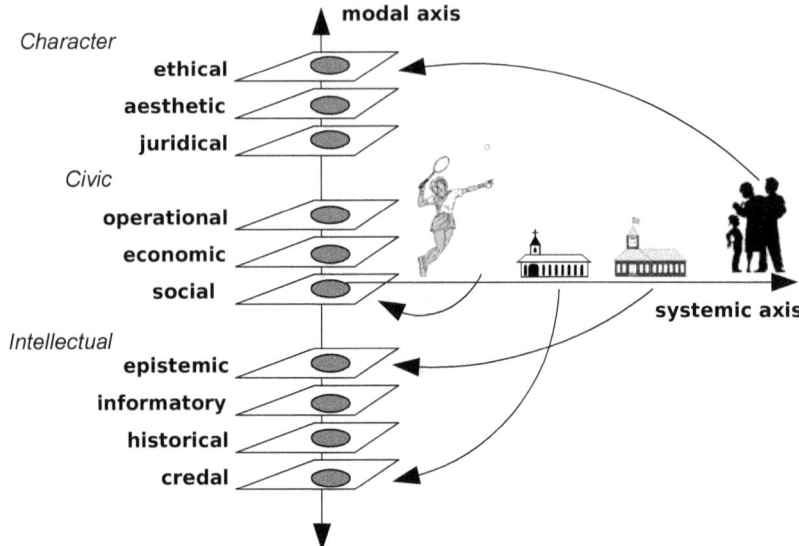

Although they might take on different attributes from community to community, there is considerable consensus in the sustainability research from around the world that non-economic factors such as these are important for long-term sustainability. This is reviewed in the sustainability literature surveyed from communities as far apart as South Africa, North America, Australia, the United Kingdom and Scandanavia[26]. Siebenhüner[27], who like others in the field of ecological economics, believes that sustainable development is essentially an ethical concept and should be defined as such. Others[28] conclude that providing economic solu-

---

[26] de Raadt, Veronica D. (2002).
[27] Siebenhuner (2000) argues for *homo sustinens*, an ethical way of living sustainably embracing nature; acting collectively; learning and creating; and being morally responsible for future generations.
[28] Schmidt (1998) and Schutte (2000) studied aid to South Africa from rich countries (the North/South divide). These projects usually take a socially engineered approach to community development and dictate to poor countries

tions to developing community – the *modus operandi* of governments – while ignoring local cultural, non-economic factors is a costly exercise that does not work in the long term anyway. Schmidt suggests that when rich countries pour money into poorer ones, sustainable development projects usually end up being white elephants or disappearing altogether once the money runs out. These results are hardly surprising as communities, to be sustainable in the long term, no matter where they are, require shared socio-cultural ideals. Equally important, they are the necessary foundation for building successful, long-term economic solutions.

To illustrate the weight and wide variety of modal demands on a system, let us think about a healthy – multi-modal – community, especially how it prepares the younger generation for the future. As children require character building to give back to their community as adults, community groups will need to lay a foundation for these youngsters in ethics, beauty and justice[29] – the intrinsic qualities (*factors*) of the first three modalities – the ethical, aesthetic and juridical. In addition, our community will need to prepare children for their future civic roles in work, management and building up social structures. These are qualities that belong to the operational, economic and social modalities respectively. We aim to orient young people to work for the community and address its most pressing needs with their talents and education and not in the corporate world which does little to prioritise community needs. To achieve this, our community will need a community-centred, rather than corporatist model of management, that allocates funds and resources to identify talent and prepare the next generation for local leadership. Likewise, social structures which build and sustain community life are needed to prepare and form youth. To achieve this, more value and support than what is given presently to families, schools, hospitals, doctors, neighbourhood houses, sports and scouting groups etc. will need to be given. Children need knowledge and understanding to carry out their adult civic

---

what sort of aid they need. They leave out the local ownership of the "what, how and when" of community needs.

[29] For a more detailed elaboration of these factors see Papers 9 and 10 and also de Raadt, J. D. R. (2000b) and de Raadt, Veronica D. (2002).

roles through education, information, heritage and vision, qualities that belong to the final four modalities – epistemic, informatory, historical and credal. Here we are not meaning mere practical training – the focus of much modern, technological education – but rather the type of education which encourages reflection, creativity and a vision for life which impacts the community and wider society, besides being transposed into a vocation and its practice.

Therefore the modalities represent both *integration* and *diversity* at the same time. For, in order for a multi-modal community to prepare the next generation, it should function as an integrated whole, while at the same time, satisfy diverse aspects of life. Modalities are differentiated according to the scientific disciplines that have historically emerged as specialised branches of science, as each science has developed distinct methods for studying a particular modality. For example, the ethical modality is studied by ethics, the science of morals; the aesthetic modality by the fine arts and classics; the juridical by the science of jurisprudence; the social modality is studied by sociology because it addresses social life; social work belongs to the operational modality because it is work. The order of the modalities in the figure is not accidental, but rather intended to show how modalities influence each other; the relationships between them; and the role we humans play, for better or worse. The way they are ordered, and the inter-modal relationships (links) formed because of their order, are crucial as these represent unity. This is intended to counteract a fragmented, and therefore destabilising, view of things because the aim of the theory is to present a complete and unified picture. This fuller understanding is tantamount to thinking normatively. Modalities influence each other either normatively or determinatively; normative influences are characterised by human responsibility so that human choice plays the most consequential role; while determinative influences are characterised by natural or other forces outside the control of people. What this bi-directional linkage (illustrated by the arrows in Figure 11-2 linking a pair of modalities) means to building community is that both have a bearing on the state of health of a community and whether or not it becomes sustainable or un-sustainable over time. If firmly established, the normative link, starting from ethics and leaping to justice at the top of Figure 11-1, becomes the inspiration for a chain-like effect that spreads ethics – agape ethic – to all the other modalities and domains of culture below them.

Figure 11-2: Linkages Between Modalities

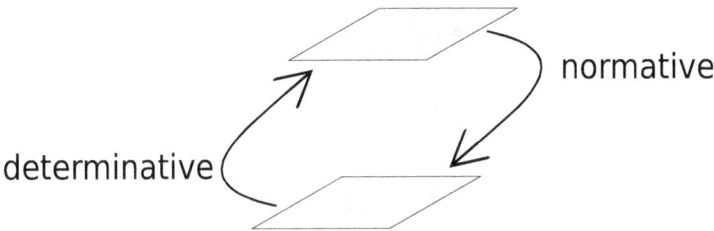

Because of the importance of ethics in sustainability and the lack of notice governments and funding bodies take of it, the normative order of human life becomes more important to understand. It emphasises that we have the power to either improve the human condition or to worsen it. This flies in the face of those who are tempted to think that social problems are insoluble, for it means we have control over the way we act and the decisions made. The dominance of positivism and utilitarianism and the dismissal of the classical humanities have deprived us of learning the skills to think normatively. To illustrate normative influences on communities let us turn to an example in Melbourne to understand how human choice favours building wealth for large corporations (represented by management in Figure 11-3) rather than building community (sense of community in the same figure). Begun in 2002, Docklands, is a new, high-rise city complex of big businesses and housing in the heart of Melbourne. However, it continues to be a controversial project and there is much criticism, even from those who initially supported it. Some have expressed concerns that Docklands – and other high rise residential buildings – may eventually become a slum[30]. Others, trying to build com-

---

[30] Chua (2014). To stop this from happening, state and local government have recently launched $300 million for funding community projects starting with

munity, are finding it hard going. Social workers from a city agency complain of the absence of community groups such as schools, libraries, kindergartens, aged and health care centres. Even setting up regular community services has proven difficult. For example, aged care personnel working with elderly residents will not make after-hours visits because they fear for their own safety. The left arrow in Figure 11-3, originating at management and linking with community sense is designed to show the lack of understanding by corporatist management to prioritize the need for communal and sociological qualities – beyond, steel, cement and glass – that must be taken into consideration when building a human habitat.

We need another type of management, one that allows modalities to reach their full potential, to harmonize with each other, to strengthen one another and contribute to each other's needs. Such management should make the community more sustainable in the long term as we show with the right arrow in Figure 11-3. A management focused on benefiting local and community interests would strengthen social structures and achieve social inclusion so as to make people feel they belong to the community. While this perfect state may not be fully attained, its pursuit is still desirable and beneficial for the community. It is questionable whether this can be achieved in Docklands because of the dominance of corporations. It appears that even those behind its development doubt whether Docklands can ever provide genuine community for people living there.

Figure 11-3: Un-sustainable and Sustainable Influences

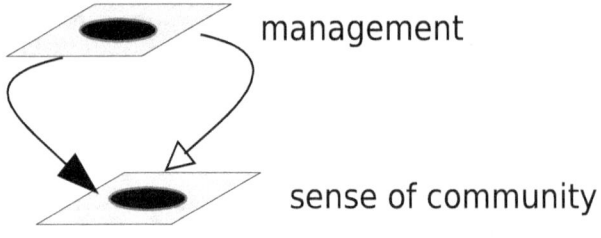

management

sense of community

---

a community garden, to breathe, as one editor put it, "heart and soul" into Docklands (Dobbin, 2012).

The case of Docklands illustrates that if diverse needs are not satisfied and there are short-falls in one or more modalities, systemic breakdown occurs and the full expression of humanity cannot be realised. If this goes on over a long period of time, the whole community has the potential to disintegrate and could disappear (which has been the fate of small country towns in Australia). While the complete disappearance of communities may be consigned to small, rather than large ones, systemic breakdown also undermines large cities, albeit later in time. It may take a generation or more to come to the surface. A study applying this methodology to inner-city Melbourne[31] suggests that social factors related to unemployment including education, ethics and social structure are already fragile and if not addressed, will cause long term, detrimental effects. This state of affairs is already affecting the most vulnerable (the homeless, aged, youth) but it has the potential to catch up with future generations. They may have to face a situation which could take decades to mend.

Because of the special position of social workers and the motives behind the exercise of their profession, this systemic framework is very suitable for their social intervention. In this context, Vinson's call for long-term intervention to address generational patterns of disadvantage at the community level is significant. This is especially important because, as the helping professions become increasingly fragmented and bureaucratized, they are in danger of losing the ability to address culture, the long term and what constitutes a humane life.

Ethics and Education

Correcting the social damage and needs of urban and rural communities requires a more demanding ethic than what it is conventionally understood; one which opposes the predominant utilitarian ethic, the self-seeking optimism and belief in progress that makes it easy for modern people to ignore the plight of those less well off. From now on, we will refer to the term ethics as it is

---

[31] Paper 10.

defined in a paper[32] that distinguishes ethics from justice. While justice imposes a duty upon us, ethics takes us beyond duty, leading us to act for the benefit – either short or long term – of others, without expecting any kind of reciprocation or recompense. Furthermore, for a community to be viable in an unjust world, there must be a sufficiently large enough number of people, working along all sectors of the community, who are committed to practise this kind of ethic in every realm of life. This is not an ethic restricted to charitable institutions, but needs to be practised by people doing all kinds of work, such as nursing, teaching, doing carpentry, practising law, running a grocery store and naturally, doing social work. That is, this is not an ethic that is injected into the community through coercive government or bureaucratic policies, but must be *worked into* the community through education. For in the humanist tradition, education was regarded as the most, if not only, legitimate way to induce social change. Teaching, without forfeiting the authority conferred by knowledge, respects the humanity of the students and the responsibility to act with the imparted knowledge as they think best. And, rather than coercion, we trust the efficacy of knowledge so that what we think best, is indeed the best.

With this ethic and vision of community in mind, we set up the Melbourne Centre for Community Development[33] in 2008 with a research and educational agenda and offered a Master of Arts degree. Although based in Melbourne, the programme was offered on-line and it attracted students from other Australian cities and overseas as well. The aim was to equip young people with a normative science. It linked together the humanities to address the vacuum left by modern science regarding norms, virtue and *oughts*. The programme began with four subjects aimed at preparing stu-

---

[32] Paper 12.

[33] We chose the term *community development* and by it meant – together with its sibling concept of *social economy* – the orientation of diverse professions, away from the capitalist, corporatist system, towards the service of integrated community life with special concern for its more vulnerable sectors. This definition is more common in Europe than English-speaking countries. Bureaucrats have borrowed the same terminology and very much distorted its meaning.

dents for the final research project. Briefly, the first subject set the Erasmian Philosophy of Christ in the context of history. We paid special attention to its being a rebirth – Renaissance – of long lost Hebrew and Greek thought to respond to the social and cultural decline of the late Middle Ages and to its demise at the hand of the Inquisition in the south of Europe and modern utilitarianism and positivism in the north. The rebirth of a lost philosophy and its application in a new era provided us with the base for the second subject. Here, we took the heritage of the Christian Renaissance – in addition to the work of those who followed it in the succeeding centuries – and gave it a rebirth for our own times incorporating the scientific advances that have taken place since. However, we imposed a major criterion upon these advances; they had to serve marginalised humanity rather than being science for the benefit of the rich. Thus we introduced our students to the systemic thought discussed above.

The third subject transferred this thought into community management. We chose a management cybernetics approach[34] because it has been inspired from nature rather than built on utilitarian and positivist assumptions. Management cybernetics aims at sustaining life rather than making profits and is useful for managing a community with the common objective of preserving its long-term viability. By now, students had assimilated a sufficient amount of methodology and learnt a method[35] to apply it. Thus in the fourth and last subject, students learnt a method of social analysis that matches the methodology. It includes mastering SmCube to store and organise qualitative data in a form that harmonises with the theory and therefore helps extracting the maximum information from it. The subject covers collection of data, establishing dynamic links between factors in different community modalities – such as work, education and social structure – and identifying how these factors, and the manner in which they are linked together, may have helped or threatened a community's long term viability. Since

---

[34] Beer (1994a; 1995).

[35] There is a tendency to use the terms methodology and method as synonyms. Here, by methodology we mean the particular epistemology of each discipline and by method the practical tools – e.g. data collection, questionnaires and software packages – used to apply this methodology.

threats are the most serious concern, students learnt to identify the type of work that needs to be carried out to dispel the threats and to design educational programmes to equip members of the community with the necessary competence to realise this work. We emphasise the word *competence* rather than the more popular *empowerment*, for the latter can be interpreted as politically coercive power. Empowerment often leads to more words and new bureaucracy rather than to action, for it ignores the necessity of education and competence required to move from ideas to their realisation. By this time, students were well prepared to carry out a larger research project in a community; we say this judging by the evaluations our students received when applying to enter into a doctoral programme. A professor and dean of social sciences at an Austrian university not only praised the theoretical and practical quality of our student's project, but judged it as already meeting doctoral standards. Similar comments were received from another professor (and dean) in an Argentinian university. We were gratified by these comments not so much for our sake, but for our students' sakes and that our programme had served them and eventually, through them, served people in communities that are falling apart.

We also participated in the continuing professional development programme of the Australian Association of Social Workers by offering one and two-day seminars. Naturally, in such a short period of time, participants were able to gain a very general view of the intricate methodology and method. And yet, despite this, participants' comments showed appreciation of the material. To illustrate, when asked what they appreciated about the seminar, a participant wrote:

> [The h]olistic approach and across all disciplines – history, ethics, sociology, philosophy, "the arts", psychology, biology, etc. Presentation style and use of history and arts; generalist approach, rather than expertise; humanist approach and community development theory (history) and practical application.

Another participant found the seminar "...[a] wonderful re-immersion into contextualising this learning in the realms of history and culture... A good reminder of the concepts of community development and systems thinking." Naturally, there were suggestions for improvement, but overall, we gained the impression that there was a need for these things in the social work agenda and we hope that, one day, young social workers studying at universities will be exposed to this methodology. We believe that it will help them be better equipped to resist the pressures from politicians and bureaucrats who wish to shape the social work vocation into a mechanistic and utilitarian straitjacket.

Re-Envisioning Social Work

Social work's vision and core principles came, at least in part, from a Christian understanding. The church initiated some of social work's first efforts and today social work is still carried out under the banner of various Christian denominations. However the church, rather than imparting a social vision to believers to change society along several fronts in the spirit of the humanists, limited itself to piety and charitable acts[36]. Rather than arresting the source of social problems, the church, by and large, engaged in mopping up the flood of problems after social conditions worsened. With secularisation, the state took up where the church left off[37] and the focus has remained on immediate needs and the short term alleviation of suffering. In addition, with the collapse of the community and the increasingly complex nature of modern social needs, large amounts of state funding and sophisticated levels of bureaucratisation have become necessary to shore up against social problems. This, combined with its historical roots in charity, has constrained social work ever more to the short-term rather than to developing long-term solutions to the social condition. The response to this dilemma should take place simultaneously along two fronts: firstly, to arrest the domination of the state – a current preoccupation among social workers – by secondly, returning social work to its roots in the community. However challenging this

---

[36] This influence goes back to the Middle Ages, when the Christian church had vast influence on European society and charity was considered to be a responsibility and a sign of one's piety.

[37] Australian Broadcasting Corporation (2012). The church, in Australia, is still an essential provider of welfare although it is heavily funded by the state.

might sound, there are grounds for hope because re-envisioning community origins has already begun. This is found in the oft-re-peated call within the profession to return to core principles. This appeal is an international one and even young social workers, new to the profession, identify pursuing core principles as the most important thing that keep them in the job.[38] The appeal of core principles represents an era in the past when social work agencies were community-based and purveyors of visionary values, social justice and respect for human life – "guiding principles"[39] which the modern state is incapable of reproducing.

However, talking nostalgically about core principles is not going to be enough. The profession is faced with the question of the most effective means of regaining these values, restoring its original context of community and arriving at new ways of operating. It must first respond by examining the kind of thinking that has led it to this state of affairs – utilitarian and positivism mixed with Kantian subjectivism – and then seek a new way of thinking and teaching, especially to the younger members of the profession. We believe that our systemic approach can be of help firstly, by stressing the normative role of science and by re-opening ethical questions such as: what is a good community; how should we live; what is a civilised life; how should we best defend social justice and human dignity? This leads to the need to discuss the nature of ethics required to achieve social justice. We need an ethic that goes beyond the call of duty for victims of injustice and because of the moral breakdown in community and consequent lack of concern among those who could help but are unwilling. Behind the call for such an ethic is an understanding that the lack of justice is inherently a moral crisis we need to face and that justice cannot be achieved through obeying laws because the law or any ethical code is unable to help society out of its moral crisis. Drawing up a list of rules or laws – the current *modus operandi* of many helping professions to tackling ethics – might be applicable to organisational charters but does little to inspire sacrificial human action.

---

[38] Asquith et al (2005).
[39] Lonne (2009).

The systemic approach can provide social work with a broad, theoretical context. It is a theory of knowledge that unifies the modalities; integrates various systems and combines the diverse scientific disciplines. Despite its interdisciplinary intentions, social work students often finish their programmes of study with a fragmented knowledge of sociology, psychology, medicine, political science, economics and other social sciences. This brings us to the important contribution of a generalist science – one which goes against the trend of increasingly specialised education. Positivist science usually limits itself to two variables whereas generalist science attempts to deal with as broad a totality as it can handle, which is certainly ambitious and challenging. Nevertheless, the value of this generalist vision would not only restore social work to its essentially systemic roots in families, schools, hospitals, neighbourhood organisations and the myriad of other community groups that prepare people for life. It would also addresses each system's complexity; how systems interact with each other; and integrate the various disciplines and fields of study that each system represents. A systemic approach would not only benefit the social work profession, but those whom it serves. It would not reduce people to abstracts, "clients", "consumers" or "customers" in an assembly line chain (e.g. the input-output model that especially dominates large government welfare providers). On the contrary, because the goal is to enable individuals to realize their humanity, it is long-term and focused on social change. One could say the spirit behind it is one of "social change through social education" for the benefit of all, including people who are very marginalised. This follows the tradition of the humanist Vives[40] who was ahead of his times and advocated employment for the mentally ill as early as the sixteenth century.

By providing a more elevated view of humanity and community than the modernist, a systemic humanist philosophy would give social work the impulse to launch it beyond charity. The focus of the social worker is towards treating social ills just as the physician treats disease. But just as the physician does not aim at merely keeping his patients alive, but seeks to restore them to full health,

---

[40] (1999).

the ultimate aim of social work must also be the full restoration of social health. It must endeavour to pull people out of misery and restore them to full citizenship, with all the benefits and responsibilities this entitles them. While this is no easy objective to attain, it must nevertheless be stubbornly pursued if we are not to give in to mediocrity, despair and cynicism. It applies not only to social work, but to every vocation. Thus, added to building relationships, informing, advocating, acting as mentor and counsellor, social workers ideally should have a communal vision and the scientific understanding to realise that vision in collaboration with other professionals. A systemic philosophy spanning and providing an integrated articulation of the natural sciences and humanities would re-open understanding the assortment of modalities that make up people's humanity and the wider cultural context that contribute to their character, virtues, beliefs, visions, language, traditions, history, knowledge and learning – cultural dimensions that are as pertinent in the social work classroom as they are in social work practice. Finally, we not only seek to provide a framework to integrate a comprehensive normative theory. We seek to promote action – especially the innovations needed in communities – by introducing new systems or community groups and the qualities, within individuals and communities, necessary to develop them. This aims at people's character and at building a foundation of systemic relations between diverse community groups and vocations. It also will also have spill-over effect, because ethical individuals create ethical communities.

12 Samaritan Ethics

J. D. R. de Raadt

Introduction

My purpose here is to explore what type of ethics our society needs and how this ethic should be incorporated into systems science and injected into our communities in a manner that is non-manipulative and that respects human dignity. We start by referring to research into communities that presents a rather disturbing picture of their ethical state and links it to several other critical factors that form an exacerbating situation. Given that there is a concern, especially within governments, for this situation, we examine three ethical approaches. The first one is utilitarian ethics which drives much of our economy and subjugates almost every other institution in society to it. Since this ethic turns out to be rather unethical, we next examine the formal approach to ethics with which governments have responded and which in turn has generated a rather oppressive situation approaching totalitarianism. We turn then to a third approach to ethics — Samaritan ethics. Samaritan ethics does not share the modernist optimism of sustained progress for humanity in a perfect world. On the contrary, it views mankind as historically oppressed through a struggle of good against evil where evil seems to be ahead most of the time, at least for the majority of people. To our knowledge, Samaritan ethics is the only form of ethics that does not turn into an oppressor of humanity, as utilitarian and formal ethics have done. On the contrary, it sustains the dignity of mankind. If its results are modest, it is not due to any fault of its own, but due to the limited number of people who are prepared to embrace it. We therefore turn to explore the most effective way to incorporate this ethic into systems science and find that to attain this, it is necessary to extend it to include the humanities. Although systems science has rejected mechanistic thinking as the only approach to scientific understanding, in practice it has not moved sufficiently away from it to be able to deal with human culture and things such as ethics. We then describe the methodology needed to attain this. We incorporate this into an appropriate framework and explain how ethics links with all levels of systemic life, both natural and ethical. We conclude by identifying education as the legitimate way to channel ethics into society and by mentioning some methods and tools available to help in this intervention.

Our Unethical Society

Due to the role the media plays in making unethical behaviour publicly known, we tend hastily to assume that such behaviour is mostly limited to our political and corporate leaders or to film and sport stars. We draw a moral line between those who are under the public eye and ourselves and, perhaps self-righteously, condemn them for their scandals. These are often amplified and even encouraged by the press which, driven by commercial interests, needs to satisfy our appetite to gloat on them. Many assume that, on our side of the moral line, we bear no responsibility for these lapses and furthermore, that we are immune from them. This assumption is not supported by our research, conducted in several regions of Europe, including Northern Sweden, Southern France, Austria and lately, Australia. What these studies reveal is that not only is public ethics linked to private ethics, but that both are interconnected to a number of systemic factors rooted in, and threatening, the local community. Chief among these factors are:

1. people's withdrawal from civic institutions and duties;
2. lack of meaning in work and its connection to service;
3. managerial practices that focus on exploiting human life, technology and the environment to generate economic resources rather than utilising economic resources and technology to sustain human life and the environment;
4. fragmentation and lack of leadership in every social group, including the family;
5. decline, and in many cases collapse, of the primary to tertiary educational system;
6. lack of vision due to a confusion and erosion of beliefs;
7. people's behaviour increasingly driven by fear;

8. the destruction of the natural environment and the dismissal of natural scientists' repeated warnings of the alarming depletion of the earth's resources.

Other studies in diverse regions of the world[1] have reached similar conclusions. Here we need only to consider briefly the links between these factors and ethics since a previous detailed discussion can be found in the preceding papers. A subset of these links is provided in Figure 12-1 to illustrate the impact that ethics has on other factors critical for a community's long-term viability, as well as how other factors have an impact on ethics. In the figure, we show how self-centred ethics has led to the abandonment of civic duties, which in turn has removed all restraints from a "managerialist" culture[2].

Figure 12-1: Ethics and Links to other Factors

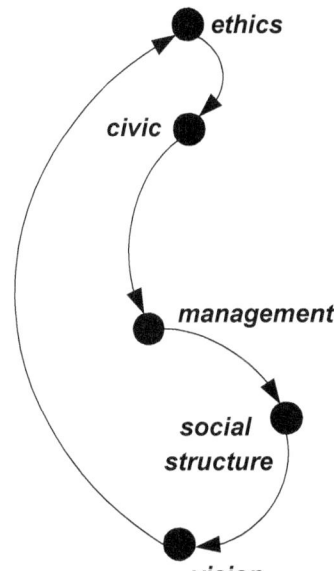

---

[1] Ahlmark (1998); Buttimer (1990, 1998); Dodds (1997); Edwards and Brown (1996); Nixon et al (1999); Ryn (1990); Råberg (1997); Schutte (2000); Smailes (1995); Sorensen and Epps (1996); Taylor et al (1997).
[2] Protherough and Pick (2002).

This, in its pursuit to manage all things like a machine, has harmed our social structures and fragmented the community. Furthermore, the fragmentation of the community has undermined its traditional beliefs and the vision that sustained it in the past. This has led it to assimilate a variety of new beliefs oriented towards an exclusive self-fulfilment and feel-good religion, feeding in turn a self-centred ethic. Of great concern in this set of links, is the loop they form: a positive feedback that progressively exacerbates the symptom of each factor rendering the community unstable and un-sustainable in the long-term. We must therefore, not only determine what sort of ethic we should adopt, but also how we should introduce it into our society to counteract the destructive feedback afflicting it. There are three main ethical frameworks — utilitarian, formal and Samaritan — that have played an active role in shaping our history. We will review each of these next.

Utilitarian Ethics

Utilitarian ethics, the idea that our actions should be determined by the pursuit of pleasure and avoidance of pain, or in economic terms, maximisation of profits, has its main origins in the work of three British thinkers Adam Smith, Jeremy Bentham and John Stuart Mill. In fairness, it must be granted that their conception substantially differed from the utilitarianism that is promoted today. They assumed that the pursuit of pleasure or economic profit took place within a just and civilised framework that not only encompassed the pleasure of the senses but also of skill, benevolence, amity and piety[3]. Modernity and post-modernity have progressively dismantled such a framework; all its constraints have been removed leading to a type of unrestrained utilitarianism, ruthless and unlike anything envisaged by either Smith, Bentham or Mill. An example of its callousness is supplied by a much-quoted statement by Milton Friedman — one the chief advocates of contemporary utilitarianism: "the social responsibility of business is to increase its profits"[4]. As might be expected, commercial enterprises have fully

---

[3] Byam (2002).
[4] (1970).

exploited this "social responsibility" and used every mode of manipulation open to them, including sex, to promote consumerism and greed among the people. The empirical evidence of such manipulation is daily provided for us on television. Moreover, in the last years we have seen "social responsibility" extend its grip beyond the boundaries of the law, such as the Australian Wheat Board's criminal collaboration with Saddam Hussein in order to secure wheat sales[5] or the notorious fraud by Enron managers. It is most disturbing to note that:

> The Enron debacle is exceptional only in its scale. Other former Wall Street favourites have engaged in creative accounting to pump up their stock prices. Lucent, Sunbeam, Waste Management, Xerox and Cendant are only some of the more notorious cases of companies forced to restate previously reported earnings, causing their stock prices to crater. People lost billions of dollars, misled by phoney numbers ratified by the accountants.[6]

The unrestrained nature of the utilitarian approach to management is in itself of great concern. However, of even greater concern is the indifference of the public to it, as shown in surveys and voting in elections[7].

Formal Ethics

The main response to this crisis has been through formal ethics, that is, a set of codes or policies that specify what ought and what ought not to be done. We have been inundated with such codes directed to corporate and professional practice and with government policies aiming to control almost every aspect of human life. Not only do such codes and policies violate freedom in order to impose a desired pattern of behaviour on people but also, rather than encouraging people to become more ethical, they have the opposite effect. For example, excessive government regulations have been blamed for driving people away from participation in volunteer organisations[8]. Furthermore, the increasing control over

---

[5] Baker (2006).
[6] New York Times (2002).
[7] Faler (2005); Bagaric (2006); Grattan (2006); Teixeira (1992).
[8] McCallum (2005); Bandow (1997).

people is carried out by politicians and civil servants who regard themselves — just as totalitarian regimes do — to be immune from the vices of the population[9]. Such an idea is not new. The law of the ancient Pharisees oppressed people in a similar way, such as when it forbade Jesus from healing a sick man on the Sabbath[10].

Since the 18th Century, modernism has added another major flaw to formalised ethics, a flaw also present in utilitarianism. It is the assumption that unethical behaviour is solely rooted in ignorance of what is right and wrong and that therefore, by specifying these in a code, people will act ethically by following it. Such an assumption is accompanied by the view that "...the world as we know it is pretty much perfect..." and inhabited by an essentially good mankind[11]. Today, we may not believe this to be universally true, but we nevertheless project the idea that it is virtually true in our occidental democracies and their institutions. Not only have countries such as the USA and its allies assumed it, but they have also taken it into their own hands — even using military force when necessary — to impose upon the rest of the world their notion of a "perfect" life. However, history points out that this assumption is false. Perhaps the greatest evidence against it, as experienced in our times, has been provided by the war in Iraq. It has shown to us an army of "liberators" carrying out, such as in the Abu Ghraib prison near Baghdad, the same brutalities performed by their enemy Saddam Hussein whom they sought to defeat.

Yet, we must resist the temptation to rush in to condemn these atrocities and overlook the commonality that exists between its perpetrators and each one of us. This commonality should shock us as much as the atrocities themselves. For most of the people who tortured prisoners in the Abu Ghraib prison, were not the hardened criminals with which we associate such cruelty. Judging from the photographs, they could have been anyone's brother, sister, son or daughter. One woman, described by her relatives "...as a kind young woman who loved athletics and the outdoors..."[12]

---

[9] Harrison (2006).
[10] Matthew 12:10.
[11] Joyce (2001).
[12] MSNBC (2004).

became a mother not long after these events. What these events tell us, is that there are undesirable properties in everyone of us which, given special circumstances and regardless of codes or rules of ethics, will lead us to perform actions associated with people such as dictators and criminals that are quite out of character from our everyday behaviour. Furthermore, we cannot necessarily blame these actions on special circumstances. We are responsible for them.

Samaritan Ethics

A third approach to ethics is by taught by Christ. He held no illusionary assumptions regarding the goodness of mankind as the incident of the woman caught in adultery reveals[13]. His challenge for anyone without sin to cast the first stone issued to the teachers of the law and Pharisees who brought her, exposed that none of these men could honestly regard himself as blameless. This exposed the inability of the law or any ethical code to help a society out of its moral crisis. Thus, he introduced a distinction between justice — as represented by laws and traditions — and *agape* love. Unfortunately, English has only one word *love* to translate three Greek words with different meanings: agape, eros and philia. According to Richardson[14] "... [agape] differs from [eros] in that the latter is brought into action by the attractiveness of the object loved, whereas agape loves even the unlovable, the repellent and those who have nothing to offer in return. According to Christ, agape is the essence of ethics, as illustrated in his story about the Samaritan[15] who helped a half-dead man fallen victim to robbers on the road. The Samaritan's ethic exhorts us to serve others even when they cannot repay us: food for the hungry, shelter for the homeless, liberation to the oppressed. It has three main qualities. Firstly, rather than based on a static codification of rules, it is founded upon systemic interactions between people. There is only one central principle that guides its action, agape. Agape is dy-

---

[13] John 8:3.
[14] (1969, p. 269n.)
[15] Luke 10:33-37.

namic; rather than following a rigid code of rule, agape leads us to respond, in a creative manner if necessary, to unforeseen circumstances of human need. Secondly, this ethic is open to all, regardless of their moral, social or legal standing. This is implied by the choice of the Samaritan character in the story; a 1st Century Jew looked down on a Samaritan and did not associate with him. Thirdly, because the ethic is oriented towards action, it has a dynamic impact on a person and his community and can thrust them forward. Through his acting ethically, a person's character will gradually improve as well as bring favourable change to his community. Many experiences point out that Samaritan ethics can be contagious; once a person starts acting ethically, others will join in. Thus, accounts of prisoners in concentration camps attest the change in attitude in a whole prison that the practice of agape by a few inmates can bring[16].

Agape, Virtue and History

In contrast to the mechanistic approach that has been associated with utilitarianism, systems science can supply a suitable methodology to incorporate Samaritan ethics and implement it in society. Systems science is focused on life, both natural and cultural, and since life is continuously threatened by death, it does not allow us to assume the naïve perspective of the utilitarian's "pretty much perfect world". On the contrary, it views living systems as being in a constant struggle against their demise. If we use a formal description of living systems such as that proposed by Ashby[17], we can represent this in terms of a system striving to maintain equilibrium in the face of continuous threats from its environment. Ashby's law stipulates that the realisation of this equilibrium depends on the regulatory capacity of the system (which he measured in terms of "variety"). The greater the regulatory variety, the greater the stability of the system and thus its viability. If the system does not have the requisite regulatory capacity, then someone must supply it to attain equilibrium. Likewise, in our un-

16 Gordon (1970); ten Boom (1971).
17 (1976).

just and turbulent world, Samaritan ethics provides the stability that draws society towards virtue and away from corruption. Stability increases to the extent to which Samaritan ethics is accepted and practised by people.

Although both natural and cultural life are linked together, there is an important difference between them. Both forms of life, natural and cultural, must struggle against disturbances that drive them out of their state of equilibrium. We may call this surviving. Yet, just as a ship that sails in a storm must not only remain afloat (survive) but also navigate towards its destination, so cultural life should transcend mere survival and journey on an historical route towards a virtuous society[18]. Given the injustices of the world, if we seek a virtuous society, then the route must be traced by an ethic that produces stability as well as an historical thrust forward. Ethics is therefore not only essential for survival but also necessary for cultural realisation. What role should systems science play in this? Prior to answering this question, we must establish an adequate methodological framework to examine this role.

The Humanist Framework

The relationship between ethics and science has not always been cordial[19]. Bellah[20] has traced the conflict to the separation made by Aristotle between intellectual and moral virtues and later by Kant between pure reason and practical reason. During the Renaissance and the Reformation, there was a school of humanists who built a bridge for ethics to reach science. In particular, we have in mind the work of scholars such as Erasmus[21] and Melanchthon[22] in Northern Europe and Luis Vives and Fray Luis de León in Spain[23] and the continental universities such as Geneva, Leiden and Heidelberg that sprang out of the Reformation. These humanists sought to uphold the dignity of mankind. Given the deplorable

---

[18] Ortega y Gasset (2004a); Unamuno (1927); de Raadt, J. D. R. (2000b).
[19] Unamuno (1912).
[20] (2000).
[21] (2000; 2004; 2011).
[22] (1999); Maag (1999).
[23] García López (1996).

state to which Europe had sank at the time, they used the new learning to reform society and its various institutions including the church and the universities. With the help of the classical languages and history, they discovered in the scriptures and ancient literature a message that aimed not only at redeeming humanity, but also at civilising it by educating it. They promoted science in order to pull people out of their misery and offer them a dignified and cultured life. They regarded this not as a luxury for the privileged, but as a vision to be fulfilled by every man and woman in order for a community to be viable. Since civilisation also required relief from disease and hunger, study of the natural sciences followed the humanities. Both remained closely linked[24] in a notion of philosophy in its etymological sense: the search for wisdom to serve humanity. These humanist ideals remained present and influenced the path of science until the rise of modernism. They inspired some of the greatest scholars, including Melanchthon himself, "the teacher of Germany", Boerhaave, "the teacher of all Europe"[25] and Linnaeus, "the prince of the botanists"[26]. In the Netherlands, they were seminal in the establishment of Dutch universities for over three hundred years, starting in Leiden in 1575 and stretching to Amsterdam in 1880, when the Free University was founded. Nearer to our own times, they strongly influenced two of Spain's greatest philosophers, Unamuno[27] and Ortega y Gasset[28] and the Dutch philosopher Dooyeweerd[29].

Sadly, the Kantian split between pure and practical reason[30], which has characterised modernism, has ultimately led to the decline of the humanities from the agenda of university teaching and research[31]. Since modernism emphasizes pure reason and undervalues practical reason, it gives prominence to the natural sciences, which it associates with the former. The humanities thus become

---

[24] Israel (1995).
[25] Knoeff (2002); Lindeboom (1968).
[26] Frängsmyr (1983); Goerke (1973).
[27] (1986, 2005).
[28] (2004a; n.d.).
[29] (1958).
[30] Kant (2007).
[31] Engell and Dangerfield (1998); Tapp (1997).

the poor sister in academia. This, in turn, has led many modern scientists — including systems scientists — to regard natural phenomena has "hard" and cultural matters as "soft" or "fuzzy". Soft systems methodology, for example, is thus presented as "a rigorous methodology to deal with non-rigorous situations"[32]. However, this is a poor definition of rigour and an application of an incompatible way of thinking to the realm of the humanities. The appellation "soft" does not reflect a trait of the humanities, but the poor humanist educational grounding of many modern scientists.

Humanist Systems Science

The next step is to incorporate this humanist tradition into a systems methodology that not only integrates the humanities with the natural sciences but also offers a method of implementing it in both natural and cultural systems. Multi-modal systems methodology is a humanist approach to systems science, which focuses especially on normative thought and the theory of design. It combines the idea of an overarching multi-dimensional philosophy, already proposed by such humanists as Melanchthon[33] and Dooyeweerd[34], with systems science. While the multi-dimensional nature of living systems was initially presented in the pioneering work of von Bertalanffy[35] it was soon abandoned and considered no further. Multi-modal systems methodology restores the humanities to their rightful place among the sciences and integrates them with the natural sciences to supply a common scientific framework and language for all disciplines. It promotes general systems theory without dismissing the specialised knowledge of each discipline. Its objective is to understand the interrelationships between all living systems, natural and cultural, and do what is necessary to sustain them.

The methodology is based on two basic assumptions. Firstly, it maintains that all thought, even the most theoretical, is not autonomous, but since it is part of our humanity, it depends on

---

[32] Checkland (1981).
[33] (1999); Frank (1995).
[34] (1958).
[35] (1971).

personal beliefs[36]. Secondly, the purpose of all thought ought ultimately to be normative: to know how to live well and realize our full humanity. Due to its systemic focus on life, it directs its study to the reciprocal and simultaneous links that form the substance of natural and cultural life rather than aspiring to a mechanical and causal understanding of the world. Instead of analysing the elements that constitute life in a fragmented manner, this methodology explores its links in the diverse living systems and the modalities in which they operate (e.g. economic, aesthetic, credal and social). The sustenance of life in its many manifestations, but especially civilised human life, is the central theme of this methodology, which studies them along two inter-linked dimensions as discussed in Paper 10 and shown diagrammatically in Figure 10-1.

Ethics and Humanist Systems Science

We must now explain how this methodology can help resolve the above-mentioned conflict between science and ethics and spread Samaritan ethics over the diverse activities of society. The determinative and normative links bind culture with nature; determinative links establish nature as the foundation of culture and the normative links provide added meaning to nature, as seen, for example, in a beautiful garden or a park. However, these links also bind in the same manner every domain and modality. Within culture and its three domains – character, community and intellect – determinative links make the intellect the foundation of civilised society and society the foundation of virtue. Conversely, normative links make virtue the purpose of society and virtuous society the purpose of intellectual pursuit. Thus the understanding of these links is of the greatest scientific importance, something that was evident to early humanists such Melanchthon[37] and more recent ones, such as de Unamuno[38] and Dooyeweerd[39].

The place of the civic or community domain in between the intellectual and character domain is of great significance. It means

---

[36] Ortega y Gasset (2004a).
[37] (1999).
[38] (1989).
[39] (1958).

that knowledge is not for knowledge's sake but for the sake of shaping a civilised society. It also means that virtue cannot be attained, in the Platonic sense, exclusively through the intellectual pursuit of wisdom. It must first be concretised in the life of the community. Conversely, neither can virtue — and therefore ethics — be attained by escaping from society. Since the role of systems science as a conveyor of ethics to society is our concern, we must point to another significant feature that emerges from the framework in Figure 10-1. If our desire is to intervene in order to attain a more virtuous society, the proper humane way to do this is by expanding the intellectual domain of a society; that is, teaching in order to enhance understanding and wisdom.

Let us examine this in more detail. The intellectual domain consists of four modalities, epistemic, informatory, historical and credal (see Figure 10-1). According to Ortega, the credal modality constitutes the "floor of our lives"[40]. Dooyeweerd[41] dedicated a third of his opus magnum to argue this same point and to reject Kant's dichotomy between pure and practical reason. If we follow the determinative arrow that points upwards, we shall find that the credal modality constitutes the foundation of the historical modality, where our creed is transformed and concretised into the many aspects of culture. History provides thus the empirical reality of culture, which are perceived as events in the next modality — the informatory. Finally, these events are comprehended in the epistemic modality where knowledge and science are built. The downwards normative arrows, within the same intellectual domain, provide the purpose of the lower modalities and especially the credal, that is, we should understand not in order to believe, but believe in order to understand[42].

However, understanding is not an end in itself, for the epistemic modality is the immediate foundation of the social modality. This means that the basis for social structure, especially authority, in a humanist civilisation, is knowledge rather than power. For example, the authority of parents over children is determined by the

---

[40] (2004a, p. 14).
[41] (1958).
[42] Augustine (n.d., p. 302).

lesser understanding of the latter, which, as it increases with education, leads also to greater independence and responsibility for self. This partly makes society like a community of students, where the senior students exercise their leadership through teaching the younger and preparing them in turn to become leaders and teachers of the next generation. Above the social modality rests the economic modality, pertaining to the management of resources necessary to sustain work in the operational modality placed over it. For it is through work that a society attains its viability and unfolds historically. The focus of this progress is inspired by the character domain where we find three modalities. The lower one — juridical — is qualified by justice. A just society by itself cannot be a virtuous society if it does not preserve the dignity of humanity, which is inspired by the aesthetic modality. Although we usually associate aesthetics with the arts such as painting and sculpture, these are only expressions of what is a human quality and endows a person with dignity. Even prisoners serving in jail should have their human dignity respected. Punishment, therefore, should not destroy the person (this constitutes an argument against the death penalty). Finally, as we have seen, in a turbulent and imperfect world, human justice and dignity cannot be assumed to flow naturally. They must be obtained at a cost through Samaritan ethics operating in the next and highest modality. Samaritan ethics constitutes therefore, the ultimate normative inspiration of culture. It has been so in classical European culture, where agape has been regarded as a divine quality: "God is agape". Mankind is challenged first to believe it and then to emulate it. Thus, this chain of normative and determinative links leaping from modality to modality provides the conduit for Samaritan ethics to spread into every domain of culture. It also spreads from there to a responsible sustenance of nature, which gratefully reciprocates by supplying the sustaining foundation for culture to unfold.

Implementation of a Samaritan Ethic in Society

Finally, we must consider how we move from thinking about Samaritan ethics — the methodological framework in Figure 10-1

— to its practical application in society. Humanists have regarded education as the civilised and humane means of influencing people's behaviour[43]. Through teaching, he who teaches can open new possibilities for him who learns. Teaching is indeed a form of leadership, perhaps the most desirable. It does not coerce the student according to what he has learnt, but rather confers a responsibility to apply it to his own life and to benefit the community. This contrasts with mechanical approaches to education that are now popular, such as "Outcomes Based Education"[44], for structuring the curriculum in schools and universities. These place the educational task in the psychic modality[45], that is, within the vital domain in nature rather than with the intellectual domain of culture. Such an approach to education leads to training for cognition rather than educating for understanding. Animals are capable of psychological cognition, but only humans have intellectual understanding. Outcomes Based Education may be useful to teach people mechanical tasks, but not to form citizens or teach them ethics[46].

Understanding by itself is not sufficient; we also require a method to implement it. Method functions in the informatory modality and provides the tools to gather data about the historical unfolding of a society, as well as to help analyse, at the epistemic level, the path that this unfolding is taking. Furthermore, it also provides tools to intervene in history in an ethical manner and alter this path if necessary. There are several examples of this method and its application[47], including SmCube, the specialised social analysis and design software package. While this work is being pioneered, a path that leads from the definition of Samaritan ethics to its implementation in society is now gradually opening.

---

[43] Melanchthon (1999); Ortega y Gasset (1992).
[44] Spady (1994).
[45] Anderson and Sosniak (1994).
[46] Berlach (2004); Donnelly (2006).
[47] See Papers 7, 8, 9 and 10.

13 Christian Social Humanism

J. D. R. de Raadt

Introduction

More than 30 years ago while living in Australia, my wife and I noticed a crisis starting with the family that branched out like poison ivy into all other civic institutions in our community. Both of us were then postgraduate students in sociology and, confronted with these circumstances, we began to direct our research towards the problem of community disintegration. Our disenchantment with positivism, which still dominates the social sciences, led us to seek the intellectual heritage and more humane foundation for science. But it was not simply a matter of reproducing the past; we needed a framework of thought that could address the particular predicament that afflicted our time in history. On discovering general systems theory, we saw in it a contemporary paradigm that would allow us to give renascence to the old humanist values.

This venture became a long journey, not only intellectually but also geographically, which took us from Australia to the U.S., then to Sweden and from Sweden back to Australia. Our research work became the systemic development of communities and the design of university programmes geared toward them. These programmes were naturally based on the methodology developed through our research. As we worked in regional universities, we designed programmes to equip our students with an ethical and professional competence to enable them to carry out their vocation in rural towns. We tried to avoid their migrating into the big city in search of money and material success. Here, I want to examine the role that the humanities must play in the systemic approach – especially in their quest to capture all essential totality[1] – to support the restoration and development of the community.

---

[1] I emphasize the focus on the totality that characterises a systemic philosophy and which unfortunately, has been partly lost in the rise of systems specialities.

The Current Crisis in the Community

I will start with a brief account of the predicament in which we found the communities we surveyed. Individualism, which is an integral element of modernity[2], has been one of the most serious threats to humanity and our natural environment. From it also emerges the destruction of our communities and pressing people into an individualist assembly-line structure of producers (human resources) and consumers. However, like wolves, humans are social creatures, we have to hunt with our pack to live. Our community is our pack, we are not like tigers that hunt and live independently; if our community disintegrates, our spirit dies. Now the destruction of the human pack has been a long historical process that is well worth studying to understand what is happening to us today. But here, I will limit myself to mention the most common factors that have emerged as threats to our present communities and which we have identified in studies of several countries in Europe, including Sweden, Spain, Italy, France, Austria and most recently Australia. In all these communities we observe the following:

- decline in ethics and charitable attitude among people;
- absence of meaning and vocation in work and its detachment from service to humanity;
- management style that exploits human life, technology and the natural environment to accumulate financial resources instead of using these resources and technology to sustain humanity and the natural environment;
- fragmentation and lack of leadership in all social groups, including the family;
- deterioration, and in many cases the collapse, of primary, secondary and higher educational institutions;
- abuse of the press and other media for commercial purposes that harm the most vulnerable sectors of society, especially youth;

---

[2] I use the word *modernity* in a manner that includes what is called *postmodernity*. This term suggests that modernity is something that was in the past, but this is not true. Modernity has found its widest expression in postmodernity, therefore, it is more appropriate to call it *hypermodernity*.

- lack of vision due to confusion and erosion of beliefs;
- mental state of fear, anxiety and depression that leads in the most extreme cases, to suicide especially among indigenous people, farmers and youth;
- destruction of the natural environment and dismissal of the repeated warnings that we are depleting the earth's natural resources.

Although each of these factors is harmful in itself, the situation is far more serious when one considers the links between one factor and the other. In systemic terms, this creates a positive feedback that destabilises the community and precipitates it towards collapse. I have drawn six of these factors and their links in Figure 13-1 with a central line (dot and dash) that hypothetically represents the equilibrium position of each of these factors. This line does not mean that social stability is rigid; my intention is only to represent graphically the principle enunciated by Ashby[3] that tells us that in a set of sub-systems, the equilibrium of the total system will not be achieved until each sub-system has reached its own equilibrium. In a social context, this amounts to saying that the community will be unviable until each of these factors are restored to their norm. This in turn requires a vision about aspects such as ethics, economics, education and justice that characterise a civilised community. It also requires knowing how to realise this vision. This knowledge corresponds to the concept of systemic cultural stability that I represent with an arrow (also dot and dash) in Figure 13-1. Stability is the ability of a system to restore equilibrium once it has been lost. Adopting this principle, we can define community development as the transformation into what we culturally[4] should be.

---

[3] (1976).
[4] de Raadt, J. D. R. (1998) explains the difference between culture, which is normative, and background, which is determinative.

Figure 13-1: Disequilibrium

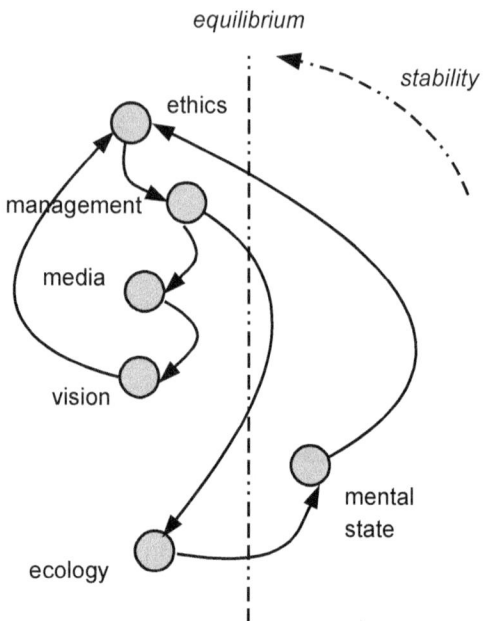

equilibrium

stability

ethics

management

media

vision

mental
state

ecology

In addition to knowing how a chaotic community becomes civilised, we also need to know historiology, which Ortega y Gasset[5] defined as the systemic science of history. This teaches us that the transition from chaos to social equilibrium is not linear, but follows an exponential pattern over time as plotted in Figure 13-2[6]. The vertical axis measures the transformation of a society and the horizontal axis stands for time. Let us assume that the dot and dash line represents states where the transformation of society is proportional to the effort invested in transforming it. This defines two stages in the development of the community: start-up and maturity. The start-up generates a deficit, the social change we obtain is proportionally less than the effort we apply. Maturity generates a surplus; the social change is proportionally greater than our effort. Unfortunately, social change is very slow, so that the start-up lasts

---

[5] (2004a).
[6] A detailed exploration of this pattern is found in de Raadt, J. D. R. (1991).

at least a generation, that is, about twenty years. This means there must be people willing to work at the beginning phase for results they will probably never fully enjoy. It is sometimes cynically said that these are people who are born before their time, but this is not true. These are people who live what Unamuno[7]and Ortega y Gasset[8] call historical lives, people who have a vision that transcends the immediate horizon and extends into the future. This projection into the future is driven by a Samaritan ethic, an ethic of *agape* love that has been discussed in detail in Paper 12. It is a type of ethics, I heard my wife recently say, that does not gather treasures on earth, but in heaven[9]. And heaven and earth do not symbolise geographic locations, but refer to these two historical periods we have defined above.

The Renaissance

In our search for a model for the development of the community we have found our inspiration in the humanist Renaissance. The word renaissance itself suggests a social transformation, but has something special: it is based on an offshoot and we need this offshoot to collect the wisdom of the past. The Renaissance furnished two types of humanism. One of them was an elitist-humanism rooted in Greek philosophy and had its greatest impact in Italy. Its major contribution was in the fine arts and architecture, but, given the elitist element inherited from the Greek, it lacked the social influence that characterised the second type of humanism. This was the Christian humanism or social humanism of northern Europe. Although this humanism did not entirely reject Greek thought, it only included those elements that harmonised with its social agenda and historic work of human emancipation introduced in the Gospels[10]. It opposed Greek thought only when it benefited the privileged and excluded those considered inferior, such as slaves and women. The father of social humanism was Erasmus of Rotterdam and although his influence was strongest in

---

[7] (1927).
[8] (2004a).
[9] Matthew 6:19-20.
[10] Erasmus (2011).

northern Europe, he also had followers in the Spanish humanist movement until it was eliminated by the Inquisition.

Figure 13-2: Social Transformation

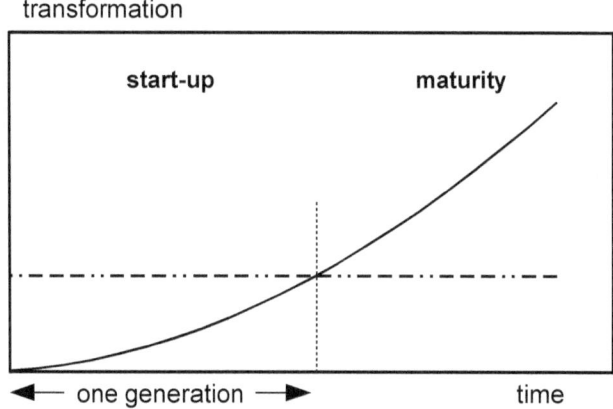

In a very subtle manner, typical of his science, Erasmus replaced medieval[11] theology with "The Philosophy of Christ"[12], a philosophy based on the Biblical concept of wisdom motivated by *agape* love for humanity. In contrast to the abstract nature of Aristotelian philosophy, Erasmus proposed a practical and social philosophy built on the natural sciences and humanities and based on empirical observation. Among the most notable disciples of Erasmus are the famous pedagogues Juan Luis Vives and Phillip Melanchthon, who already in their time talked about a systemic philosophy which, like the trunk of a tree, united the sap from its various roots. Each of these roots represent a specific scientific discipline[13]. This humanist philosophy gave northern Europe a great social and cultural impulse and the Dutch Republic was one of the most remarkable epicentres, especially during the seven-

---

[11] Theology is a discipline of Greek origin, which Aristotle (2007) placed alongside the speculative sciences together with mathematics and physics. It is quite foreign to the Bible, the thoughts of which become far more transparent when examined from an historiological perspective as defined by Ortega y Gasset (2004a).

[12] (1529).

[13] Erasmus (1978); Melanchthon (1999); Vives (1971).

teenth century. Not only did the human sciences blossom, but through the development of empirical methods, great break-throughs were provided by Boerhaave in medicine, Carl Linnaeus in botany, van Leeuwenhoek and Swammerdam in biology and use of the microscope, Beeckman in mathematics, Stevin in engineering and Grotius in international and maritime law. We must also include here the statesmen Johan de Witt and Johan van Olde-barnevelt. The humanist philosophy gave conscience, vision and method. Through it, Northern Europe became aware firstly of the decrepit state of its society, secondly of a vision for a civilised community and thirdly of the science and technology which could realise this vision. This also replaced the authority exercised by the ecclesiastical hierarchy and the aristocracy with the study of the Bible both in the scriptures and in nature because, according to the humanists, God spoke through both.[14] The humanities in particular, said the humanist Juan Luis Vives, "... restore our humanity."[15] With this restoration, the progress of the natural sciences – neg-lected by medievalism – was stimulated. Nevertheless, they always remained integrated with the humanities in a reciprocal relation-ship, or in cybernetic jargon, *in a mutual feedback*. This led to an elegant, cultured and fully human science, as evidenced by the fol-lowing passage from the book *Praeludia Sponsalarium Plantarum* about the sexuality of plants written by Linnaeus, the "prince of botany" and one of the most brilliant scientists that has ever lived:

> Words cannot express the joy that the sun brings to all living things. Now the blackcock and the capercailzie begin to frolic, the fish to sport. Every animal feels the sexual urge. Yes, Love comes even to the plants. Males and females, even the hermaph-rodites, hold their nuptials...showing by their sexual organs which are males, which females, which hermaphrodite.... The actual petals of a flower contribute nothing to generation, serving as a bridal bed which the great Creator has so gloriously prepared, adorned with such precious bed curtains, and per-fumed with so many sweet scents in order that the bridegroom and bride may therein celebrate their nuptials with the greater

---

[14] Jorink (2004). The revelation of God through nature was the foundation of the empirical method used both in the humanities and the natural sciences.
[15] (1971).

> solemnity. When the bed has thus been made ready, then it is the
> time for the bridegroom to embrace his beloved bride and sur-
> render himself to her....[16]

Language, said Linnaeus, should adorn science, and here he
combines love and pedagogy and illustrates "a learned piety and a
pious learning" of the civilised life to which the Erasmists as-
pired[17]. This pedagogy was, for the humanist, the only legitimate
way to change the direction of society and develop the community. For them, a civilised community was an educated and
compassionate community. This required giving access to education to all citizens. Therefore, in the Netherlands, teachers in Reformed schools were required to provide free education to children from poor households, which explains the high level of Dutch
literacy when compared with the rest of Europe[18]. In England,
Thomas More, Erasmus and Juan Luis Vives founded Saint Paul[19]
school especially for children from poor families. Also during his
stay in England, Juan Luis Vives wrote the first manual for the
education of the woman[20].

The humanists added to pedagogy a social structure modelled
on the family. Not only was the family the basic unit of society, but
following the teachings of Jesus, they considered the totality of the
community like a family where all were members, from the
humblest to the most noble. This was a family socialism or a "social humanism"[21] that dismissed all social rank or caste; the hierarchy was exclusively formed by age tiers corresponding to children, parents and grandparents based on respect for wisdom and
experience. Each tier was being educated to assume the responsibility of the next tier. Family love was spread through all institutions; orphanages and old people's homes were managed not by
executives, but by a *House-father* and a *House-mother*[22]. Science
also reflected the solidarity of family, like Rembrandt in his first

---

[16] Cited in Blunt (2001, p. 33).
[17] Olin (1987).
[18] Israel (1995).
[19] Phau (1995).
[20] (2000).
[21] Hurtado (1992).
[22] In Dutch: *binnenvader* and *binnenmoeder*.

masterpiece: *The Anatomy Lesson of Dr. Tulp* (Figure 13-3). The central place in the canvas is occupied by the body of Adriaan Adriaans, who had been executed for his crime the day of the autopsy. Rembrandt causes the light to drop on his body, to communicate to us that despite his crime, this body is God's work[23]. There is a line that starts in the body and spreads out towards the face of the students who observe, with awe, the tendons of the arm exposed by Dr. Tulp. Thus, Rembrandt shows with his brush the wonder that Linnaeus found impossible to express with words.

Figure 13-3: *The Anatomy Lecture of Dr. Nicolaes Tulp*; Rembrandt, Harmenszoon van Rijn (1632); The Hague, Mauritshuis

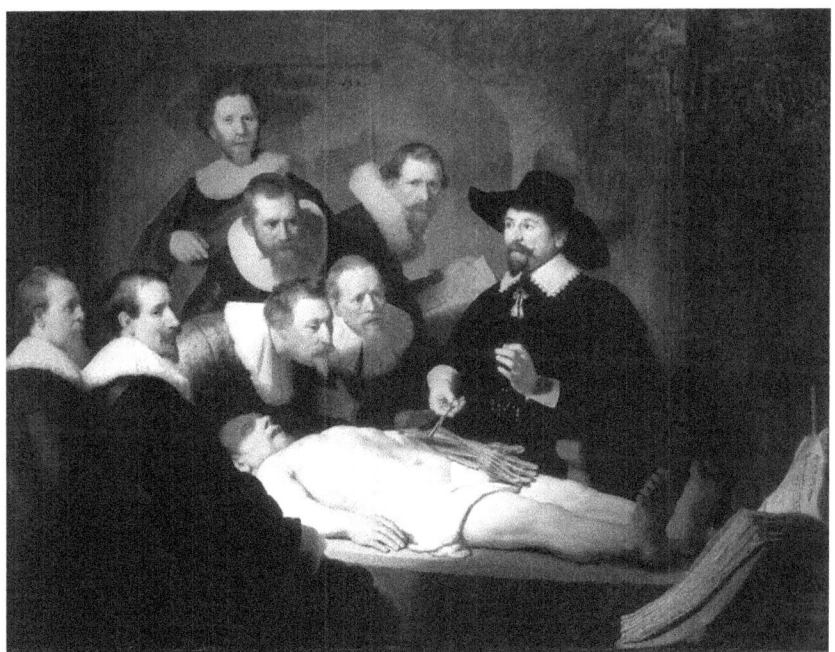

A second line also starts from the body but now heads towards Dr. Tulp's hat. The Doctor is the only one who has his hat on, something that is typical of this period in the Netherlands. Foreigners visiting the Netherlands in the seventeenth century were

---

[23] Rembrandt creates a similar effect in his painting *Christ and the Woman Taken in Adultery* (1644) National Gallery, London.

surprised that Dutch men kept their hats on all the time, even in church and when sitting down to dinner[24]. The hat was for them a symbol of freedom and they kept it on not as a gesture of superiority or arrogance but on the contrary, as an indication of humility. By keeping their hat on they declared that Christ had freed them morally and politically. With this second line, Rembrandt connects Adriaans' death with the death of Jesus making it the line of human brotherhood. Although Dr. Tulp was a famous doctor and held important civic positions, he shared the same human nature with Adriaans, and thus Rembrandt painted him with his hat on, with a more sober-coloured suit and with a more modestly embroidered collar than his students. This is not just in the painting, in real life Dr. Tulp was a very modest man devoted to his patients, compassionate and regarded as "a true physician who was aware of his responsibility in dealing with mental troubles as well as bodily ills"[25].

There is a marked difference between Rembrandt and the painting of the same subject produced a century later by Cornelis Troost (Figure 13-4). This art work belongs to the transition period that takes us from humanism to modernism and that is – when we carefully think of it – ironically referred to as "Enlightenment". Judging by the lack of interest in the faces of the students, this enlightened anatomy class does not generate wonder in its students. On the contrary, the somewhat precarious position of the cadaver shows a measure of disdain. The characters are dressed like French aristocrats with their powdered wig affecting wealth and power. Finally and in contrast to Dr. Tulp who is looking at his students in a pedagogical attitude, Dr. Röell appears quite oblivious of them and his pose betrays far more interest in conveying a sense of his own importance.

At this point in history, compassion and human conscience had been replaced with rationalism and materialism. As one would expect, in the absence of love and education to transform society, people had no other resort than to grovel for power and violence as the only route out of their misery and to achieve "freedom, equality and fraternity." Thus the French Revolution marks the be-

---

[24] van de Wetering (2005).
[25] Goldwyn (1961, p. 274).

ginning of modernity with power as the primary method for social change. In a giant painting, Jacques-Louis David portrays the tyrant Napoleon crowning his wife Josephine after having crowned himself emperor (Figure 13-5).

Figure 13-4: Anatomy Lesson of Dr Willem Röell, Troost, Cornelis (1728) Amsterdam Museum

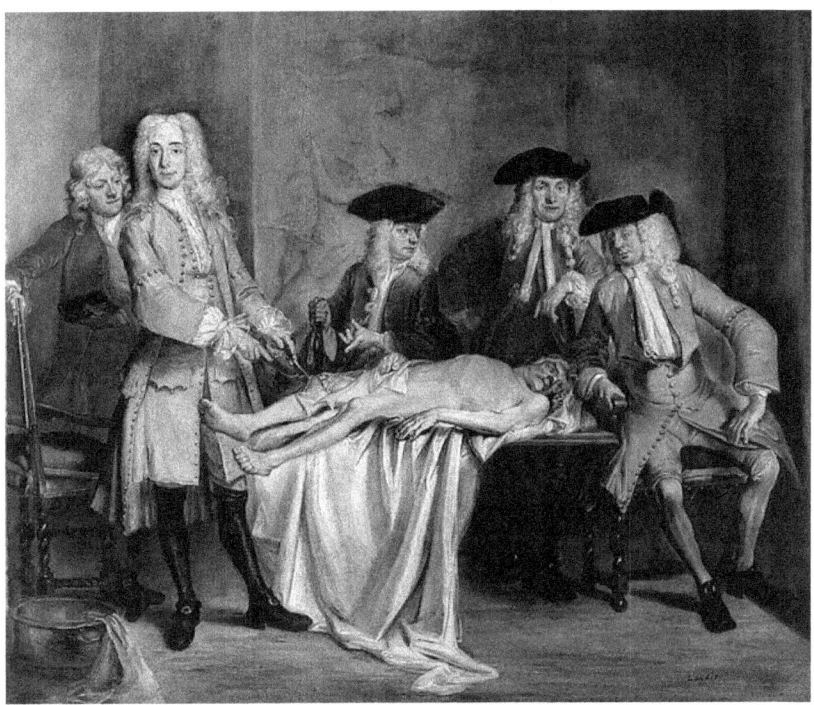

This is not a charitable Doctor Tulp with his black hat, but it is a new Domitian who proclaims himself Dominus et Deus (Lord and God) in order to modernise Europe, not with compassion and pedagogy, but with power and violence. From now on, it is the ambition for power that reigns in ideology, politics, science and all human endeavour. Even the contemporary Josephine, having discovered that power has replaced love and pedagogy, casts her empress crown away and covets the emperor's crown.

But power not only replaces the humanist pedagogical love, it also attempts to discredit it. Militarism, the main tool to convert communities into empires, despises compassion as a sign of weakness.

Figure 13-5: *Consecration of the Emperor Napoleon I* **(detail) David, Jacques-Louis (1805-1807) Paris, Louvre Museum**

This contempt, according to Blasco Ibañez, was expressed in the First World War as a:

… blasphemies against humanity, against justice, against all that makes life sweet and bearable. "Might is superior to Right!" ... "The weak should not exist."... "Be harsh in order to be great." [and] "...Kultur is the spiritual organization of the world, it does not exclude bloody savagery when that becomes necessary. Kultur sanctifies the demon within us, and is above morality, reason and science. We are going to impose Kultur by force of the cannon."[26]

These "blasphemies" are not things of the past, they are still part of the politics of nations, even those that are considered democratic are not mortified by getting rid of "everything that makes life tolerable and sweet." According to Donald Rumsfeld, "[t]oday, it should be clear that not only is weakness provocative...but the perception of weakness on our part can be provocative as well..." and "...[f]reedom's untidy, and free people are free to make mistakes and commit crimes and do bad things"... "Stuff happens..."[27].

There are other ways of exercising violence and of discrediting humanism and although they may not physically hurt, they can inflict deep psychological damage. Socio-economic coercion may be applied in a very sophisticated and effective manner to subdue people. Huntford[28] tells how the Swedish Social Democratic Party used totalitarianism based on socio-economic blackmail to achieve desired social changes. Through this method, it subordinated the Swedish people with the same effectiveness as the Soviet Union, but without the physical brutality. Thus it mastered all Swedish institutions. This socio-economic violence discredits the humanist ethic not only by regarding it as weakness, but by considering it impracticable and by threatening people with alienation. However, this type of control is not an instrument of state socialism only. Capitalism has also dismissed love, arguing that utilitarianism and egoism, when guided by the invisible hand of greed, generate more social benefit than what can be achieved by altruism[29].

---

[26] (2008).
[27] Rutenberg (2006); Loughlin (2003).
[28] (1971).
[29] Smith (1970).

Finally, the humanities have been cast away by subjectivity, the father of which is Kant. Kantian doctrine, which assures us that reality is a projection of our thinking, is very seductive, for it robs science of its conscience and gives us license to do whatever we please. What a charming philosophy, it allows us to pretend that all are saints when in fact we are all sinners! Subjectivism has left its legacy in soft systems methodology. This approach, which today is the most popular, was designed for executives who must address issues that they consider tangled and unclear ("fuzzy")[30]. In regarding them as fuzzy, it ignored the profound erudition of the humanities and their incisiveness to discern the problems of society and culture. With great convenience for business executives, subjective systems approaches have cast an epistemological cloud over the human suffering and desolation that surrounds today's capitalist corporations. It is an open invitation to turn a blind eye and continue with the slogan "les affaires sont les affaires." Let us not forget how Rumsfeld emphatically declared that freedom is messy and that crime and bad things just happen. How does soft systems methodology respond to Rumsfeld's "rich picture"?

Moreover, removing the humanities from the reach of the people and the students, is to abandon them to individualism and help commerce to turn them into "infantilized adults"[31] living in an "idiot culture"[32]. It is like impeding wolves to hunt in packs and forcing each to fend on its own, declaring them free wolves. Subjectivism leaves people, especially the young, confused and helpless, ready to be considered as human material for the use of capitalism. We should not be surprised, therefore, that there has been no resistance to the introduction of the concept Human Resources into management, a notion consonant with Nazism and Stalinism and which originates from de La Mettrie's notion of man:

> Let us then conclude boldly that man is a machine, and that in the whole universe there is but a single substance differently modified.[33]

---

[30] Checkland (1991). A detailed critique of the subjective systems methodology is found in Flood & Ulrich (1990).
[31] Barber (2007).
[32] Bernstein (1992).
[33] (2009).

Captivated by economies of scale and greed to dominate the market, executives have promoted the growth of the metropolis as a gigantic human factory and supermarket of human resources at one end and consumers on the other. Hence, we have a continuously growing number of cities passing the ten million inhabitants mark. To satisfy the cities' insatiable appetite for people and talent, rural and remote regions have had to sacrifice their populations. Most who emigrate from them are young with talents that rural communities desperately need to retain in order to stabilise and develop. True, the metropolis offers privileges that rural areas cannot provide, but these benefits are accessible only to a small proportion of the population. Most do not have access to these privileges and reside in the metropolis because it is the only way for them to survive. But there is another argument against the expansion of the metropolis. As we have maintained, human beings are social beings who need a community to realise themselves. Moreover, a community must have a systemically appropriate structure and size to allow civic engagement. The structure and size of a metropolis prevents citizens from exercising their rights and assuming their civic and democratic responsibilities. Therefore, the metropolis is not a community and its inhabitants will never be citizens but only a mass of men and women[34].

Towards a New Systemic and Humanist Transition

We have reached a point where we must move from critical thinking to creative thinking and ask ourselves: What should we do now? To restore the equilibrium in a fragmented community we must do three things simultaneously: (1) share the knowledge of the humanities and free people from ignorance, (2) reintegrate the community and (3) turn knowledge into work, for life is a task[35]. This task cannot be done through the bureaucracy, because this is mostly a redundancy that wastes lives and resources and yields almost nothing in return. Nor can we rely purely on politics, for its goal is to exercise justice and not to dictate to people how they

---

[34] Ortega y Gasset (2004b).
[35] Ortega y Gasset (2004a).

should live. We must adopt the humanist path of pedagogy and educate a new generation willing to work with sacrifice in the start-up stage of history shown in Figure 13-2. My wife and I have devoted much of our lives to this work. With the help of our colleagues, we devised a multi-modal path to restore the humanities into general systems theory. We have also developed qualitative methods to integrate methodology with method – ideas with action – in research. Here, I wish to conclude by giving a brief account of our educational venture. Our work began to take shape, concretely, during our years in Norrbotten (in the north of Sweden). All the factors of social disequilibrium I mentioned above were present in this remote region, yet the educational programmes were mainly oriented towards industry in the metropolitan centres of Sweden and the rest of Europe. They were programmes that belonged to the mature stage of social change (Figure 13-2) and as a result, most of the students, after graduation, left the region in search of the good life in the major cities.

To counteract this trend, we established an undergraduate degree programme and endeavoured to turn our department into an *universitas scholarium*, a community of students. To generate this sense of community, we sought to create a family atmosphere and to integrate ourselves to the community outside the campus. We established a connection with a local village where the leadership was sympathetic to our project in order to realise Tolstoy's scientific vision:

> Science is entirely arranged for the wealthy classes... The service of the people by science and art will only be performed when people, dwelling in the midst of the common folk, and, like the common folk, putting forward no demands, claiming no rights, shall offer to the common folk their scientific and artistic services; the acceptance or rejection of which shall depend wholly on the will of the common folk.[36]

We considered it important that both teachers and students integrate with the people; not to agitate them politically, but to know their troubles and share our scientific knowledge for their resolution. In our visits to this village, where we stayed for a night

---

[36] (2003).

or two, the students collected data and interviewed families and leaders. We also invited the local press to write articles to encourage our students and show that their interest in the community was appreciated. The students built analytical models to identify the critical factors affecting the community and designed activities to help stabilise it. For our purpose was not just to pass on knowledge, but also to turn this knowledge into work, real work for the benefit of the community.

During the years I worked at universities, I observed that a large proportion of the budget was absorbed by the administration[37] and this increased year after year. At the same time, the contribution of the administration to the advancement of science and the quality of education was minimal. Moreover, university autonomy and academic freedom had disappeared, since the direction of the university was dictated by government bureaucrats and implemented by their counterparts within the university administration. Since most bureaucrats have proven to know little about science and education but much about bureaucracy, the university was becoming a metro-university with commercial interests but of mediocre intellectual quality. On the other hand, the cost of information and communication technology was decreasing while its potential increased. The Internet, the digitisation of literature, the emergence of open source software like Linux and Ubuntu, eliminated the need for centralisation of the university. A new opportunity opened for us to become independent of the metropolitan university and create a true *universitas* (academic community) made up of small academic groups located in regional communities. The Internet allowed us to form an academic federation to share knowledge and provide an independent peer review similar to that adopted by scientific journals and thus help improve the quality of our work. Such collegiality made it also possible for community to combine localised education with distance education and expand opportunities for students. Thus later we formed a centre, Melbourne Centre for Community Development, that at present offers a master's degree in community development and carries out research integrated with teaching. The centre resides in Melbourne

---

[37] Cain and Hewett (2004).

in name only, because students are in various locations and teaching is done through the Internet from our home in Batemans Bay on the south-east coast of Australia. The centre is affiliated with two academic institutions, one of which awards the degree to students and, outside the normal academic regulations, the centre operates with ample scientific autonomy.

There has always been great difficulty in establishing systems programmes in the university. Programs are started with the same speed that they are discontinued and this instability has prevented the systemic sciences from reaching their intellectual maturity. Part of this is due to the fragmentation of traditional science that is imposed on the structure of the university and prevents systems science from finding a permanent home in the faculty structure. Part is also due to systems science being unable to generate the level of profits attained by other programmes that are incorporated into the university for their commercial value rather than their scientific and humanitarian merit. But now technology offers us a historic opportunity to create a federated system integrated into the community. I have watched with great interest the extensive systemic activity in Latin America and it seems likely that this is where the most fertile ground for this vision lies. Perhaps the time has come to be in Latin America where such systemic initiative will emerge and lead us to remark: "Here are those who speak as they live, and live as they speak."[38]

---

[38] Vives (1971, p. 287).

References[12]

ABC Online (2006) Farmer suicide rates worry GPs. <http://www.abc.net.au/news/newsitems/200610/s1771783.htm> (Accessed 28 March 2008)

Ahlmark, Per (1998) Swedish Myopias. *Society*, 36: 72-77.

Anderson, D (2001) Submission to Senate Inquiry into Higher Education: How Can Anyone Know About The Intellectual Standards Of University Degrees And Does It Matter Anyway? <http://www.aph.gov.au/Senate/committee/eet_ctte/completed_inquiries/1999-02/public_uni/submissions/sub092.doc> (Accessed 28 March 2008).

Anderson, Don; Johnson Richard and Sarah, Lawrence (2002) Changes in Academic Work: Implications for Universities of the Changing Age Distribution and Work Roles of Academic Staff. Department of Education, Science and Training, Australian Government.

Anderson, Lorin W. and Sosniak, Lauren A. (eds.) (1994) *Bloom's taxonomy: a forty-year retrospective.* Chicago, Illinois, University of Chicago.

Aquinas, St. Thomas (1955) *Contra Gentiles: On the Truth of the Catholic Faith*. Edited, with English, especially Scriptural references, updated by Joseph Kenny, O.P. New York: Hanover House, <http://dhspriory.org/thomas/ContraGentiles.htm> (Accessed 19 August 2014).

Aristotle (2007) *Metaphysics*. Translated by W. D. Ross. <http://ebooks.adelaide.edu.au/a/aristotle/metaphysics/complete.html> (Accessed 11 August 2011).

Ashby, W. Ross (1976) *An Introduction to Cybernetics*. London, Methuen.

Asquith, Stewart; Clark, Chris and Waterhouse, Lorraine (2005) The Role of the Social Worker in the 21st Century. *The Scottish Executive*, December. <http://www.scotland.gov.uk/Resource/Doc/47121/0020821.pdf> (Accessed 17 May 2014).

---

[1] When making reference to Spanish authors, I have made use of the original Castilian version. If available, I have provided a reference to an English translation in a footnote.

[2] Where possible, I have listed references to digitalised versions in the public domain and on the Internet.

Associated Press (2007) Carl Bernstein laments U.S.'s 'idiot culture ': Reporter raps media, reader infatuation with celebrity news. MSNBC. <http://www.msnbc.msn.com/id/21595196/> (Accessed 2 November 2007).

Australian Broadcasting Corporation (2012) Church welfare groups and the hazards of state money. 29 August. <http://www.abc.net.au/radionational/programs/religionandethicsreport/church-welfare-groups-and-the-hazards-of-state-money/4231006> (Accessed 17 May 2014).

Australian Bureau of Statistics (2013) 6523.0 - Household Income and Income Distribution, Australia, 2011-12. <http://www.abs.gov.au/ausstats/abs@.nsf/Latestproducts/6523.0Main%20Features22011-12?opendocument&tabname=Summary&prodno=6523.0&issue=2011-12&num=&view=> (Accessed 16 May 2014).

Bachelard, Michael (2007) Workers badly done by as managers strip rights. *The Melbourne Age*, 13 September.

Bagaric, Mirko (2006) Telling us what we already know. Online Opinion - Australia's e-journal of social and political debate. <http://www.onlineopinion.com.au/print.asp?article=4380>

Baker, Richard (2006) The odd stray shot: photos reveal our men at work. *The Melbourne Age*, February 3. <http://www.theage.com.au/news/national/photos-reveal-our-men-at-work/2006/02/02/1138836372830.html> (Accessed 14 August 2014).

Bandow, Doug (1997) Service to Whom? The Future of Freedom Foundation. <http://fff.org/explore-freedom/article/service-part-1/> (Accessed 14 August 2014).

Barber, Benjamin R. (2007) *Consumed: How Markets Corrupt Children, Infantilize Adults, and Swallow Citizens Whole*. New York, Norton.

BBC News (2002) Schroeder calls for schools reforms. 14 June.

BBC News (2003a) EU values - united in diversity? <http://news.bbc.co.uk/go/pr/fr/-/2/hi/europe/3280697.stm> (Accessed 19 November 2003).

BBC News (2003b) What the EU constitution says. <http://news-.bbc.co.uk/go/pr/fr/-/2/hi/europe/2950276.stm> (Accessed 14 November 2003).

BBC News (2003c) Worshipping celebrities 'brings success'. <http://news.bbc.co.uk/go/pr/fr/-/2/hi/health/3147343.stm> (Accessed 13 August 2002).

BBC News (2003d) We were not at all prepared <http://news.b-bc.co.uk/go/pr/fr/-/2/hi/europe/3150997.stm> (Accessed 8 August 2003).

Beer, Stafford (1994a) *Brain of the Firm*. (2nd. ed.) Classic Beer Series. Chichester, Wiley.

Beer, Stafford (1994b) *Platform for Change*. Classic Beer Series. Chichester, Wiley.

Beer, Stafford (1995) *The Heart of Enterprise*. Classic Beer Series. London, Wiley.

Bell, Lynn (2005) Port Phillip Bay dredging hits obstacle. *ABC Online*. <http://www.abc.net.au/pm/content/2005/s1335630.htm> (Accessed 31 March 2005).

Bellah, Robert N. (2000) The True Scholar. Academe Online, Volume 86:1.

Bentham, Jeremy (1781) The Principles of Morals and Legislation. Utilitarianism Resources. <http://www.utilitarianism.com/jeremy-bentham/index.html> (Accessed 13 May 2008).

Berlach, Richard G. (2004) Outcomes-based Education and the Death of Knowledge. *Proceedings*, The Australian Association for Research in Education Conference, The University of Melbourne, Australia. 28th November to 2nd December.

Bernstein, Carl (1992) The Idiot Culture. *The New Republic*, 8 June. <http://carlbernstein.com/magazines_the_idiot_culture.pdf> (Accessed 28 January 2013).

Birrell, Bob and Healy, Ernest (2008) Melbourne's Population Surge. Centre for Population and Urban Research Bulletin. Monash University. <http://arts.monash.edu.au/cpur/publications/cpur.pdf> (Accessed 28 March 2008).

Blasco Ibáñez, Vicente (2008) *Los Cuatro Jinetes del Apocalipsis*. Project Gutenberg. <http://www.gutenberg.org/wiki/Main_Page> (Accessed 20 August 2014).

Bloom, Allan (1987) *The Closing of the American Mind*. New York, Simon and Schuster. <http://iwcenglish1.typepad.com/Documents/14434540-The-Closing-of-the-American-Mind.pdf> (Accessed 07 March 2013).

Blunt, Wilfrid (2001) *The Compleat Naturalist: A Life of Linnaeus*. London, Frances Lincoln.

Boulding, K. E. (1956a) General Systems Theory - The Skeleton of Science. *Management Science*, 2: 197-208. <http://www.panarchy.org/boulding/systems.1956.html> (Accessed 15 October 2008).

Boulding, Kenneth E. (1956b) *The Image: Knowledge in Life and Society*. Michigan, Ann Arbor Paperbacks.

Boulding, Kenneth (1969) Technology and the Love-Hate System. In (Scott, William G. (Ed.) *Organization Concepts and Analysis*. Belmont, California, Dickenson; p. 109-121).

Boulding, Kenneth E. (1970) *Beyond Economics*. Ann Arbor, University of Michigan.

Boulding, K. E. (1987) Systems Profile: Some Origins. *Systems Research*, 4: 283-288.

Bunge, Mario (1959) *Metascientific Queries*. Springfield, Illinois, Charles C. Thomas.

Buttimer, Anne (1990) Geography, Humanism, and Global Concern. *Annals of the Association of American Geographers*, 80: 1-33.

Buttimer, Anne (1998) Close to home. *Environment*, 40: 12-24.

Byam, Sarah (2002) Adam Smith's Dead Hand. <http://www.tuppenceworth.ie/Politics/smithhand.html> (Accessed 14 August 2014).

Cain, John and Hewitt, John (2004) *Off Course: from Public Place to Marketplace at Melbourne University*. Melbourne, Australia, Scribe.

Caldwell, Alison (2004) The World Today - Woman alleges rape by former AFL player. *ABC Online*. <http://www.abc.net.au/worldtoday/content/2004/s1100400.htm> (Accessed 3 May 2004).

Calvin, John (n.d.)[3] *The Institutes of Christian Religion*. 2 Volumes. Christian Classics Ethereal Library, Grand Rapids, MI. <http://www.ccel.org/ccel/calvin/institutes.pdf> (Accessed 25 April 2012).

Chaucer (2000) *The Canterbury Tales and Other Poems*. <http://www.gutenberg.org/ebooks/2383> (Accessed 20 August 2014).

Checkland, Peter (1981) *Systems Thinking, Systems Practice*. Chichester, Wiley.

Checkland, Peter (1999) Soft Systems Methodology: A Thirty Year Retrospective. *Systems Research and Behavioral Science*, 17: S11–S58. <http://citeseerx.ist.psu.edu/viewdoc/download?doi=10.1.1.133.7381&rep=rep1&type=pdf> (Accessed 22 April 2014).

Chesterton, G. K. 1994. *Orthodoxy*. Harold Shaw, Illinois.

Chossudovsky, Michel (1998) Global Poverty in the Late 20th Century. *Journal of International Affairs*. 52, 1. <http://www.mtholyoke.edu/acad/intrel/chossu.htm> (Accessed 19 August 2014).

Chrisafis, Angelique (2002) Widespread cheating devalues school tests. London, *The Guardian*, 28 October.

Chua, Geraldine (2014) Sky-high slum fears in Melbourne prompt design rule rethink by state government. <http://www.architectureanddesign.com.au/news/sky-high-slum-fears-in-melbourne-prompt-design-rul> (Accessed 16 May 2014).

Churchman, C. West (1968) *Challenge to Reason*. New York, McGraw-Hill.

Churchman, C. West (1987) Systems Profile: Discoveries in an Exploration into Systems Thinking. *Systems Research*, 4: 139-146.

Clark, Gordon H. (1974) *The Philosophy of Science and Belief in God*. Nutley, New Jersey, Craig.

[3] n.d. = non dated digitalised document published on the Internet.

Cleary, Phil (2004) It's time to recognise and deal with footy's silent subculture of misogyny. *Online Opinion*. <http://www.onlineopinion.com.au/print.asp?article=2094> (Accessed 26 March 2004)

Colebatch, Tim (2006) Revealed: a nation of drop-outs. *The Melbourne Age*, 17 April.

Colebatch, Tim and Topsfield, Jewel (2007) Australia scores badly on emissions growth report. *The Melbourne Age*, 1 November.

Comte, Auguste (1896) *The Positive Philosophy*. 3 Volumes. Translated and Condensed by Harriet Martineau. London, George Bell & Sons. <http://socserv2.mcmaster.ca/~econ/ugcm/3ll3/comte> (Accessed 17 May 2007).

Coomarasamy, James (2002) France considers TV porn ban. BBC News Online, 16 August.

de La Mettrie, Julien Offray (2009) *Man a Machine*. Translated by Jonathan Bennet. <http://www.earlymoderntexts.com> (Accessed 23 December 2011)

de Raadt, J. D. R. (1989a) Dis-information and Time Lags in Information Systems. *Cybernetics and Systems*, 20: 321-342.

de Raadt, J. D. R. (1989b) Information Machines and The Brave New World. *The Information Society*, 6: 139-152.

de Raadt, J. D. R. (1989c) Multi-modal Systems Design: A Concern for the Issues That Matter. *Systems Research*, 6: 17-25.

de Raadt, J. D. R. (1991) *Information and Managerial Wisdom*. Idaho, Paradigm.

de Raadt, J. D. R. (1995) Expanding the Horizon of Information Systems Design. *Systems Research*, 12: 185-199.

de Raadt, J. D. R. (1997a) A Multi-Modal Systems Approach to O.R. Fourth Conference of the Association of Asian-Pacific Operational Research Societies, Melbourne.

de Raadt, J. D. R. (1997b) A Sketch for Humane Operational Research in a Technological Society. *Systems Practice*, 10: 421-441.

de Raadt, J. D. R. (1997c) Design of an Undergraduate Programme in Informatics and Systems Science. *Proceedings*, 14th International Conference of the World Association for Case Research Methods and Case Methods Application, Universidad Complutense de Madrid.

de Raadt, J. D. R. (1997d) Faith and the Normative Foundation of Systems Science. *Systems Practice*, 10: 13-35.

de Raadt, J. D. R. (1997e) A Celebration of Professor Stafford Beer's 70th Birthday. *Systems Practice*, 10: 361-363.

de Raadt, J. D. R. (1998a) *A New Management of Life*. Toronto Series in Theology (Vol. 75). Lampeter, Wales, Edwin Mellen.

de Raadt, J. D. R. (2000a) Multi-Modal Modelling Method Manual. FMV, Swedish Defence Forces.

de Raadt, J. D. R. (2000b) *Redesign and Management of Communities in Crisis*. Parkland, Universal Publishers.

de Raadt, J. D. R. (2001) *A Method and Software for Designing Viable Social Systems*. Parkland, Universal Publishers. <http://www.melbourneccd.com/publications.html> (Accessed 11 June 2014).

de Raadt, J. D. R. (2006) Samaritan Ethics, Systems Science and Society. *Systemic Practice and Action Research*, 19: 489-500.

de Raadt, J. D. R. (2010) Community Development and Renaissance Social Humanism - Some Lessons for Systems Science. *Systemic Practice and Action Research*, 24: 509- 521.

de Raadt, J. D. R. and de Raadt, Veronica D. (2004a) Normative Evaluation of Community Projects: A Multimodal Systems Approach. *Systemic Practice and Action Research*, 17: 83-102.

de Raadt, J. D. R. and de Raadt, Veronica D. (2004b) Where there is No Vision the People Perish: Ethical Vision and Community Sustainability. *Systems Research and Behavioral Science*, 22: 233-247.

de Raadt, J. D. R. and de Raadt, Veronica D. (2008) Arresting the Collapse of the City Through Systemic Education: A Case Study of Melbourne. *Systemic Practice and Action Research*, 21: 299-322.

de Raadt, Veronica D. (2001a) Multi-Modal Systems Method: The Impact of Normative Factors on Community Viability. *Systems Research and Behavioral Science*, 18: 171 - 180.

de Raadt, Veronica D. (2001b) Normative Application of Multi-Modal Systems Thinking to a Non-Viable Social System. Doctoral thesis, Luleå University of Technology.

de Raadt, Veronica D. (2002) *Ethics and Sustainable Community Development*. Parkland, Florida, Universal Publishers.

de Raadt, J. D. R. (2013) *Intelligent Christianity for an Age of Folly*. Melbourne, Melbourne Centre for Community Development. <http://www.amazon.com/Intelligent-Christianity-Age-Folly-Raadt-ebook/dp/B00C89GLZ4> (Accessed 21 August 2014).

Dickens, Charles (1997) *Hard Times*. Project Gutenberg <http://www.gutenberg.org/dirs/etext97/hardt10.txt> (Accessed 18 May 2008).

Dobbin, Marika (2012) Garden breathes life into Docklands. *The Melbourne Age*, 15 July. <http://www.theage.com.au/victoria/garden-breathes-life-into-docklands-20120715-223v9.html> (Accessed 16 May 2014).

Dockery, A. M. and Barns, A. (2005) Who'd be a Nurse? Some evidence on career choice in Australia. Curtin University of Technology, Perth Western Australia, Working Paper No 39.

Dodds S. (1997) Towards a 'Science of Sustainability': Improving the Way Ecological Economics Understands Human Well-Being. *Ecological Economics*, 23: 95-111.

Donnelly, Kevin (2006) Gobbledygook a poor swap for old school ways: On how outcomes-based education has infected the curriculum. *The Australian*, 16th June.

Dooyeweerd, Herman (1958) *A New Critique of Theoretical Thought*. 4 Volumes. Philadelphia, Pennsylvania, Presbyterian and Reformed.

Dooyeweerd, Herman (1975) *In the Twilight of Western Thought*. Nutley, New Jersey, Craig.

Dowling, Jason (2012) Jobs shift from suburbs to CBD. *The Melbourne Age*, 5 December. <http://www.theage.com.au/victoria/jobs-shift-from-suburbs-to-cbd-20121204-2at8n.html> (Accessed 16 May 2014).

Dubecki, Larissa (2008) Why 10 is too young for your first Brazilian. *The Melbourne Age*, 8 January.

d'Holbach, Baron Paul Henri Thiry (2005) *Systeme de la Nature*. 2 Volumes. Translated by Samuel Wilkinson. Project Gutenberg. <http://www.gutenberg.org/etext/8909> (Accessed 17 May 2008).

Eagle, Gerard (2002) Morin alerta de que la política "del día a día " alimenta a la extrema derecha. Madrid, *El País*, 17 de Junio.

Edwards, Hannah and Rumble, Chantal (2006) We pay, you pay: bullying students turn on academics. *The Melbourne Age*, 12 November.

Edwards, Pat K. and Brown, Duane R. (1996) Schools as Community Centres for Rebuilding Community. *National Civic Review*, 85: 48-51.

Engell, James and Dangerfield, Anthony (1998) The Market-Model University. Humanities in *The Melbourne Age* of Money. *Harvard Magazine*, May-June. <http://www.harvardmag.com/issues/mj98/forum.html> (Accessed 06 February 2013).

Erasmus, Desiderius (1529) *An Exhortation to the Diligent Study of Scripture*. Edited Frank Luttmer. <http://history.hanover.edu/courses/excerpts/346erasmus.html> (Accessed 21 July 2008).

Erasmus, Desiderius (1978) *The Antibarbarians*. Translated by Margaret Mann Phillips. Collected Works of Erasmus: Literary and Educational Writings 1. University of Toronto.

Erasmus, Desiderius (2000) *Praise of Folly*. Grand Rapids,MI:Christian Classics Ethereal Library. <http://www.ccel.org/ccel/erasmus/folly.html> (Accessed 23 April 2008)

Erasmus, Desiderius (2004) *The Colloquies*. Volume 1. The Online Library of Liberty. <http://files.libertyfund.org/epub/726_Erasmus_0046-01.epub> (Accessed 4 September 2010).

Erasmus, Desiderius (2011) *The Manual of the Christian Knight*. The Online Library of Liberty. <http://oll.libertyfund.org/Texts/Erasmus0096/ManualChristianKnight/0048_Bk.html> (Accessed 11 February 2013).

Erasmus, Desiderius (n.d.) *Antipolemus; or, the Plea of Reason, Religion, and Humanity, against War*. <http://www.bookyard-

s.com/en/book/details/9472/Antipolemus#.U-x7LtSSxLU>
(Accessed 14 August 2014).

European Commission (1998) Adapting and promoting the Social
Dialogue at Community Level. Commission Communication.

European Commission (2001) Preparatory measures for a local
commitment for employment. Call for proposals VP/2001/015.
Applicants guide. ESF, DGBudget Article B5-5030.

European Employment Observatory (2002) National Labour Market Policies - Trends: Germany.

Evans, C. Stephen (1971) *Despair: A Moment or a Way of Life -
An Existential Quest for Hope*. Illinois, Inter-Varsity.

Faler, Brian (2005) Census Details Voter Turnout for 2004. *The
Washington Post*, 26th May.

Flood, Robert L. and Romm, N.R.A. (1995) Diversity Management. *Systems Practice*, 8:469-482.

Flood, Robert L. and Ulrich, Werner (1990) Testament to Conver-
sations on Critical Systems Thinking Between Two Systems
Practitioners. *Systems Practice*, 3: 7-29.

Frängsmyr, Tore (1983) *Linnaeus: The Man and His Work*.
Uppsala Studies in History of Science, 18. Berkeley, University
of California.

Frank, Günter (1995) *Die theologische Philosophie Philipp Mel-
anchthons* (1497-1560), Leipzig, Benno.

Friedman, Milton (1970) The Social Responsibility of Business is
to Increase its Profits. *The New York Times Magazine*, September 13.

Friends of the Earth (2002) Briefing: Climate change and the
Earth Summit <http://www.foe.co.uk/resource/briefings/cli-
mate_change_summit.pdf> (Accessed 28 March 2008).

Frye, Sally; Dawe, Sharon; Harnett, Paul; Kowalenko, Sascha and
Harlen, Moana (2008) Supporting the families of young people
with problematic drug use: investigating support options. Australian National Council of Drugs research paper 15.
<https://www.families.org.au/article_files/ANCD%20Press
%20Release%202008.pdf> (Accessed 15 August 2014).

García López J. (1996) *Historia de la Literatura Española*.
(Vigésima edición). Barcelona, Vicens Vives.

Gaskell, Elizabeth (2000) *Mary Barton*. The Project Gutenberg. <http://www.gutenberg.org> (Accessed 25 August 2010).

Geis, Don and Kutzmark, Tammy (1995) Developing Sustainable Communities. *Public Management (US)*, 77: 4-13.

Gettler, Leon (2007) Australian dream fades as cost sends some to ghetto. *The Melbourne Age*, 30 July.

Goerke, Heinz (1973) *Linnaeus* (Translated by Denver Lindley). New York, Charles Scribner's Sons.

Goldsmith, Merle (1994) *The Trail Blazers*. Ryde, New South Wales, South American Missionary Soicety.

Goldwyn, Robert M (1961) Nicolaas Tulp (1593-I674). *Medical History*, 5: 270 - 276. <http://www.ncbi.nlm.nih.gov/pmc/articles/PMC1034629/?page=1> (Accessed 28 September 2010).

Gordon, Ernest (1970) *Miracle in the River Kwai*. London, Fontana.

Gordon, Josh and Rood, David (2008) City turning ugly: Baillieu. *The Melbourne Age*, 25 February.

Goudzwaard, Bob (1979) *Capitalism and Progress: A Diagnosis of Western Society*. Toronto, Wedge.

Gould, A. (1988) *Conflict and Control in Welfare and Policy: The Swedish Experience*. London, Longman.

Graham, Gordon (2002) *Universities: The Recovery of an Idea*. Thoverton, UK, Imprint Academic.

Grattan, Michelle (2006) Howard's might beats Costello's 'truth'. *The Melbourne Age*, 17th July.

Griffioen, Sander (1987) *The Problem of Progress*. Iowa, Dort College.

Grotius, Hugo (1901) *The Rights of War and Peace*. The Online Library of Liberty. <http://oll.libertyfund.org/EBooks/Grotius_0138.pdf> (Accessed 23 April 2008).

Grotius, Hugo (1916) *The Freedom of the Seas*. Translated by Ralph Van Deman Magoffin. New York. Oxford University Press. <http://socserv2.mcmaster.ca/~econ/ugcm/3ll3/grotius/Seas.pdf> (Accessed 20 August 2014).

Hanson, Kjell and de Raadt, Veronica (1995) Immigration and Social Instability. *Proceedings*, 39th Annual Meeting, International Society for the Systems Sciences, Free University, Amsterdam.

Harnden, Roger and Leonard, Allena (eds.) (1994) *How Many Grapes Went into the Wine: Stafford Beer on the Art and Science of Holistic Management.* Chichester, Wiley.

Harrison, Dan (2006) Police corruption not endemic: chief. *The Melbourne Age*, 6th July.

Hayek, F. A. (2006) *The Road to Serfdom.* London, Routledge.

Held, David (1997) Introduction to Critical Theory. Cambridge, UK, Polity.

Hellard, Peta (2007) Paris Hilton scared of prison. *The Daily Telegraph*, 4 June.

Higgins, Ann (1995) Teaching as a Moral Activity - Listening to Teachers in Russia and the United States. *Journal of Moral Education*, 24: 143-158.

Hill, Jason (2007) Ethical dilemmas. *The Melbourne Age*, 20 September.

Holroyd, Jane (2008) Adults' attitude leads to binging. *The Melbourne Age*, 25 February.

Hooykaas, R. (1974) *Religion and the Rise of Modern Science.* Grand Rapids, Michigan, Eerdmans.

Houston, Cameron; Johnston, Chris and Austin, Paul (2008) This is Melbourne at night: 'anarchy'. *The Melbourne Age*, 23 February.

Huizinga, Johan (2007) *Erasmus and the Age of Reformation.* Project Gutenberg. <http://www.gutenberg.org/etext/22900> (Accessed 21 July 2008).

Huntford, Roland. (1971) *The New Totalitarians.* London, Allen Lane.

Hurtado Cruchaga, Alberto (2004) *Humanismo Social.* 4 ed. Santiago de Chile, Fundación Padre Hurtado.

Huxley, Aldous (1946) *Brave New World.* New York, Harper & Row.

Huxley, Aldous (1993) A Defence of the Intellect. *UNESCO Courier*, 46: 42-43.

Israel, Jonathan (1995) *The Dutch Republic: Its Rise, Greatness and Fall*. 1477- 1806. Oxford, Clarendon.

Jackson, M.C. (1991) The Origins and Nature of Critical Systems Thinking. Systems Practice, 4: 131-149.

Jameson, Fredric (1991) *Postmodernism, or, the Cultural Logic of Late Capitalism*. London, Verso.

Jones, Albert. S. (2000) *The Crisis of Governments*. Melbourne, Aristo.

Jorink, Henricus Gerardus Maria (2004) Het boeck der natuere : Nederlandse geleerden en de wonderen van Gods schepping, 1575-1715. Dissertaties - Rijksuniversiteit Groningen. <http://dissertations.ub.rug.nl/faculties/arts/2004/h.g.m.jorink/> (Accessed 20 August 2014).

Joyce, Helen (2001) Adam Smith and the invisible hand. <http://plus.maths.org/issue14/features/smith/> (Accessed 15 August 2014).

Kant, Immanuel (2007) *Critique of Pure Reason*. Translated by J. M. D. Meiklejohn. Project Gutenberg. <http://www.gutenberg.org/etext/4280> (Accessed 12 July 2008).

Kaplan, E. Ann (1990) Feminism/Oedipus/Postmodernism: The Case of MTV. In Kaplan, E. Ann (ed.) *Postmodernism and its Discontents: Theories and Practices*. New York, Verso.

Khadem, Nassim (2007) Housing pressure bites poor. *The Melbourne Age*, 6 March

Kirby, Emma J. (2002) France's clean break with sexy past. BBC News Online, 27 October.

Klapwijk, J.,Griffioen, S. and Groenewoud, G. (1991) *Bringing Into Captivity Every Thought*. New York, University Press of America.

Kleinman, Rachel (2006) Climate set to go from bad to worse. *The Melbourne Age*, 23 December.

Kleinman, Rachel (2007) Climate calamity forecast. *The Melbourne Age*, 7 April.

Knoeff, Rina (2002) *Herman Boerhaave (1668-1738): Calvinist Chemist and Physician*. Amsterdam, Royal Netherlands Academy of Arts and Sciences. <http://www.knaw.nl/publicaties/pdf/20011109.pdf> (Accessed 24 February 2009).

Kostas, Jasmine (2006) Students turn to sex industry work to pay for degrees. *ABC Online*. <http://www.abc.net.au/am/content/2006/s1785727.htm > (Accessed 28 March 2008).

Kuyper, Abraham (1950) *Christianity and the Class Struggle*. Translated by Dirk Jellema. Grand Rapids, Michigan, Piet Hein. <http://www.reformationalpublishingproject.com/pdf_books/Sc anned_Books_PDF/ChristianityandtheClassStruggle.pdf> (Accessed 12 February).

Lantz, Sarah (2005) Students Working in the Melbourne Sex Industry: Education, Human Capital and the Changing Patterns of the Youth Labour Market. *Journal of Youth Studies*, 8: 385-401.

Lewis, C.S. (1955) *Mere Christianity*. London, Fontana.

Lewis, C. S. (1960) *The Four Loves*. New York, Harcourt Brace. <http://www.scribd.com/doc/515895/The-Four-Loves> (Accessed 18 May 2008).

Lewis, C.S. (1994) *God in the Dock*. Eerdmans, Michigan, Grand Rapids.

Lindbom, Tage (1996) *The Myth of Democracy*. Grand Rapids, Michigan, Eerdmans.

Lindeboom, G. A. (1968) *Herman Boerhaave: The Man and His Work*. London, Methuen.

Lonne, Bob (2007) Facing our Future. *Australian Association of Social Workers National Bulletin*, Vol 17, No. 5: 3-5.

Lonne, Bob (2009) Social Justice and High-Quality Human Services: Visioning the Place of a Contemporary Professional Association. *Australian Social Work*, 62: 1-9.

Loughlin, Sean (2003) Rumsfeld on Looting in Iraq: 'Stuff happens'. <http://articles.cnn.com/2003-04-11/us/sprj.irq.pentagon_1_looting-defense-secretary-donald-rumsfeld-coalition-forces?_s=PM:US> (Accessed 9 October 2010).

Lunn, Stephen (2008) Teenage drink and drug abuse rife. *The Melbourne Age*, 25 February.

Lyon, David (1994) *Postmodernity*. Buckingham, Open University.

Lyons, John (2007) *Of freedom and fascism in America*. The Australian, 5 October.

Maag, Karin (ed.) (1999) *Melanchthon in Europe: His Work and Influence Beyond Wittenberg*. Grand Rapids, Michigan, Baker.

Mackay, Hugh (2007) RIP: Australia's egalitarian ideal. *The Melbourne Age*, 24 November.

Marín Ibáñez, Ricardo (1994) *Juan Luis Vives* (1492?-1540). *Prospects: The Quarterly Review of Comparative Education*. Paris, UNESCO: International Bureau of Education, 24: 743-759. <http://www.ibe.unesco.org/publications/ThinkersPdf/vivese.pdf> (Accessed 15 August 2014).

Marx, Karl and Engels, Friedrich (2005) *The Communist Manifesto*. <http://www.gutenberg.org/> (Accessed 21 July 2014).

Maskell, Duke and Robinson, Ian (2002) The New idea of the University. Thoverton, UK, Imprint Academic.

McCallum, Jan (2005) How over-regulation is killing off volunteerism. *The Melbourne Age*, April 18.

McDougall, Dan and Doward, Jamie (2007) The human cost of cheap high street clothes. *The Observer*, 22 April.

Medew, Julia (2006) Elderly assaults ignored, court told. *The Melbourne Age*, 11 July.

Melanchthon, Philipp (1999) *Orations on Philosophy and Education*. (Sachiko Kusukawa, ed.) Cambridge, Cambridge UP.

Midgley, Gerald (1992) The Sacred and Profane in Critical Systems Thinking. *Systems Practice*, 5: 5-16.

Migulez, Fausto (2002) Controversy over new definition for measuring unemployment. Dublin, European Foundation for the Improvement of Living and Working Conditions, 28 February.

Miletic, Daniella (2008) Teens 'can't taste' liquor in alcopops. *The Melbourne Age*, 27 February. <http://www.theage.com.au/news/national/teens-cant-taste-liquor-in-alcopops/2008/02/26/1203788345714.html> (Accessed 18 August 2014).

Mill, John Stuart (1969) *The Six Great Humanistic Essays*. New York, Washington Square.

Mill, John Stuart (2004) *Utilitarianism*. Project Gutenberg.
<http://www.gutenberg.org/files/11224/11224-h/11224-h.htm>
(Accessed 13 May 2008)

Millar, Royce (2003) Call to allow social housing at Docklands.
The Melbourne Age, 7 July.

Millar, Royce (2007a) Drought hitting rural councils. *The Melbourne Age*, 14 November.

Millar, Royce (2007b) Rural Australians to pay price for climate
change. *The Melbourne Age*, 27 November.

Millar, Royce and Boulton, Martin (2005) Young embrace the
high life. *The Melbourne Age*, 11 June.

Millar, Royce and Lucas, Clay (2007) Melbourne comes alive - at
a price. *The Melbourne Age*, 27 June.

Millennium Ecosystem Assessment Board (2005) Living Beyond
Our Means: Natural Assets and Human Well-Being.
<http://www.millenniumassessment.org/en/BoardState-
ment.aspx> (Accessed 28 March 2008).

Miller, James Grier (1978) *Living Systems*. New York, Mc-
Graw-Hill.

Mitchell, Bill (2002) The hidden truth about unemployment. Australia, Centre of Full Employment and Equity, University of
Newcastle.
<http://e1.newcastle.edu.au/coffee/pubs/oped/nh_11_07_02_cl
mi.pdf> (Accessed 15 August 2014).

Moreno, Valentín and Calero, Francisco (2006) Juan Luis Vives.
Obras completas y Epistolario: Estudio introductorio. Bibli-
oteca Valenciana Digital. <http://bv2.gva.es/es/estaticos/conten-
ido.cmd?pagina=estaticos/vives/vives_introduccion> (Accessed
06 February 2013).

Morris, Leon. (1964) *Ministers of God*. London, Inter-Varsity.

Morton, Adam (2007) 640 University staff lose jobs. *The Melbourne Age*, 26 February.

MSNBC (2004) Soldier charged with abusing Iraqi prisoners. 7th
May. <http://www.msnbc.msn.com/id/4927273/print/1/display-
mode/1098/> (Accessed 15 August 2014).

Multinational Monitor (1995) Media Monopoly: An Interview
with Nicolas Johnson.

<http://www.multinationalmonitor.org/hyper/mm0595.html#int
> (Accessed 28 March 2008).

New York Times (2002) A Failure to Account. 14 January.

Nixon, Jon, Sankey, Kate, Furay, Victor and Simmons, Malcolm (1999) Education for Sustainability in Scottish Secondary Schools: Boundary Maintenance or Professional Reorientation? *Environmental Education Research*, 5: 305-318.

Olin, John C. (1987) *Christian Humanism and the Reformation: Selected Writings*, 3rd Edition. New York, Fordham University.

Ortega y Gasset, José (1924) *Kant - Hegel - Scheler*. <http://www.librodot.com> (Accessed 30 May 2008).

Ortega y Gasset, José (1992) *Misión de la Universidad*. Madrid, Alianza Editorial.[4]

Ortega y Gasset, José (1993) *Estudios Sobre el Amor*. Madrid, Alianza Editorial.

Ortega y Gasset, José (2004a) *Historia como Sistema: Sobre la razón histórica como nueva revelación*. <http://www.laeditorialvirtual.com.ar/Pages/Ortega_y_Gasset/Ortega_HistoriaComoSistema.htm> (Accessed 14 January 2012).[5]

Ortega y Gasset, José (2004b) *La Rebelión de Las Masas. La Editorial Virtual*. <http://www.laeditorialvirtual.com.ar/Pages/Ortega_y_Gasset/Ortega_LaRebelionDeLasMasas01.htm#PageTop> (Accessed 20 April 2009).[6]

Ortega y Gasset, José (n.d.) *El Tema de Nuestro Tiempo*. <http://idd00qaa.eresmas.net/ortega/biblio/biblio.htm> (Accessed 28 January 2013).[7]

---

[4] Ortega y Gasset, José (1991) *Mission of the University*. Somerset, NJ, Transaction.

[5] Ortega y Gasset, José (1961) *History as a System, and other Essays Toward a Philosophy of History*. New York, Norton.

[6] Ortega y Gasset, José (1996) *The Revolt of the Masses*. World Library. <http://www.19.5degs.com/ebook/revolt-of-the-masses/1419/read#list> (Accessed 23 April 2008).

[7] Ortega y Gasset, José (2012) *The Modern Theme*. Forgotten Books. <http://www.forgottenbooks.com/books/Modern_Theme_1000277235> (Accessed 18 August 2014).

Pacala, S. and Socolow, R. (2004) Stabilization Wedges: Solving the Climate Problem for the Next 50 Years with Current Technologies. *Science*, 305: 968-972.

Pelikan, Jaroslav (1992) *The Idea of the University*. New Haven, Yale University.

Phau, Donald (1995) Erasmus of Rotterdam, The Educator's Educator. Fidelio, 4: no. 2. <http://www.schillerinstitute.org/fid_91-96/952_erasmus.html> (Accessed 24 Fabruary 2010).

Philo (1890) *Complete Works*. Translated by Charles Duke Yonge. <http://www.utom.org/library/books/Philo.pdf> (Accessed 8 November 2012).

Piccone, Paul (1998) The End of Public Education? *Telos*, 111: 123-138.

Plato (1987) *Theaetetus*. Translated by Waterfield, Robin. London, Penguin.

Plato (1993) *The Last Days of Socrates.* Translated by Tredennick, H. and Tarrant, H. London, Penguin.

Plato (2008a) *The Republic*. Translated by Benjamin Jowett. <http://www.gutenberg.org/> (Accessed 25 January 2013).

Plato (2008b) *Timaeus and Critias*. Translated by Benjamin Jowett. <www.gutenberg.org> (Accessed 15 January 2012).

Polanyi, Michael. (1973) Personal Knowledge. London, Routledge and Kegan Paul.

Protherough, Robert and Pick, John (2002) *Managing Britannia*. Exeter, UK, Imprint Academia.

Råberg, Per (1997) *The Life Region: The Social and Cultural Ecology of Sustainable Development*. London, Routledge.

Raven, John (2005) Designing a Learning Society. Society in Sync Conference, Aberdeen. <http://www.dln.org.uk/JohnRavenPaper.htm> (Accessed 28 March 2008).

Reilly, Tom (2008) Students turn to sex work to help pay for university. *The Melbourne Age*, 2 March.

Richardson, Alan (1969) *An Introduction to the Theology of the New Testament*. London, SCM.

Ritchie, John (1986) *Lachlan Macquarie: a Biography*. Carlton, Victoria. Melbourne University Press.

Rood, David (2007) Numbers fall short in maths. *The Melbourne Age*, 8 February.

Rookmaaker, Hans (1994) *Modern Art and the Death of a Culture*. Illinois, Crossways.

Rush, Emma and La Nauze, Andrea (2006) Corporate Paedophilia: Sexualisation of Children in Australia. The Australian Institute, Discussion Paper No. 90. <http://www.tai.org.au/documents/dp_fulltext/DP90.pdf> (Accessed 28 March 2008).

Ruswick, Brent (2013) *Almost Worthy - The Poor, Paupers, and the Science of Charity in America, 1877 -1917*. Indiana, Indiana University.

Rutenberg, Jim (2006) In Farewell, Rumsfeld Warns Weakness Is 'Provocative'. *New York Times*. 16 December. <http://www.nytimes.com/2006/12/16/washington/16prexy.html> (Accessed 9 October 2010).

Ryn, Claes G. (1981) The Work of Community. In (Ryn, Claes G. (1981) The Work of Community. (In Lawler, Philip (1981) *Papal Economics*. Washington DC, Heritage Foundation; p. 8-18).

Ryn, Claes G. (1990) *Democracy and the Ethical Life: A Philosophy of Politics and Community*. Washington DC, The Catholic University of America.

Ryn, Claes G. (1994) A Question of Class. *National Review*, 46: 50-52.

Sandkvist, Johnny (1984) *Rosvik under 3500 år* Piteå, Norrbotten, Sweden.

Scailliérez, Cécile (n. d.) Mona Lisa – Portrait of Lisa Gherardini, Wife of Francesco del Giocondo.
<http://www.louvre.fr/en/oeuvre-notices/mona-lisa-%E2%80%93-portrait-lisa-gherardini-wife-francesco-del-giocondo> (Accessed 23 June 2014).

Schaff, P. (Ed.) (1986) *The Nicene and Post Nicene Fathers*. 1st series, 8 Vols. Grand Rapids, Michigan, Eerdmans.

Scherman, Tove (2002) Dåliga studieresultat för ingenjörsstudenter. *Uppsala Nya Tidning*, 2 August.

Schmidt, Bettina (1998) Impact of Culture on Development: Making Sustainable Development Human. *South African Journal of Ethnology*, 21: 41-53.

Schubert, Misha (2007) Plea for action to help the poor. *The Melbourne Age*, 26 February.

Schutte, De Wet (2000) Community Development and Community Participation: a Conceptual Revisit. *Entwicklungsethnologie*, 9: 12-25.

Scott, William G. (Ed.) (1969) *Organization Concepts and Analysis*. Belmont, California, Dickenson.

Shanahan, Angela (2003) The children of middle Australia are in crisis. *The Melbourne Age*, 8 December. <http://www.theage.com.au/articles/2003/12/07/1070732069765.html> (Accessed 05 August 2014).

Sharp, Ari (2007) Lenders let teens notch up massive debts. *The Melbourne Age*, 9 December. <Sharp, Ari (2007) Lenders let teens notch up massive debts.> (Accessed 18 August 2014).

Shaw, Meaghan and Cooke, Dewi (2007) Families struggling to balance life and work. *The Melbourne Age*, 7 March.

Siebenhuner, B (2000) Homo Sustinens - Towards a New Conception of Humans for the Science of Sustainability. *Ecological Economics*, 32: 15-25.

Smailes, Peter J. (1995) The Enigma of Social Sustainability in Rural Australia. *Australian Geographer*, 26: 140-150.

Smith, Adam (1970) *The Wealth of Nations*. Project Gutenberg. <http://www.gutenberg.org/dirs/etext02/wltnt10.txt> (Accessed 15 July 2008).

Solzhenitsyn, Alexander (1974) *Letter to Soviet Leaders*. London, Collins.

Sorensen, Tony and Epps, Roger (1996) Leadership and Local Development: Dimensions of Leadership in Four Central Queensland Towns. *Journal of Rural Studies*, 12: 113-125.

Spady, W. (1994). *Outcome-based education: Critical issues and answers*. Arlington, VA: American Association of School Administrators.

St. Augustine (1910) *The Soliloquies*. Translated by Rose Elizabeth Cleveland. Boston, Little Brown. <http://oll.libertyfund.org/titles/1153> (Accessed 06 June 2014).

St. Augustine (2002) *Confessions*. Translated by Translator: E. B. Pusey. <http://www.gutenberg.org> (Accessed 06 June 2014).

St. Augustine (2014) *The City of God*. Volumes I & II. Translated by Marcus Dods. <http://www.gutenberg.org> (Accessed 06 June 2014).

St. Augustine (n.d.) *Homilies on the Gospel of John; Homilies on the First Epistle of John; Soliloquies*. Translated by John Gibb and James Innes. Grand Rapids, MI: Christian Classics Ethereal Library. <http://www.ccel.org/ccel/schaff/npnf107.pdf> (Accessed 20 August 2014).

Stafford, Annabel (2007) How Suicide is Ripping Aboriginal Lives Apart. *The Melbourne Age*, 18 June.

Stark, Jill (2007) Revealed: how alcopops lure the young. The *Sydney Morning Herald*, 6 August.

Stern, Nicholas (2006) The Economics of Climate Change: The Stern Review. HM Treasury. <http://www.hm-treasury.gov.uk/independent_reviews/stern_review_economics_climate_change/stern_review_report.cfm> (Accessed 28 March 2008).

Swinburne, Richard (1991) *The Existence of God* (Revised ed.). Oxford, Clarendon.

Swinburne, Richard (1993) *The Coherence of Theism* (Revised Ed.). Oxford, Clarendon.

Tapp, Robert B. (1997) The Demise of the Humanities Department at the University of Minnesota. *Humanism Today*, 11. <http://www.humanismtoday.org/vol11/tapp.html> (Accessed 06 February 2013).

Tar, Zoltán (1985) *The Frankfurt School*. New York, Schocken.

Taylor, Paige (2007) Cousins arrested, car searched. *The Australian*, 16 October.

Taylor, Thomas C., Kazakov, Alexander Y. and Thompson, Michael C. (1997) Business Ethics and Civil Society in Russia. *International Studies of Management & Organization*, 27: 5-18.

Teixeira, Ruy (1992) *The Disappearing American Voter*. Washington D.C., Brookings Institution.

ten Boom, Corrie (1971) *The Hiding Place*. London, Hodder and Stoughton.

The Holy Bible (1995) New International Version. London, Hodder and Stoughton.

The Melbourne Age (2002a) Earth summit sold out environment: Greens.
<http://www.theage.com.au/articles/2002/09/03/103095345472 7.html> (Accessed 4 September 2002).

The Melbourne Age (2002b) Poorest regions slip further behind: report. 29 October.

The Melbourne Age (2003) Developmental problems by five: study. 26 November.

The Melbourne Age (2004) The global warming sceptics.
<http://www.theage.com.au/articles/ 2004/11/26/1101219743320.html> (Accessed 27 November 2004).

The Melbourne Age (2005) Opinion: The most mortal sin of all - growing old. 10 January.

The Melbourne Age (2006) Qantas to axe 300 IT jobs. 1 October.

The Melbourne Age (2007a) Free speech being whittled away. 5 November.

The Melbourne Age (2007b) Online 'safe sex passport' coming.
<http://www.theage.com.au/articles/2007/11/29/119603704396 7.html> (Accessed 29 November 2007).

The Melbourne Age (2007c) PM disputes poverty report. 30 August.

The Melbourne Age (2007d) Supermarkets 'promoting smokes to young'. 16 November.

The Melbourne Age (2007e) Sutherland jailed for drink-driving.
<http://www.theage.com.au/articles/2007/12/06/119681288787 2.html> (Accessed 6 December 2007).

The Scotsman (2003) Christianity Must Be in European Constitution Says Pope. 7 November.

The Senate Employment, Workplace Relations and Education References Committee (2005) Student income support. Common-

wealth of Australia.
<http://www.aph.gov.au/senate/committee/eet_ctte/studentin-come04/report/report.pdf> (Accessed 28 March 2008).

Tolstoy, Leo (2003) *On the Significance of Science and Art*. Project Gutenberg. <http://www.gutenberg.org/etext/3631> (Accessed 9 June 2010).

Tomazin, Farrah (2008) One in five students falling short in maths. *The Melbourne Age*, 2 February.

Topsfield, Jewel (2007) Schools produce illiterate students. *The Melbourne Age*, 13 September.

Tritter, Jonathan (1992) An Educated Change in Moral Values: Some Effect of Religious and State Schools on their Students. *Oxford Review of Education*, 18: 29-43.

Unamuno, Miguel (1989) *Amor y Pedagogía*. Madrid, Espasa-Calpe.

Unamuno, Miguel de (1912) *Del Sentimiento Trágico de la Vida*. <http://literatura.itematika.com/descargar/libro/301/del-sentimiento-tragico-de-la-vida.html> (Accessed 27 January 2013).[8]

Unamuno, Miguel de (1927) Cómo se hace una novela. Ciudad Seva. <http://www.ciudadseva.com/textos/teoria/opin/unamuno2.htm> (Accessed 06 February 2013).

UNINEWS (2001) Older men get pensions, not jobs. Australia, University of Newcastle, 20 August.

van de Wetering, Ernst (2005) *A Corpus of Rembrandt Paintings IV: The Self-Portraits*. Dordrecht, Netherlands, Springer.

van der Stoep, J. (1995) Hypermobility as a Challenge for Systems Thinking and Government Policy. *Proceedings*, 39th Annual Meeting, International Society for the Systems Sciences, Free University, Amsterdam.

van Voss, Lex Heerma and van Leeuwen, Marco H. D. (2012) Charity in the Dutch Republic: an Introduction. *Continuity and Change*, 27: 195-197.
<http://socialhistory.org/sites/default/files/docs/publications/201

---

[8] Unamuno, Miguel de (1954) *The Tragic Sense of Life*. Translated by J. Crawford Flitch. New York, Dover. <http://www.gutenberg.org/etext/14636> (Accessed 11 April 2008).

2introcharityheerma_van_voss_and_van_leeuwen.pdf> (Accessed 31 March 2014).

Vinson, Tony (2007) Dropping of the Edge: The Distribution of Disadvantage in Australia. Jesuit Social Services and Catholic Social Service Australia.

Vives, Juan Luis (1971) *On Education*. Totowa, New Jersey, Rowman and Littlefield.

Vives, Juan Luis (1999) *On Assistance to the Poor*. Translated by Alice Tobriner. Toronto, University of Toronto.

Vives, Juan Luis (2000) *The Education of a Christian Woman*. Translated by Charles Fantazzi. University of Chicago.

von Bertalanffy, Ludwig (1971) *General Systems Theory*. London, Penguin.

von Bertalanffy, Ludwig and LaViolette, Paul A. (ed.) (1981) *A Systems View of Man*. Boulder, Colorado, Praeger.

Vos, Geerhardus (1971) *Biblical Theology*. Grand Rapids, Michigan, WM. B. Eeerdmans.

Wintour, Patrick; Watt, Nicholas and Ward, Lucy (2002) Morris quits: 'I've not done as well as I should have' Education secretary rejects Blair plea to stay. London, *The Guardian*, 24 October.

Wray, Lyle & Hauer, Jody (1997) Performance Measurement to Achieve Quality of Life: Adding Value through Citizens. *Public Management (U.S.)*, 79: 4-7.

Zwartz, Barney (2008) Family values threatened, says panel. *The Melbourne Age*, 9 January.

Index

www.ingramcontent.com/pod-product-compliance
Lightning Source LLC
Chambersburg PA
CBHW060234290526
45789CB00001B/50